Substantial discounts on bulk quantities of Jossey-Bass books are available to corporations, professional associations, and other organizations. For details and discount information, contact the special sales department at Jossey-Bass Inc., Publishers. (415) 433-1740; Fax (415) 433-0499.

For international orders, please contact your local Paramount Publishing International office.

Manufactured in the United States of America. Nearly all Jossey-Bass books and jackets are printed on recycled paper that contains at least 50 percent recycled waste, including 10 percent postconsumer waste. Many of our materials are also printed with vegetable-based ink; during the printing process these inks emit fewer volatile organic compounds (VOCs) than petroleum-based inks. VOCs contribute to the formation of smog.

Library of Congress Cataloging-in-Publication Data

Dryfoos, Joy G.
    Full-service schools : a revolution in health and social services for children, youth, and families / Joy G. Dryfoos. — 1st ed.
        p. cm.
    "A joint publication in the Jossey-Bass health series, the Jossey-Bass social and behavioral science series, and the Jossey-Bass education series" — CIP data sheet.
    Includes bibliographical references (p.) and index.
    ISBN 1-55542-601-8
    1. School health services—United States. 2. Students—Services for—United States. 3. Human services—United States. I. Title.
LB3409.U5D79   1994
371.7'0973—dc20   93-41936
                                                                            CIP

FIRST EDITION
HB Printing   10 9 8 7 6 5 4 3 2   Code 9437

FULL-SERVICE
SCHOOLS

▲▲▲

Foreword by David A. Hamburg

▲▲▲

FULL-SERVICE SCHOOLS

▲▲

A Revolution in
Health and Social Services for
Children, Youth, and Families

▲▲▲

JOY G. DRYFOOS

 Jossey-Bass Publishers • San Francisco

Contents

▲▲▲

▲▲

Foreword

▲▲▲

Deep commitment is a fundamental attribute of humanity. But drastic social changes, reflecting the transformation of modern economies, are disrupting established family patterns and the conditions that affect powerfully the way children grow up. In recent years, through the work of courageous scholars such as Joy G. Dryfoos, we have been waking to the scope of serious casualties in child and adolescent development.

The United States is a very large, heterogeneous, and individualistic country. These strong assets also make it difficult to reach a shared understanding on complicated social problems and to arrive at widely acceptable decisions. Thus, we are struggling to reach consensus on fundamental questions about improving the life chances of today's children. Within the scientific and professional communities, a remarkable degree of consensus on the core facts has been emerging in recent years, and no one has done more to clarify it than Dryfoos. This consensus is only beginning to be understood by the general public and by policymakers in the public and private sectors.

Therefore, it is crucial now to have the kind of well-informed analysis and bold yet practical vision presented in this book.

How can we translate scholarly research into practice? How can we better coordinate services that are now fragmented among different bureaucracies? How can professionals with different training backgrounds learn to cooperate to help families? Research and practice provide insights into these questions. We can use experience from the programs thus far undertaken and draw out the implications of research in child development, health, and education to ascertain which programs are the most effective, which need the most attention, and how we can proliferate the best models for broad-scale benefit. That is what *Full-Service Schools* does.

This book expands on the author's prior work. Her thorough 1990 review of research, *Adolescents at Risk: Prevalence and Prevention*, indicates that successful programs to prevent delinquency, substance abuse, teenage pregnancy, and school failure share several common elements. Efforts to help high-risk children avoid these difficulties primarily require sustained individual attention as well as communitywide, multiagency, collaborative approaches in order to reach children and their families early in the development of problem behaviors. Many successful programs are located in schools, including not only those aimed at educational improvement but also those aimed at substance abuse, delinquency, and pregnancy prevention. Successful school programs are typically administered by agencies outside of schools. Exemplary programs make provision for adequate staff training in the protocol or curricula they use. Many make effective use of social-skills training, and many use peers in their interventions. A variety of programs have demonstrated success by directing interventions toward parents, whether by home visiting or by employing parents as parent aides. Finally, many successful prevention programs have a link to the world of work, introducing career planning and exposing youngsters to the work experience. From these earlier findings, there is a logical progression to Dryfoos's present formulation of full-service schools.

One can envision how schools, the media, churches, business, community organizations, government at various levels, and organizations of the scientific community might cooperate in addressing the developmental needs of youth. Many parents view schools as trustworthy institutions that are easy to locate in any community. Elementary schools are usually in the immediate neighborhood. An authentic community program in the schools could provide a universal, integrating experience. School building space is available in many areas, and services could use existing transportation systems.

A school-based approach requires that schools connect strongly with the health and social services systems. As a practical matter, it will be necessary to achieve cooperation among several institutions in a particular community—and the mix might well differ from one to another. Schools, universities, clinics, social service agencies, the media, churches, business, community organizations, government at various levels, and professional organizations—all could be highly constructive in cooperative efforts.

Any such combination of institutions would need to serve several valuable functions:

- Clarifying the nature of child and adolescent problems.
- Stimulating interest and hope in the possibility of useful interventions.
- Facilitating the delivery of appropriate services.
- Providing resources—not only money but also people, organization, and technical skills. Participating institutions would need to have a steady flow of the most reliable and up-to-date information about what works for whom in fostering healthy, constructive, problem-solving child and adolescent development.

Schools will have to broaden their mission considerably to be effective in full-service functions. New Jersey's recent experience in implementing school-based health and social services for adolescents suggests that schools will respond when offered funding to expand their services in unaccustomed directions. Evidently, tying funding to certain critical requirements (such as coordination with community agencies), while allowing schools the independence to design the details of their own programs, is likely to produce good results.

Dryfoos's formulation recognizes that schools are now required, as a practical matter, to take on more responsibilities than ever before. They must cope with drug abuse, violence, and other problems. They must make education more inclusive and technically competent than ever before. They cannot do so without sustained intellectual, organizational, technical, financial, and political support. Finding such resources and linking them in sustained collaborative partnerships with schools is a formidable task, but many working models now exist that demonstrate the feasibility of this approach.

For instance, many functional links exist between, on the one hand, the scientific assets of universities, colleges, corporate laboratories, and national laboratories and, on the other, the elementary and secondary schools; these links strengthen the national capability for education in mathematics, science, and technology. The past decade has seen the rapid growth of the schools' links with the nation's colleges and universities, business organizations, and a great variety of community organizations. Such partnerships are situations of mutual benefit for the schools and the cooperating organizations, but they are not sufficiently extensive. Can we now make a serious commitment to this approach?

The integrated interventions in education, health, and social services considered in this book have much to do with the kind of future we will all have. Sadly, few complete models of full-service schools are available so far, but those that we have are encouraging. Crucial components do exist all across the country and in other nations as well. We can learn how to put these components together in ways that provide our children with the full range of developmental opportunities permitted by today's knowledge and emerging research findings. A

comprehensive sequence of developmentally useful opportunities can
be applied in a concerted way even in poor and disadvantaged communities. *Full-Service Schools* provides bright illumination of one path
on which such a vision can be brought to realization.

January 1993   DAVID A. HAMBURG
New York   President
                                  Carnegie Corporation

Preface

▲▲▲

A merican schools are failing because they cannot meet the complex needs of today's students. Teachers cannot teach hungry children or cope with young people who are too distraught to learn. Anyone working in an inner-city school, in a marginal rural area, or even on the fringes of suburbia will tell you how impossible her or his job has become. The cumulative effects of poverty have created social environments that challenge educators, community leaders, and practitioners of health, mental health, and social services to invent new kinds of institutional responses.

One of the responses has been the creation of school-based clinics, primary health care centers in schools operated by local health agencies. The idea of delivering health services to low-income students in schools is an old one, a concept that emerges and disappears with the swings of the social pendulum. In the 1980s, as conditions worsened for young people, school-based clinics began to pop up serendipitously around the country. The first wave, designed to prevent teen pregnancy, was rapidly superseded by a more comprehensive model. These new centers were seen as an answer to the lack of access to primary health services in general, as well as places to prevent substance abuse, depression, sexually transmitted diseases, and other "new morbidities" that were striking down millions of American youngsters. Mental health counseling emerged as a high priority for the troubled adolescents who flocked to the centers as soon as the doors opened. As the concept of coordinated integrated services in school gained acceptance, it was put forward as a major component of school restructuring. Today, most school reformers recognize that you can't fix the schools without paying attention to the students, their families, and their communities.

This book attempts to describe this emerging phenomenon of school-based services. The first time I visited a school-based clinic in Jackson, Mississippi, in 1983, I became an ardent advocate of the idea. In this case, the site was a high school and the provider was a community health center. Since then, I have seen almost every variant of program run by health departments, hospitals, medical schools, physicians' groups, visiting nurses' associations, and even school systems. I decided to write a book about school-based clinics because they made so much sense to me, bringing committed and skilled practitioners into schools who want to help school-communities become healthier physical and social climates for disadvantaged young people. No book had been written on this subject before.

In taking on this task, I got much more than I bargained for. While I was writing the book, the idea of school-based services caught on all across the country, but the models that were proliferating did not fall neatly into my simple definition of school-based health clinics. The broader definition, shaped largely by state initiatives, has become a school center in which health, mental health, social, and/or family services may be co-located, depending on the needs of the particular school and community—hence the label in the title, "full-service schools." If that label still puzzles you, substitute "settlement house in a school" or "community-school," phrases in the new vocabulary of advocates of school-based services. In this discussion, you will also hear about "family resource centers," another variant of service integration that focuses on parents and young children and that often takes place on school sites.

Audience

In a sense, this book is about the transition from school-based clinics to full-service schools. For people who are interested in "what's happening," I have described a new way of looking at the school as a piece of real estate that we all own, where our most precious future assets are trained to become responsible adults, schools which could be so vastly enriched by the addition of a whole array of community resources. For educators and school board members, I have given specific examples of programs that are now being provided in schools, with a detailed analysis of the benefits and limitations of partnerships between schools and community agencies. For health, mental health, and social service practitioners in schools and outside, I have presented many variations of collaborative arrangements for working in schools, with emphasis on the rich diversity of programs. For parents, who must ultimately decide whether to permit their children to utilize these new service structures, I have presented evidence of how young people have been helped and how supportive parents have been in maintaining these programs. For federal, state, and local legislators and administrators, I have given specific recommendations for rapidly expanding full-service schools so that the school staff, practitioners, and parents will be able to do their jobs with enthusiasm and effectiveness. For the media, enough material is presented here that they can stop writing about "sex clinics" in schools and start helping the public understand the possibilities for institutional change. University people can use this book in courses on child and adolescent development, educational innovation, social and community psychology, social work, public health, nursing, and medicine.

Organization of This Book

Full-Service Schools was conceived as a relatively short work on school-based clinics. But rapidly changing social developments made this limited scope impossible. It seemed important to capture both the past and the present, the rich detail of school-based clinics and the flavor of all the emerging models, the diversity in state programs and the potential of federal efforts. Thus, the knowledge base is broad, covering hundreds of sources including books, articles, task force reports, legislation, program reviews, budgets, proposals, site visits, formal interviews, and conversations with people all over the country.

Chapter One introduces the subject, reviewing why the movements for educational reform and access to health services have come together in recent years. A vision of the full-service school is presented as a framework for the book, showing the two strands of interest here, quality education and support services. Chapter Two presents a brief history of this nation's experience with support services, exemplified by school-based health services, to show the remarkable correspondence between the problems encountered and the solutions proposed a century ago and now. Chapter Three offers two categories of program examples that could serve as components of the full-service school; support services, including health, mental health, family services, recreation, and culture; and quality education, including school remediation, dropout prevention, school-restructuring efforts, and comprehensive, multicomponent programs. Following this overview, Chapter Four focuses on school-based health clinics. "Pioneer" programs are described and the current scene is surveyed, with a general description of how health and social services are provided in schools. Chapter Five reports on two schools that come close to the vision of the full-service school, characterized here as the "settlement house in the school" and the "community-school." The question always comes up, "Do these programs work?" Chapter Six reviews and summarizes the evidence from emerging research about the effects of school-based services on a range of behaviors.

Chapter Seven opens up a broad discussion of organizational and service delivery issues that practitioners trying to move toward these various full-service models experience. We look at the roles of schools, community agencies, and parents in collaborative arrangements and at the turf, staffing, and quality of care issues that must be confronted during implementation. Of course, long-term financing is the major barrier to broad replication. Chapter Eight looks at specific funding problems at the local level, at how states have been the prime movers in the development and financial support of school-based programs so far, and at how the federal government might move to promote the concept of full-service schools in the future.

In Chapter Nine, the final chapter, I address the following questions: Are school-based services the wave of the future? All schools or only some? How can the need for thousands of new centers be met? Recommendations for actions at the community, state, and national levels follow. Appendix A presents brief profiles of twelve states that are supporting school-based services with different kinds of initiatives. Appendix B describes federal programs that could be tapped as funding sources for creating new school-based programs if regulations were made more "consumer-friendly." Appendix C is a glossary of acronyms—the alphabet soup of bureaucracy.

I hope that this book will strengthen the conviction that full-service schools are the way to go and will inspire readers to get involved in the movement that will change the vision into the reality.

Acknowledgments

This work has been made possible by the Carnegie Corporation of New York. This foundation has been supporting me for many years for a long-term "youth-at-risk" project, leaving me free to independently explore all avenues toward helping adolescents grow into responsible and productive adults. I deeply appreciate the encouragement and commitment of David Hamburg, president; Vivien Stewart, chair of the program on Education and Healthy Development of Children and Youth; and Gloria Primm Brown, program officer. Ruby Takanishi, executive director of the Carnegie Council on Adolescent Development, has also been a sympathetic colleague who has offered guidance and stimulation throughout this project. (The content of this book does not necessarily reflect the views of the Carnegie Corporation.)

Hundreds of people contributed to these pages. For almost every program mentioned, a person invited me to visit, talked to me on the telephone, or sent me material. Substantial assistance was provided by Debra Lipson, who acted as a consultant on the state and federal chapters, and Philip Coltoff, Pat Logan, and Pete Moses, who reviewed Chapter Five. I appreciate the help of Christel Brellochs, Paul Dryfoos, Kate Fothergill, Marc Freedman, Robert Haggerty, Debra Hauser, Tia Melaville, Philip Nader, Susan Philliber, Philip Porter, Ann Segal, Richard Silva, Lorraine Tiezzi, Deborah Von Zinkernagel, and Alfred Yankauer for reviewing and commenting on various chapters and supplying resource materials. State program advisors included Marie Sandusky Peterson (Arkansas); Lynn DeLapp, Jane Henderson, and Amy Loomis (California); Lynn Letarte (Connecticut); Lynn Graves (Florida); Becky Wilson (Georgia); Ronnie Dunn, Patricia Nickle, and Dee Swain (Kentucky); Sandra White (Michigan); Roberta Knowlton (New Jersey); Karen Gaylord (New Mexico); and Michelle Kravitz (New York). I also wish to thank David Kaplan, Jonathan Klein, the National School Boards Association, and the Support Center for School-Based Services of the Center for Population Options for sharing data bases. Mary Rose Puthiyamadam came in at the finish to straighten out the references and to help generate the manuscript. Christie Hakim, Lesley Iura, and Frank Welsch at Jossey-Bass contributed to the production process with their enthusiasm, support, and patience. Finally, I am deeply indebted to George Dryfoos, who read every page, saved me from egregious errors, and held my hand throughout.

This book is dedicated to our granddaughter, Amy Li Hua Rodgers-Dryfoos, who came into our lives as the culminating chapter. I know she will grow into a responsible and productive adult, and I hope she will always be on the cutting edge of social change. That's what this book is all about: stimulating committed people to move ahead to create new solutions to old problems, new institutions, new approaches to youth work, and new hope for the future.

January 1994   JOY G. DRYFOOS
Hastings-on-Hudson, New York

The Author

▲▲▲

J oy G. Dryfoos is an independent researcher, writer, and lecturer from Hastings-on-Hudson, New York. She received her B.A. degree (1951) from Antioch College in sociology and her M.A. degree (1967) from Sarah Lawrence College in urban sociology. She has received grants from the Carnegie Corporation of New York since 1984 for the Youth-at-Risk Project, synthesizing the "state of the art" on planning and evaluating programs for disadvantaged youth. Her primary research focus has been on programs for adolescents, particularly those aimed at prevention of teen pregnancy, substance abuse, delinquency, and school dropout.

Dryfoos was appointed by the National Research Council of the National Academy of Sciences to the panels on Adolescent Pregnancy and Childbearing (1987) and High-Risk Youth (1993). In 1992, she received the Carl Shultz Award from the American Public Health Association for her work in the field of reproductive health care. She serves on the editorial board of the *Journal of Adolescent Health*. Dryfoos's books include *Adolescents at Risk:*

Prevalence and Prevention (1990) and *Putting the Boys in the Picture* (1988).

Dryfoos is also adjunct professor, Columbia University School of Public Health. From 1969 to 1981, she was director of research and planning and fellow at the Alan Guttmacher Institute.

FULL-SERVICE
SCHOOLS

▲▲▲

1

▲▲▲

The Full-Service Vision: Responding to Critical Needs

T he last decade of the twentieth century will be a hazardous time for many children and their families in the United States. A measurable segment of the society is not going to "make it" without massive changes in the way that they are educated, supported, and cared for. Families and schools, the primary institutions that have traditionally carried the responsibilities for raising and teaching children, cannot fulfill their obligations without immediate and intensive transformation. New kinds of arrangements of community resources have to be brought together to ensure that children can grow up to be responsible, productive, and fully participating members of this society.

Family structure has shifted away from the idealized Ozzie-and-Harriet model of Dad in the workplace and Mom at home in their suburban ranch house with the two children. Today, three-fourths of all mothers of school-age children are in the labor force, up from about half in 1970.[1] One in four children live in families with only one parent, more than double the rate of two decades ago. However, even two-parent families are feeling the pressure of poor economic conditions and excessive housing and health insurance costs that require them to concentrate heavily on making a living and supporting their children.

The decade of the 1980s is now being characterized for its glorification of the "me-first" doctrine. We saw the rise and fall of the junk-bond artists and savings-and-loan bandits; the media exposed us to the excessive "life-styles of the rich and famous." But during this same decade, poverty increased and the number of poor children grew. By 1991, more than fourteen million children—22 percent of all children—lived in families below the poverty line, the highest number and rate since 1965.[2] As in no other period of time, disadvantage shifted from the oldest people to the youngest. And those children living in mother-only households have become the most deprived of all, with more than 55 percent living in poverty.

The demand for basic social programs continues to grow as budgeting crises mount. Many states are coping with horrendous budget crises that have produced drastic cuts in human services of all kinds, and many cities are teetering on the brink of financial disaster.

Impacts on Children

As a result of the deteriorating social environment and growing fiscal crises, children are suffering. Many face substantial barriers to growing into responsible adults who will be able to enter the workforce, become effective parents, and participate in the political process. Throughout this book, I will refer to the "new morbidities"—unprotected sex, drugs, violence, and depression—that threaten the future of today's children. (In contrast, the "old morbidities" were chronic diseases, nutritional deficiencies, acne, and infestations of head lice.) The factors leading to substance abuse, teen pregnancy, delinquency, and school failure are highly interrelated and are much more likely to affect children who live in disadvantaged social environments.[3] My estimate is that about one in four children and youth (aged ten to seventeen) in the United States "do it all"—use drugs, have early unprotected intercourse, are truant, and fall far behind in school—and as a result, these seven million young people will never be able to "make it" without massive changes in their current circumstances.

We know a great deal about "high-risk" children. Their status is defined by their families; they lack attention from parents who can provide nurturing and attention. From a rich literature about effective parenting, we can conclude that children who have "authoritative" parents do a lot better than those whose parents are too "permissive" or too "authoritarian."[4] Parental substance abuse adversely affects offspring, not only genetically, as in the case of children of alcoholics; addicted parents are also poor role models and may be negligent and even abusive. We know, too, that poverty erodes expectations and that families have difficulty raising children in stressful, dangerous, and unhealthy environments. And, of course, children of absent parents suffer most of all, unless they are attached to a strong adult who can act as a surrogate parent.

Certain children start getting into trouble at early ages, usually with aggressive "acting out" behavior that gets translated fairly soon into truancy, destructiveness, and other conduct disorders. Early involvement with one problem behavior frequently predicts involvement in other domains; for example, smoking at age ten can precede unprotected intercourse, heavy alcohol use, and trouble in school. High-risk children cannot resist peer influences, and they become easily distracted or enticed by friends and acquaintances into dangerous behaviors.

Evidence is accumulating that young people who are prone to these problem behaviors are frequently depressed and suffering from symptoms of stress. "Suicidal ideation" is on the rise: in a recent national survey, one in seven young people (eighth- and tenth-graders) reported having attempted suicide.[5] Many children are exposed to violence at very early ages and grow up with many fears about their own security and the safety of their families. Many young people respond to violence by purchasing firearms and knives; one-third of high school students report that they could obtain a handgun if they wanted one.

The most recognizable symptom of high-risk status is school failure. Children who are older than their classmates because they have been left back are in a precarious position. Being two or more years behind almost always leads to dropping out of school prior to high school graduation. And high school completion is a significant marker for future success. It should be noted, however, that a high school diploma alone does not guarantee success, since increasing numbers of graduates lack basic skills in numeracy and literacy. Acquisition of basic cognitive skills is the proverbial bottom line for all children.

A recent report from the Panel on High-Risk Youth of the National Academy of Sciences stressed the importance of redirecting attention away from the individuals affected to the institutional settings creating the risk status.[6] The children are "at risk" because they live in high-risk environments. Thus, immediate interventions are called for in the realms of family, school, and community, with particular urgency for both creating jobs and overcoming the educational and social barriers to employment.

Implications for Schools

Every day, forty million children are expected to arrive at the U.S.'s eighty-two thousand public elementary and secondary schools. Based on the one-in-four estimate, fully ten million of those children are at high risk of failure.[7] In some schools, almost all of the children arrive with social, emotional, and health handicaps that stand in the way of success. One principal described his school-community as an "under-developed country," isolated from and abandoned by the mainstream society. In other schools, almost all of the children arrive ready to learn and securely attached to a supportive home and family environment. In some states, the difference between school systems is dramatic. One educational task force found that "two different systems of education have been created in our State. One encompasses effective schools holding high expectations for their students and located in affluent or stable communities; the other, ineffective schools which communicate low expectations and aspirations for their students, who are not given full opportunity to succeed. They are too often located in large urban areas and the inner cities. Our society's acceptance of two unequal educational systems is putting us at risk of creating a permanent underclass."[8]

Our interest here is primarily directed toward the roles of schools and community agencies in responding to the needs of high-risk children and their families and equalizing access to future opportunities. Schools are increasingly being called on to be those "surrogate parents" that can increase the "teachability" of children who arrive on their doorsteps in poor shape. Today's schools feel pressured to feed children; provide psychological support services; offer health screening; establish referral networks related to substance abuse, child welfare, and sexual abuse; cooperate with the local police and probation officers; add curricula for prevention of substance abuse, teen pregnancy, suicide, and violence (the new morbidities); and actively promote social skills, good nutrition, safety, and general health.

Around the country, school administrators are crying for help. They acknowledge that they cannot attend to all the needs of the current crop of students and at the same time respond to the demands for quality education. The educational institution's first order of priority is to ensure that all children gain the basic skills required for full participation in our society. Because school financing and governance are structured around this very specific and essential mission, other institutions have to share the responsibility for "everything else"—all those health and social services needy children and their families require to use the basic skills and participate in the society.

Consensus on the Need for Collaborative School-Based Services

This book is about bringing service systems into schools to respond to the needs of today's children and their families. A significant consensus is emerging that schools cannot do it alone, that the interests of the educational establishment and the health and social service systems must be joined in order to shape powerful new institutions. Demands for more comprehensive, collaborative, unfragmented programs located in schools are coming from a wide spectrum of organizations and individuals that advocate for educational reform and adolescent health and on the behalf of young children and families.

Educational Reform

Michael Kirst, one the most articulate advocates for innovative school-based programs recognizes the multidimensionality of the situation: "What's needed is a complete overhaul of children's services, bringing together public and private organizations to meet the comprehensive needs of children, adolescents, and parents. Schools should constitute one of the centers of a coordinated network of total children's services."[9] Kirst's strategy calls for grouping a number of services in one place, generally, but not always, with the school as the hub. But, as he is careful to point out, not with the school in charge—the parties should be coequals, participating in planned communitywide collaborative programming.

Studies of school-restructuring issues have highlighted the relationship between good health and educational achievement, as well as the importance of bringing health services into schools. *Turning Points*, the challenge of the Carnegie Council Task Force on Education of Young Adolescents to middle school reform, called for, among other interventions, the placement in every school of a health coordinator who can marshal the necessary resources so that young adolescents will be healthy and can learn.[10] The task force recognized, however, that the needs of some students might exceed the available resources and that therefore schools should consider options such as school-based and school-linked health centers. They envision a comprehensive services network with the school as the center and community agencies acting as the lead coordinating organizations.

The proposed "reinvention" of America's schools has generated a lot of media attention and discussion among educational gurus. Much of the emphasis has been on raising academic performance and developing standardized testing methods. Unfortunately, the plight of high-risk students and their families has received short shrift in all of this discourse. As Sid Gardner, an authority on service integration projects, pointed out, "the tone . . . is still 'let's fix the kids,' with an assumption that fixing the *institutions* that serve the kids will all be taken care of by vouchers and more rhetoric. Budget constraints have been allowed to overwhelm the parallel reforms in children's services that are needed to make education reforms a reality."[11] Gardner stressed that schools ought to work with other public and private agencies to help students already targeted as needy by several agencies. In his view, city and county governments should help schools by encouraging local leaders to integrate their often fragmented and disconnected federal grants into locally designed comprehensive programs.

Edward Meade, who led the Ford Foundation's school reform initiatives, found that proposed strategies disregarded the documented interrelationships among good health, good support services, and good education and failed to offer specific steps to bring about more effectiveness in providing *comprehensive* services. Over the years, Meade observed that "schools that have solid working links with agencies that provide other services for students, such as health and social supports, are more effective in educating the students who need these services."[12]

Increasingly, educational experts are espousing the language of collaboration. In this book, we will be visiting with a few states and local school systems that have moved in the direction of structuring school reform broadly and incorporating requirements that school districts and public health and social service agencies work together to create more effective institutions.

Adolescent Health

In an unprecedented move, two organizations representing diverse major interest groups, the American Medical Association and the National Association of State Boards of Education, issued *Code Blue: Uniting for Healthier Youth*.[13] Code Blue is the parlance used in medicine to signify a life-threatening emergency, which is how the organizations' joint commission characterized contemporary health problems of youth. Their recommendations stem from their agreement that *education and health are inextricably intertwined*, that efforts to improve school performance that ignore health would be ill conceived, as would health improvement efforts that ignore education. Thus, the commission strongly supported the establishment of health centers in schools, attention to the school climate and to issues related to achievement, and the restructuring of public and private health insurance to ensure access to services. They pointed out that "families, schools, neighborhoods, the health community, and the public and private sectors will need to forge new partnerships to address the interconnected health and education problems our young people are experiencing."[14]

The Office of Technology Assessment (OTA), when charged by Congress to review the health status of American adolescents and present options for congressional consideration, came up with similar recommendations to support the development of comprehensive health centers in schools and communities, to create a central locus in the federal government for addressing adolescent health issues, and to improve adolescents' social and economic environments in general.[15] The OTA report was particularly persuasive on the subject of school-linked services, referring to school clinics as the "most promising recent innovation to improve access to health." They add a note of caution, however, pointing out that systematic evidence that school centers improve health outcomes is still somewhat limited.

Although it is not my intent here to cite a lot of statistics about adolescent health issues, it is important to note that adolescents' access to health care is severely restricted by a number of barriers, among which lack of health insurance is significant. It has been estimated that close to five million adolescents aged ten to eighteen, 15 percent of the total, have no public or private health coverage.[16] Of those who live in low-income families, however, at least one-third lack coverage.

Young Children and Their Families

A number of social commentators have argued that the most urgent task facing this society is to regenerate families. Roger Wilkins contends that "while employment, early childhood education, and child-care programs are critical parts of such an effort, it is essential that the public schools become the focus of special remedies... the centers of the community for the children they serve and for their parents and grandparents."[17] Concern about troubled families has clearly led to a resurgence of interest in family-oriented early childhood development programs. Heather Weiss's study of school-based family support and education programs found examples of comprehensive networks that provided parent education, referral to community agencies, home visiting, peer support groups, child care, health screening, and counseling.[18]

One of the most promising interventions, "Schools of the Twenty-First Century," created by Edward Zigler of Yale University, promotes schools that function as community centers, linking family support systems with child care systems.[19] Zigler argues eloquently that the community already "owns" the school buildings, having invested one to two *trillion* dollars in these properties. He would open the doors of the schools from 7 A.M. to 6 P.M., all day, every day. In the building, he would establish full-day child care for three- to five-year-olds, insuring high-quality developmentally appropriate services. He would also provide before- and after-school care to six- to twelve-year-olds that included recreation and "fun." In addition, these schools would offer home visitors to all parents of newborns, incorporating the Parents as Teachers model (from Missouri), and organize and supervise family day care for children from birth to three years. The center would be run by early childhood educators trained to garner the resources and referrals needed by "new American families."

Jane Knitzer and colleagues' study of the implementation of the Education of the Handicapped Act, which required schools to educate large numbers of children identified as having behavioral and emotional disorders, yielded strong recommendations for bringing mental health services into schools.[20] They found a growing recognition in both regular education and special education that access to school-based mental health services can have a positive impact on students, on teachers, and on school climate and that "for the most seriously troubled children and adolescents—those at risk of residential placement—school involvement in multi-system collaboration is an essential ingredient to keeping children in their own communities." They advised local mental health agencies to explore with the schools the range of services they could offer, including working with teachers to devise joint programs.

One organization, Joining Forces, sponsored by the American Public Welfare Association and the Council of Chief State School Officers, sought to foster communication among the educational and human service systems, identify barriers to collaboration, and assist federal and state agencies in development, implementation, and evaluation of emerging collaborative models. At the end of the first year of Joining Forces, director Janet Levy (now at the Danforth Foundation) documented an impressive array of joint ventures but pointed toward the absence of replications of the models and the lack of incorporation of unique models into larger systems.[21] She warned that though new arrangements cannot be put in place with "quick fix" actions, "this is a propitious time for collaboration because education and human services face *common* challenges as they try to help the *same* people and respond to the *same* problems."

William Morrill, director of the Center for Service Integration, and Martin Gerry, former assistant secretary for planning and evaluation, Department of Health and Human Services (DHHS), have contributed substantially to discussions about integration of services for children and families. They have observed that fragmented, separately organized, and physically scattered services create serious access problems for school-aged children. Even where all the requisite services are available, barriers to access are caused by different eligibility rules and lack of communication between professionals. They conclude that "the schools as central institutions in the community provide an important, if not critical, organizing focus for the coordination and integration of services. This hypothesis does not necessarily assume that the schools need be the organizer or operator of all services to be delivered, but the physical facility or the cooperation of the school administration is usually critical to integration and coordination efforts."[22]

A powerful consensus is emerging from the recommendations of diverse groups and experts in educational reform, child and adolescent health, and family welfare reform. A universal call has been issued for one-stop unfragmented health and social service systems that are consumer-oriented, developmentally appropriate, and culturally relevant. Agreement is strong that the school should be an active partner in collaborative efforts, and the idea that school facilities should serve as the *place* for the provision of noneducational support services of all kinds is rapidly gaining support.

Components of the Full-Service School

The vision of the full-service school puts the best of school reform together with all other services that children, youth, and their families need, most of which can be located in a school building. The educational mandate places responsibility on the school system to reorganize and innovate. The charge to community agencies is to bring into the school: health, mental health, employment services, child care, parent education, case management, recreation, cultural events, welfare, community policing, and whatever else may fit into the picture. The result is a new kind of "seamless" institution, a community-oriented school with a joint governance structure that allows maximum responsiveness to the community, as well as accessibility and continuity for those most in need of services. The theme of integration of educational, health, and social welfare services reverberates through local, state, and national dialogues. A century of demonstration projects may finally be leading to the combination of the settlement house with the school. Though this sounds like a tall order, fraught with political and practical barriers, successful models in dozens of communities show that it can happen.

Exhibit 1.1 presents an idealized model of the full-service school, listing some of the components that might be incorporated into a quality education initiative and those support services that could be provided by community agencies. The components listed are based on the program experiences cited in Chapter 3 and on findings of a study of one hundred successful prevention programs in the separate fields of substance abuse, teen pregnancy, delinquency, and school failure.[23] The model reflects the belief that no single component, no magic bullet, can significantly change the lives of disadvantaged children, youth, and families. Rather, it is the cumulative impact of a package of interventions that will result in measurable changes in life scripts.

Exhibit 1.1. Full-Service Schools: One-Stop, Collaborative Institutions.

**Quality Education Provided
by Schools**
Effective basic skills
Individualized instruction
Team teaching
Cooperative learning
School-based management
Healthy school climate
Alternatives to tracking
Parent involvement
Effective discipline

**Provided by Schools or
Community Agencies**
Comprehensive health education
Health promotion
Social skills training
Preparation for the world of
work (life planning)

**Support Services Provided by
Community Agencies**
Health screening and services
Dental services
Family planning
Individual counseling
Substance abuse treatment
Mental health services
Nutrition/weight management
Referral with follow-up
Basic services: housing, food, clothes
Recreation, sports, culture
Mentoring
Family welfare services
Parent education, literacy
Child care
Employment training/jobs
Case management
Crisis intervention
Community policing

The Reality

The current reality is an ill-defined assortment of school-based programs
spread out across a continuum, from simple one-component partnerships between a school and an outside agency or business to sophisticated, complex, multicomponent, multiagency collaboratives.
Marked differences exist in program orientation. Family-oriented
programs start with meeting the needs of parents and infants and
move toward services for young children. Youth-oriented programs
are formulated around the needs of older children and adolescents
and move cautiously toward family involvement. This book focuses
primarily on experience with programs for youth at the middle

and high school levels. However, the organizing principles, service delivery issues, and funding problems are applicable to school-community partnerships in general.

No one model of school-based services predominates. New programs are called school-based health clinics, youth service centers, family resource centers, full-service schools, wellness centers, student service centers, and community-schools. What they all have in common is their location in or near the school, opening up access to students and their families for health and social services of all kinds. In practice, "full service" is defined by the particular community and school, with a mix of services that are needed, feasible to provide in school facilities, and acceptable to the school system and the community. State initiatives have strongly influenced the composition of school-based services.

The burst of activity, the "bubbling up" of experimentation, in communities across America reflects a growing consensus that the major institutions in society must change. It should be acknowledged, however, that simple changes in service delivery arrangements are more evident than radical changes in systems of governance. Although many educational systems are in the process of restructuring through site-based management and changes in teaching practices, this process is seldom integrated with the movement to develop comprehensive health and social services for children, youth, and families. With the exception of a few community-schools, a governing structure has yet to be devised that draws these strands together into a collaborative system. In a few unique prototypes, a new nonprofit coordinating agency or council has been organized; in others, governance is taken over by an existing agency such as the United Way or a youth bureau of city or county government. And around the country, one can find innovative schools with comprehensive services being created entirely by school personnel.

Throughout the country, community agencies are locating programs in school buildings, mainly in low-income areas both urban and rural. Close to five hundred comprehensive school-based clinics have been identified, and many more are in the planning stage. School-based health clinics currently have the capacity to provide the primary health and mental health services listed in the support services section of the full-service schools model (Exhibit 1.1). Hundreds of family resource centers (the number is unknown) provide other support services, including parent education, Head Start, after-school child care, case management, meals, crisis intervention, and whatever else is needed by parents and young children. Many community-schools are locations for evening, weekend, and summer educational enrichment and recreation programs provided by voluntary agencies. Other schools have received grants to hire coordinators to work with community agencies either to bring services into the building or to facilitate referrals.

Although we have identified many efforts that fall into the category of school-based services, only a tiny fraction of the population has access to these new programs. We do not know how many families are served by centers. About 750,000 students are currently enrolled in the 500 schools that have clinics, mostly in middle and high schools, and only 70 percent of these students are registered in the clinics. Thus, only one-tenth of the seven million youth in the highest-risk settings currently have access to health and social services in middle and high school sites. Millions of children and their families need access to the full range of programs that can be located at full-service schools.

The Need for Full-Service Schools

Of the twenty thousand senior highs, twelve thousand middle schools, and fifty thousand elementary schools in the country, how many need a center into which community agencies can bring health and social services? An estimate of the number of units needed would greatly facilitate future planning. It would probably benefit most schools to have a specific procedure for coordinating with community agencies for support services. In every school, a few students and families require special attention. Given the limited availability of new resources, however, we should start with those schools and communities where children, youth, and families have the least opportunity to succeed without a great deal of support.

Using the indicator "percent of schools in which more than 50 percent of students are eligible for a free or reduced cost lunch," we can derive a rough approximation of very needy schools. About 20 percent of all U.S. public schools fit into that category, and in 8 percent of all schools, at least 75 percent of students are eligible (and, obviously, poor).[24] Applying these indicators to schools, at least sixteen thousand clinics or centers should be organized, with highest priority given to the 6,500 schools (8 percent) where most of the students are from families of exceedingly low income.

Significant Questions

While there is clearly a strong movement toward the creation of institutions that look like full-service schools, the problem is how to put these complex systems together, how to adapt models that work, how to build documentation that they do work and are cost-effective. Many issues must be addressed if the concept of school-based services is to "go to scale" with the broad replication of demonstration models. A sense of urgency drives this new movement because of the growing needs among disadvantaged families and their children. At the same time, plans for health care reform have given a new visibility and legitimation to school-based clinics as delivery sites for primary health care. Given this boost, can we conclude that full-service schools are the wave of the future? Should every school become full-service, or is this concept only meaningful in low-income communities? If 16,000 centers is a reasonable goal, how can it be met? Is it really possible for a marriage to take place between educational systems and health and social systems to create new kinds of governance?

We begin this exploration with a look at the past. A century ago, similar questions were being asked. The society was confronted with problems of integrating millions of new immigrants while adjusting to the impacts of urbanization and industrialization. Educators, health officials, and settlement house workers came together to seek solutions, with prescriptions that are not significantly different from the proposals you will find on these pages.

School-Linked Services: The Historical Precedents

The vision of a full-service school is not a new idea. For more than one hundred years, community agencies have been bringing services into schools to augment whatever the educational system could provide to maintain health standards within the school. The pendulum has swung back and forth in regard to the assignment of responsibility for the welfare of school children. A century ago, "do-gooders" worked hard to establish the concept that health screening, dental health, mental health, food services, and family visits were all necessary adjuncts to educational programs. The history of school services is rich and well documented. In this chapter, the focus is primarily on school health services; with the recognition that excellent sources exist for further research in the other parallel areas.[1]

The Progressive Era

The story of school-based services starts in what is referred to as the Progressive Era, roughly between 1890 and 1917. During this period, the full impact of immigration, industrialization, and urbanization hit our society and forced many social changes. This early period is of particular interest now because many of the problems and proposed remedies are mirrored a century later in today's social dialogue about conditions and solutions. The powerful combination of compulsory school attendance and child labor laws pushed many immigrant children into traditional and rigid schools for the first time, schools that had been geared to the education of the wealthier classes. Because this kind of elitist education was inappropriate for disadvantaged children, many were held back and labeled as retarded. Concern was expressed that the inability of lower-class children to make it in school would lead to the creation of more juvenile delinquents. City schools particularly felt the burden of this new type of school population, most of whom came from foreign parentage. In some city schools, the class size was sixty or more; the buildings were old, poorly lit, cold, and unsanitary; and the teachers were totally ill equipped to deal with these different kinds of students.[2]

Social reformers, distressed by the poor health and the terrible living conditions of the immigrant children, initiated efforts to transform schools from places that concentrated strictly on the Three R's to places that tried to make up for the impact of poverty. Early on, the inadequate school buildings were recognized as health hazards to children because of overcrowding and lack of ventilation and heat. Journalists such as Jacob Riis and settlement house workers such as Jane Addams and Lillian Wald urged the government to play a key role in the upgrading of the health of children and youth to eliminate handicaps to successful educational achievement. The earliest health interventions came in the guise of "medical inspection"—examining immigrant children for contagious diseases. Almost all modern professional community-based services for children were established during this era of reform. This beginning of the "century of the child" produced "an endless stream of new services justified in the name of child welfare and community uplift."[3] By the end of this era, school medical inspection and dental clinics flourished in hundreds of schools.

In 1872, an epidemic of smallpox in Elmira, New York, caused the Board of Education to hire a health officer for enforcement of laws on vaccination. Following the crisis, the health officer was kept on to examine all children for diseases and defects and periodic surveys of health conditions in the school. The first citywide system of medical inspection was started in Boston in 1894. Following epidemics of diphtheria and scarlet fever, the Boston commissioner of health appointed fifty school physicians as medical visitors, one to each of the fifty school districts. They visited the schools daily and examined all the children selected by the teachers. Communicable disease rates decreased, and other cities (Chicago, New York, and Philadelphia) set up similar medical inspection systems.[4]

New York City has a rich and well-documented history of the development of school health services during the reform period. A Board of Health was first established in 1866 to deal with a cholera epidemic. The emerging health department faced incredible challenges in dealing with the health of thousands of newly arrived people living in unlit and unsanitary housing with open privies and filthy streets. The department worked to get sewers laid and streets cleaned, control the disposal of tons of horse manure, gain support for public transportation, develop public baths, and regulate prostitution and public markets.[5] Beginning in 1870, the health department began to collaborate with the Board of Education in providing vaccinations to all school children. The health department appointed assistant medical health inspectors whose duty was to visit each school and home in the tenement areas to offer free vaccinations. From that point on, whenever there was an epidemic, special funds were provided to send physicians into schools.

Support for the health department's school health programs rose and fell (and still does) with the changing of health department commissioners and the vagaries of New York City politics. Before the turn of the century, with support from the Medical Society of New York and the New York Academy of Medicine, the health department appointed a chief medical school inspector and, ultimately, 150 part-time inspectors. In 1895, schools were identified as the major source for transmission of infectious and contagious diseases. Medical inspectors were to give a daily examination to all children in school but to exclude from school only those children with communicable diseases. If treatment was necessary, care was to be provided by family physicians, hospitals, and dispensaries. In one year, hundreds of cases of diphtheria, mumps, measles, scarlet fever, and whooping cough were diagnosed, as were more than 5,000 cases of head and body lice and 1,346 cases of contagious eye diseases. This careful documentation of case finding paved the way for the development of more comprehensive programming which was to follow.

By 1898, the number of part-time school medical inspectors increased to 192, who in one year examined 140,000 students and excluded 7,600 from school. The inspectors, all physicians, worked for one hour per day making a cursory exam of all children whom teachers thought had a communicable disease. As a result of medical inspections, many children were sent home from school because of skin diseases. Lillian Wald loaned one of the Henry Street Settlement visiting nurses to the schools to visit parents to encourage them to secure treatment for their children. This led to the formation of the first school nursing service in New York in 1902. (Los Angeles's school nursing program started five years earlier.) As the demand increased, more school nurses were added to the program to treat pediculosis and minor skin diseases, reducing the number of children excluded from school. One observer remarked, "Those early nurses must have had noble spirits indeed. Nearly all of them acquired head lice in the process of inspecting children and their visits to the childrens' homes must have taken a strong stomach and an incredible faith in mankind."[6] Later, routine weekly inspection of children was turned over to school nurses, allowing the physicians to devote their time to more thorough exams. The latter involved testing eyes, ears, nose, and throat; checking for cardiac, pulmonary, glandular, and skin disorders; and noting the child's nutritional status. Nurses were much better able to assure follow-up of identified defects; the rate increased from 6 percent to 43 percent treated in the year after nurses began doing the routine inspections.[7]

Around that time, a group of ophthalmologists examined a large number of school children and discovered that 12 percent had contagious eye diseases and 4 percent trachoma. To deal with the trachoma, the health department opened an old hospital on an emergency basis to provide surgical treatment and outpatient care. New York was the first American city to establish a formal connection between its school medical inspection program and a hospital. During the same period, several physicians volunteered to perform operations to remove tonsils and adenoids on the school premises. In 1906, eighty-three children were operated on at PS 75. After a rumor was spread that the school doctors were slitting the throats of school children as a prelude to a general massacre of Jews, two thousand parents stormed the school. The riots were attributed to rumor mongering among the "snip doctors" who were in private practice to remove tonsils or adenoids for 25 to 50 cents and resented the health department doing the work free of charge.

Reformers used research findings effectively to develop advocacy for school health programs for needy children. In 1906, the Board of Estimate voted $250,000 for school health, enough to pay for examination of all children in Manhattan but not the other boroughs. In 1908, the New York City health department organized its Division of Child Hygiene to handle school inspection and a summer corps that included the 192 medical inspectors and 195 nurses and administrators. Just before World War I, New York City could claim a model school health inspection system. In a typical school of 2,500 students, a special doctor and nurse were assigned to work with teachers and parents, with a view toward identifying and correcting defects and decreasing communicable diseases. In addition to specialized dental and eye clinics, the school offered special instruction to the blind, mentally deficient, and physically handicapped, and had open-air classrooms on the roof for children with weak lungs. This was the height of school health in New York City, but all of this was too costly. Toward the end of the Progressive Era, resistance to providing health services to children in schools began to build on all sides. When the school superintendent suggested an eye exam for every child and free glasses, his proposal was greeted with cries of socialism. School medical inspection in New York City was swept away in a wave of political turmoil and social neglect and did not reemerge as an issue until the Depression.

Other cities and states experienced similar developments in school health programs. By 1911, medical inspection was required in 300 city school systems, and school nurses were employed in 102 cities.[8] Nine states had mandatory school health inspection laws, and in ten states, local agencies were permitted to hire school health inspectors. In some cities, a "squad system" incorporated a team of physicians who moved from school to school examining all kindergartners and first-graders. Social reformers and settlement workers appealed to health departments and school boards to create new free treatment to aid students not being served in the private sector. Typically, poor urban school children got complete medical exams at regular intervals. Physicians and nurses were brought in to inspect children daily for evidence of contagious diseases. They found many noninfectious ailments—hearing and vision problems, malnutrition, rickets, physical handicaps, mental retardation, and emotional illness—but the most common complaints were dental caries and other oral diseases.

Many early studies made the connection between health and education. In 1911, the American Medical Association (AMA) and the National Education Association (NEA) formed the Joint Commission on School Health Policies as a means of marshaling the power of the professions of education and medicine to aid in developing and expanding health education in schools. A later report made by a joint committee of these two organizations discussed factors influencing changes in school health services, including the shift in educational emphasis at the turn of the century from subject matter to child development, rapid expansion and specialization in social services, discovery of the linkages between poverty and educational need, and the expansion of public health programs. The AMA supported school-based health services throughout the Progressive Era and did not succumb to negative pressures from private physicians until the 1920s.

The early child advocates, such as Jane Addams, Florence Kelley, and Lillian Wald, were particularly concerned about child labor and the importance of compulsory education. They were influential in persuading Theodore Roosevelt to organize the first White House Conference on Children in 1909 to address the problems of children who "make no trouble but are simply unfortunate."[9] Recommendations from this "Conference on the Care of Dependent Children" gave strong impetus to the movement for mothers' pensions (ultimately Aid to Families with Dependent Children) and resulted in the creation of the Childrens' Bureau (CB) in 1912. It took six years to pass the legislation creating the CB, calling specifically for research on child welfare, infant mortality, child employment, and neglect. This unique bureau responsible for child well-being in the federal government was never authorized to provide services. Even this agency was opposed by some who thought it threatened the sanctity of the family and by others because it shifted responsibility for children's health and welfare from the states to the federal government. Later White House Conferences on Children were held every decade up until 1970, but none had the impact of the first.

After the Progressive period, a distinction was made between the practice of medicine (diagnosis and treatment of disease) and the provision of school health services (screening, health education, and school environment).

Between the Wars

The innovation and social concern of the Progressive period was abruptly halted by World War I. The country was overtaken by a conservative sweep and reaction against government intervention at any level. The "Red scares" in the early twenties and the regressive administrations of Harding and Coolidge put the damper on further development of children's services. Many school-based health and social services were under attack as an opening wedge to socialism. Nevertheless, in 1921, the Maternal and Infancy Care Act, the oldest and most important federal child health initiative in our nation's erratic history, was passed by Congress. In keeping with the temper of the times, the act was opposed by the AMA as an "imported socialistic scheme," and by 1929, the legislation was allowed to lapse.

While this period was politically and socially conservative, a much wider range of individual behavior was considered acceptable. With the acquisition of the vote by women, freer access to birth control, rising interest in sexuality, and popularization of Freud and psychoanalysis, the "Roaring Twenties" offered sharp contrasts between public and private behaviors. Immigration came to a dead stop as a result of restrictive legislation in 1921, 1924, and 1927. Yet even during the twenties, significant contributions were made to the movement to bring health and social services into the schools. Lewis Terman, of IQ test fame, the coauthor of the leading text published in 1929 on educational hygiene, called for a greatly expanded role of medical personnel in schools to preserve the child from all dangers inherent in the environment of poor families. Earlier he asserted, "The school must be the educational center, the social center, and the hygiene center of the community in which it is located—a hub from which will radiate influences for social betterment in many lives."[10] Challenging the medical profession's concern about "socialism," Terman maintained that supporting free medical and dental clinics with public dollars was no different from supporting public education. But the AMA rejected this reform ideology and launched a contentious campaign to discourage the medical profession and the society at large from supporting any proposals that might threaten private fee-for-service medicine.

The frenetic twenties rapidly led to the dreary thirties, culminating in the Depression years. By the end of this period, the country experienced another dramatic shift in the pendulum between federal intervention and private control with the passage of Roosevelt's package of legislation. The Social Security Act, approved in 1935, gave grants to states for Maternal and Child Health (MCH) programs, making funds available for child welfare and the handicapped children's program. Aid to Dependent Children (welfare) was also created under this significant act. Much of the MCH funding was used to set up pre- and postnatal and child health clinics for low-income families (and became, as we will see, a major source for supporting school-based clinics.)

Under the Works Progress Administration (WPA), unemployed health workers were made available to emergency nursery schools for screening and to other schools to test hearing with audiometers. By the 1930s, twenty-six states had laws related to school medical inspection, a development hastened by the discovery of many physical defects among World War I recruits. By this time, the allied AMA and NEA shifted positions and strongly discouraged delivery of any treatment services in schools.[11] Direct service of any kind was frowned on unless no local practitioners were threatened or the service was just not lucrative. During this period, the acceptable form of intervention became health education and promotion. Didactic presentations about health were not threatening to the private sector, and some of the materials used fit well with the avant-garde educational pedagogy of the time. For example, cartoon characters were used to tell stories about health promotion, cleanliness, and tooth care.

Attempts to provide direct health services on school sites were terminated in many parts of the country because of funding cutbacks, opposition from the medical profession, changing concepts about the responsibility of the schools for meeting the social needs of children, the upgrading of the role of the school nurse, and the availability of collaborative arrangements with outside medical providers.[12] School systems maintained medical directors, but they were largely responsible for making sure that school nurses did their jobs and that immunizations were completed. According to Kort, school health services during the twenties and thirties were limited to health inspection, assessment, and first aid.[13] Only those children whose parents were too poor to pay would be examined by school physicians, and even then one medical group complained that school physical exams were an indication of a trend toward "state medicine." In any case, school exams uncovered few defects, and even if problems were identified, they were rarely referred for medical treatment.[14] It was suggested that priority be given to providing services to preschoolers, before the problems set in.

During this period, the medical profession staked out the claim for the provision of all health care through the medium of private practice. Their view was that the provision of preventive services in schools should supplement their practices but not substitute for private care or compete with it. The regulations governing schools tended to institutionalize this dichotomy, requiring a strict separation between preventive and curative services. The provision of health and other ancillary services received low priority, giving way to the emerging doctrine that the only purpose of schools was to educate. Back to the Three R's.

Nevertheless, by 1923, almost all of the major cities surveyed by the American Child Health Association had established nursing services in their schools, and in many, physicians still conducted some physical examinations.[15] However, most (70 percent) of the school health services were administered by boards of education, representing a shift away from public health services. Child advocates believed that school boards were less easily influenced by political pressures than were local health departments run by city-appointed politicians. Annette Lynch, director of school programs in the state of Pennsylvania, asserted that "institutionalization placed a millstone of incredible deadening weight around the neck of school health. Health professionals carried out (menial) tasks, while persons without any health training made school health policy and program decisions.... School nurses were denied the smallest change in, or expansion of, their professional role."[16] While health departments continued to claim that their personnel were the most appropriate providers of school health services, they lost out to state laws that limited school health services to health appraisal, emergency care, and counseling. The American School Physicians Association, formed in 1927, became the American School Health Association in 1933 and shifted its emphasis to health education and school nursing.

In 1936, a resurgence of public health services in New York City schools was attributed to the reform government of Fiorello LaGuardia and the emergence of federal grants. The Bureau of Child Hygiene and School Health merged with the Bureau of District Health Administration and was able to employ 493 half-time physicians to examine all children entering school for the first time, students in the eighth grade, and those specifically referred by their teachers. The bureau began working more closely with the very active parent association and recruited more than 2,500 mothers to volunteer their services as health registrars in the schools.

During the Depression, the idea of the "community-school," first proposed during the Progressive Era, began to gain increased attention. The term at that time referred to a school in which both the curriculum and the ancillary activities were designed to interact with the needs of the community.[17] Rather than developing as an outgrowth of either health or social services, community-schools were a response to a perceived need for developing additional recreational and educational outlets for youth and adults who lived in the school-community. According to Barbara Hunt, common characteristics of a community-school were the use of the school building as a center all year round for leisure-time activities and intellectual stimulation; willingness to accommodate space requirements for health clinics, counseling services, and employment and legal aid centers; provision of opportunities for citizens to get involved with solving community problems; and facilitation of open communication between the school and the community. As Hunt says, "it had something for everyone."

One version of community schools focused on school curriculum, involving students with the "real-life" community through course work, field trips, and visiting experts. Community job experience was made available to students as well. The value of community improvement was heavily stressed, along with projects that could engage parents and children in working together.

The most frequently cited model was located in Flint, Michigan. By 1935, fifty school buildings had been designated as part of the Flint Community Schools initiative, fostered by the Charles Mott Foundation. These "lighted schools" were supposed to respond to such problems as poor health, unemployment, and poverty during the Depression years. At first they concentrated on after-school and summer recreation, later on health and nutrition services. Eventually, this movement became a vast adult education program, with 1,200 course offerings of every description.

The most idealistic view of the community-schools saw the school as an agent of social change, "the social nexus for a whole range of reforms to change the quality of life."[18] But the social change goal was rarely achieved, and the concept that emerged was primarily one of using the school as a shared facility. Observers attributed this failure to the tendency of researchers to "lay on" concepts without adequate involvement of either the community or the school staff. Much of the community-schools ideology survives today in the design of alternative schools and new versions of the model.

After World War II

If the problems of urbanization and immigration set off the first wave of a movement toward school-based health services at the turn of the century, a second wave was created after World War II following analyses of the high rejection rate among Selective Service registrants. In 1944, William Schmidt, a consultant to the Children's Bureau, urged the American Public Health Association and the American School Health Association to support health services in schools to remedy the situation.[19] The rejection rate among eighteen- and nineteen-year-olds was 25 percent, higher among rural, low-income, and minority youth. Most of the problems identified (eye and ear conditions, emotional problems, cardiac, skeletal, and neurological conditions, hernia, syphilis, underweight, and tuberculosis) could have been identified and treated long before military service. Schmidt found this clear evidence that health supervision and adequate medical care from infancy throughout childhood and adolescence were required. While acknowledging the need for early intervention, he specifically advocated a high school health plan that included needs assessments, services provided directly to students without parents being present, beefed-up health education, preemployment physicals, continuity of care, and follow-up of referrals. His model, to be developed in close association with the local health agency, called for one physician and two nurses working with individuals and in classrooms for each school of three thousand students. He pointed out that the annual cost of $3 per student was minimal when related to the median annual educational expenditure per pupil in 1944—$90![20] Schmidt recognized that there were not enough resources to establish these high-quality services in every school and recommended that the model first be implemented in the schools with the most needs (rather than targeting individuals within all schools).

These Selective Service findings stimulated no less than twelve new bills affecting school health submitted to the Seventy-ninth Congress in 1945 (none passed that year or later). Leona Baumgartner, long an advocate for children's health services, portrayed this period as one that shifted from mass health efforts to building programs around individual children. "The new aim of the school is to fit the child for living and if medicine has contributions to make to positive health—then educator, medical staff, and the home must work together."[21] She advocated closer coordination of whatever medical inspection program went on in schools with treatment facilities and private physicians. In her view, school health programs should encompass mental hygiene, and children should be taught to assume more responsibility for their own health. She described schools emerging all over the country where principals; classroom teachers; teachers of health, physical education, and nutrition; school nurses; physicians; janitors; guidance experts; cafeteria managers; and parents were joining together to plan health programs. Baumgartner's list of "players" gives evidence of the expansion of the school personnel roster beginning in the 1940s and the emergence of the concept of school health planning councils.

During this time, a significant demonstration project—the Astoria Plan—was launched to evaluate the effectiveness of a new approach to school health services. According to Harold Jacobziner, a prominent pediatrician, an earlier evaluation of the New York City school health services found that less than 22 percent of the defects identified by health inspection had been corrected: "In the constant search for defects, the child was almost lost in the shuffle."[22] The routine exams of the past had little effect without guidance to the parents, the teachers, or the individual child and without coordination between educators and health workers. In this new model, the annual physical exams (medical inspections) by schools or private physicians were replaced with only one medical exam conducted at the time of entrance into school, a parent's presence at the exam, annual (or more frequent) conferences between teachers and school nurses, and longitudinal record keeping on each child. The conferences were used to identify students' problems and select those cases that would be followed up with referral to a school physician for diagnosis and referral. A public health nurse actively assisted parents in gaining access to the treatment agency or private physician where the case would then be treated. Each teacher was trained to keep a "pupil's health record," logging in observations to be used in the conference. A medical record was kept in the medical office for use in conferences and for referral and follow-up. Considerable effort was put into training public health physicians, nurses, and the teachers who were central to the case finding.

After being tested in a few schools, the Astoria Plan was adopted by the entire New York City system and in many other cities. Evaluations found the system to be very effective in improving services, follow-up, coordination, parent involvement, and record keeping. One of the shortcomings noted was overreliance on teachers as the primary case finders, who might note only obvious defects. Jacobziner was concerned that of nine hundred thousand students in the system, only eighty thousand were identified for screenings, and of those, thirty-seven thousand were referred for treatment. He recommended two additional routine examinations during the elementary school years to insure a higher rate of case finding. He also noted that the occurrence of unidentified defects among students who were examined by private physicians was much higher than among those examined by school physicians.

Jacobziner concluded that his predictions for the future might "sound visionary, improbable, or at best unrealistic" in light of a report from the American Academy of Pediatrics that in 1946 more than 50 percent of the counties in the U.S. had no system of medical examinations in their public elementary schools and over one-third had neither medical nor nursing services.[23] Someday, he reflected, all children in all schools would have full and adequate health supervision, with attention to their physical, mental, emotional, and social needs. Every school would have a doctor and nurse present daily, and school health services would be integrated with public and nonprofit community health services.

Alfred Yankauer, a public health administrator and later editor of the *American Journal of Public Health*, contributed significantly to the literature on school-based health services with seven articles published between 1947 and 1962. A series of evaluations of the Astoria Plan in New York and other programs in Rochester and Albany focused on the issue of the annual medical examination.[24] He demonstrated in various studies that elementary school students showed little evidence of illness and that after an initial physical exam, defects could be determined just as well by teachers and nurses as long as attention was paid to consistent observation and careful record keeping. In this model, physicians' time would be freed up for the most severely handicapped students and those with emotional disorders that parents could not or would not deal with. Yankauer proposed that parents of elementary school children, after careful orientation, be required to fill in an annual health appraisal questionnaire and that junior and senior high school students (not their parents) do the same. This work is still cited as evidence that an annual physical exam for children is not a cost-effective intervention and that case finding can be done more efficiently using other techniques such as teacher nurse conferences and annual needs assessments.

By the 1960s, the federal role in the delivery of child health services was well established, although there was never a consensus (and there still is none) about who should get what services and how they should be paid for. In 1961, a National Institute of Child Health and Human Development was added to the National Institutes of Health to conduct more basic research than that produced by the Children's Bureau. The short Kennedy administration focused heavily on mental retardation, shepherding the passage of important legislation in 1963 with virtually no opposition. Funds were authorized for maternal health programs to lower the rate of infant mortality and increase access to early intervention.

The Johnson administration was responsible for a host of significant legislation that shapes our current delivery systems today. Most important were the 1965 amendments to the Social Security Act creating Medicaid and Medicare. In addition, new kinds of maternal and child health efforts were formulated, called Children and Youth (C&Y) Projects, to develop systems of comprehensive care through grants to local agencies such as hospitals and medical schools. These funds could be used for screening, diagnosis, preventive services, treatment, correction of defects, and aftercare, both medical and dental. However, according to Gilbert Steiner, C&Y just barely survived as the "ignored stepchild," a fact he attributes to "the inability of the child health cause to attract a fair share of attention in an environment dominated by complex issues of social security, unemployment insurance and public assistance."[25] Nevertheless, the concept of the C&Y grants was translated into a vast new Medicaid initiative in 1967 called EPSDT, Early Periodic Screening Diagnosis and Treatment, for all Medicaid-eligible children.

The 1960s "War on Poverty," administered by the Office of Economic Opportunity (OEO), produced an alternative delivery system to public health departments in the creation of specially funded centers for community health, migrant health, family planning, and mental health. Head Start programs were initiated across the country in low-income communities. Project grants were created that went directly to community-based agencies. By 1975, with the exception of Head Start, which moved to the Office of Child Development in the Department of Health Education and Welfare (DHEW, Education, became a separate department shortly thereafter), all of these OEO health programs were folded into the vastly expanding and increasingly complex public health service. Responsibility for child health services was spread across the giant bureaucracy, and in fact, no central locus could be identified for child health issues. And school health was completely buried, with only a small office in the Education agency.

The Elementary and Secondary Act (ESEA) was another invention of the 1960s, for the first time providing funds for schools with disadvantaged populations. In its earliest incarnation, funds could be used for salaries for school nurses and physicians, but by 1974, school health was downgraded in the legislation. During the Nixon administration, child advocates tried (once again) to pass a Comprehensive Child Development Act calling for community services and day-care centers. Nixon's veto message decried using the national government to favor "communal approaches to child-rearing over family-centered approaches."[26] In 1975, the Office of Education funded a few demonstration projects that provided medical and dental screening, nutrition, and social and mental health services. In the same year, the Education for All Handicapped Children Act was passed, which guaranteed education and related services for all children from preschool to age twenty-one and set the stage for special education (now called the Individuals with Disabilities Education Act).

Throughout the 1960s, the nation was caught up in turmoil surrounding our involvement in the Vietnam War. Many young people were affected by this issue and began "acting out," demonstrating their sense of alienation from the establishment goals of the country. Different life-styles proliferated. Sex and drugs emerged as both symbols of independence and grave threats to health. Because young people were so estranged from their families, a new kind of health service evolved built around "free clinics," comprehensive, community-based, largely volunteer-run shelters.[27] Schools were not perceived to be places that would respect the confidentiality of a "turned off" generation; in any case, many young people had dropped out of schools and taken to the streets.

Forerunners of Today's School-Based Programs

We have unique insights into the 1970s because of a tiny volume, *400 Navels: The Future of School Health in America*. Written by Godfrey Cronin and William Young, it describes the development of one of the first modern school-based clinic programs, at the Posen-Robbins Elementary School District in suburban Cook County, Illinois.[28] Posen-Robbins was a very disadvantaged neighborhood where a new school administrator in the early 1970s brought in an array of services such as free lunches, mobile libraries, and school remediation. In collaboration with the authors of the book and with the approval of the school board, this district opened several clinics in elementary schools. A model medical unit was carved out of old kindergarten space, with a waiting area, secretarial space, two treatment rooms, a small laboratory, and storage. The program was operated by two full-time school nurse practitioners, four health aides, a lab technician, and four outreach workers. Medical backup was provided by two pediatricians from a neighboring hospital who came into the clinic twice a week. Arrangements were made for them to refer to medical specialists at the university medical school and hospital. A nonprofit corporation was set up to administer this program to avoid the school's bureaucratic issues of malpractice, tenure, certification, and union membership.

The Posen-Robbins program was modeled on the experience of three other programs that preceded it, in Cambridge, Massachusetts; Galveston, Texas; and Hartford, Connecticut. The Cambridge program, started by Philip Porter, brought together efforts of the Cambridge Department of Health (where he was director of Maternal and Child Health) and Cambridge Hospital. Comprehensive services were located in four schools and one municipal building adjacent to a school. Porter trained and employed fifteen pediatric nurse practitioners, who staffed the clinics along with social workers. This model demonstrated that it was possible to centralize administrative functions while decentralizing services.

The Hartford project developed school health service models in one urban and one suburban school. The city model delivered primary health and dental health care to all students, utilizing specially trained school nurse practitioners who had previously been school nurses. Medical backup was supplied by the University of Connecticut. In the other Hartford school, with less need among the children (and more concern about competition with the private sector), services were primarily for health screening and referral. Philip Nader, another pioneer in school health services, attempted to link the health screening done by the Galveston School District (of which he was medical director) to the primary health care that could be obtained at the hospital of the University of Texas Medical Branch. This program relied heavily on new categories of personnel; in addition to nurse practitioners, there were health aides to assist in the clinic and ten "home-school agents," trained outreach workers to act as child and family advocates.

The four innovative school-based health programs were all funded at one time or another by the Robert Wood Johnson Foundation, a very early supporter of the concept of integration of services at school sites. A new wave of interest in school-based health services programs resulted in the creation of a new category of health professional, the school nurse practitioner, pioneered by George Silver at the University of Colorado. These school nurse practitioners were given training for one year beyond their baccalaureate nursing degree to gain skills in conducting physical examinations, diagnosis, treatment, and patient management. In Seattle, with a history of school nursing that went back to 1908, school nurses were routinely employed in giving inoculations, conducting hearing and vision screening, checking for orthopedic defects and skin diseases, treating allergies, and dispensing medicine to students if authorized by a physician. After retraining as nurse practitioners, the same staff were able to conduct in-depth assessments, work in special education programs, and give more advanced health care to students. By 1979, an estimated thirty thousand school nurses were employed in the U.S., one for every three school buildings. Throughout the country, about five hundred full-time school physicians were employed, but half were purely administrators in large districts. In one-third of the then 16,500 school districts, public health personnel worked in schools.

At the end of the 1970s, despite these pioneer programs and innovative developments, one observer, Annette Lynch, complained to the American School Health Association that "there is no health in school health!"[29] Instead, the movement was perceived as bogged down in poor communications between health professionals and educators, exacerbated by "the incomplete, garbled, and irrational message transmitted by health professionals from the health field." Evidence for this complaint included the fact that at the highest national levels (then DHEW), no staff was committed to working on school health, and this was true in most state health departments, university departments of pediatrics and nursing, and boards of medical specialists. It was widely believed that school health should be implemented primarily through educational activities. Advocates for a broader view defined the limitations of school health as a static system of input activities (often legally mandated) with little relevance to the needs of students—for example, continuation of useless screening exams and referral of students to nonexistent community resources. Lynch proposed a school health system that paid attention to gathering data on needs, using the data to make decisions about what services were needed, and then providing the services. She endorsed the concept of expanding the role of the school nurse to that of school nurse practitioner as the key to developing her ideal.

Many objections were raised to the idea of school-based health services in both the health professions and the educational establishment. The AMA spokesperson on health education observed, "Schools are not proper settings in which to practice medicine. That should be done in a hospital clinic, or doctor's office where you have the proper staff and equipment. Children should be treated by their family physician or, if they don't have one, at a clinic or through Medicaid. The schools can fill a health role by having nurses, teachers, or technicians provide screening for vision and hearing."[30]

In the late 1970s, Cronin and Young asked John Marshall, then director of community health services for DHEW, whether "we might wake up 20 years from now and find health programs fully established in all our schools." Marshall replied,"If you had asked me five years ago...I would have said, yes, because it looked as though schools were branching out, increasingly teaching kids to be socially responsible and getting into new areas. But during the last few years, there has been a reaction and increasingly schools are going back to basics. School systems... [look toward]... strict disciplinarians with 40 kids in the class and never mind about the fuzzy-minded liberal who's worried about their development and wants only 25 kids per class, with a reading specialist, a science specialist and now a health specialist."

In 1976, the Carter administration moved into Washington with high hopes of improving conditions for children and families. DHEW Secretary Joseph Califano told participants of a National School Health Conference that improved school health programs would be a key element in the comprehensive national child health policy of the future.[31] "As Secretary of Health, Education and Welfare, I will assist in bridging the historic gap between health professionals and educators.... At least at the federal level, I will see that our federal agencies in health and education reinforce what you are planning at the state and community levels." He pointed toward Head Start as a model of integrated services and mentioned the need for school nutrition, driver education and safety, and juvenile justice programs to be included in expanded school health programs. "The challenge before us will be to pull all of these worthwhile efforts together.... The President is interested in exploring these possibilities for using schools to provide a full range of services to children and families, including health and social services as well as education."[32]

Participants at the conference responded to the statement by Secretary Califano with a call for the establishment of an entity within DHEW to support school health programs by collecting and disseminating data, providing a central contact point, and identifying more effective federal policies and programs. They also called for the development of state administrative authorities for school health to stimulate planning. It is interesting to note that no one called for additional funding. In 1980, President Reagan brought with him a giant wave of budget cuts in human service programs. Funding for

Maternal and Child Health services, which might have been able to support school health programs, was reduced 30 percent, giving states more responsibility and less money to take care of what turned out be growing numbers of dependent families.

Reviewing this situation in the mid 1980s, Michael Sedlak and Stephen Schlossman expressed regrets that the movement to create comprehensive school health services would never overcome the pressure from private physicians to limit the scope of school services to minimal screening and referral. "The prospects for reorganizing the delivery of services to children via the schools seem slight indeed."[33]

Moving into the 1990s

Over the years, the supply of services within schools has been turned on and off. The demand has fluctuated, reflecting the social environment for families. In periods of poverty, unrest, and disadvantage, service provision in schools has risen. In periods of relative affluence and in the absence of new immigrant populations, provision has been limited. The private sector, which authorizes the supply through policy control, has been willing to allow public agencies to go into schools during crisis periods (epidemics, economic depressions) but has withdrawn approval whenever school services loomed as competition. This is most evident among physicians whose sporadic presence in school has mirrored the fluctuating approval of the American Medical Association.

The mode of delivery of school health services has reflected the roller coaster of the political situation compounded by the state of the art of medical technology. The earliest approach, health inspection, responding to the fear of contagious diseases, focused on providing immunizations and excluding diseased children from school. With the availability of mass vision and hearing tests, the model evolved into screening and health assessments, seeking to identify defects among targeted populations. The work could be divided between nurses, who could screen and home-visit, and physicians, who could diagnose and treat, following up on defects. Schools became referral agencies for physicians in private practice. Control of school health services shifted from public health agencies, which had a commitment to case finding and treatment, to school systems, in which health services had no priority.

In the thirties, educational psychology took over, and the rhetoric began to focus on the whole child. The strategy shifted from treatment to prevention, from case finding to universal interventions, from medical care to health education. It was believed that school-based annual physical examinations were not cost-effective and could be replaced with careful observations by teachers and nurses. All that was left in the school was the nursing office, with first aid and referral for emergency care, and teachers, who would be trained to implement health education curricula. And in some states, school nurses were prohibited even from laying on hands and were relegated to the role of minimal health screening. In any case, schools were for educating youth, not for nurturing, and surely not for treatment.

During the final decade of this century, the pendulum is swinging far back to school-based programs as schools struggle to educate children who can only be educated if they also receive a wide array of health and social services. Currently, the AMA, as well as every other major national social and health organization, supports the concept that community agencies should bring services into schools. This does not imply that the arrangements that produce collaborative school-community programs are easily organized and implemented, but merely that there is little opposition in the private sector to developing innovative responses to what are increasingly viewed as crisis situations. Along with these changes in perceptions about roles, there is a growing demand for "integration" of services, reducing the fragmentation of existing service systems for families. Many of the new "family-centered" programs are being placed in schools to facilitate "one-stop shopping" for whatever families and their children need to overcome the enormous odds with which they are confronted in disadvantaged communities. A new vision of full-service schools is emerging a hundred years after similar efforts were made to bring the settlement house into the school. Today, we encounter the same rhetoric about the crises confronting families, the school as the only viable institution for reaching the children, and the possibilities for development of comprehensive services in the school building. Many separate health, welfare, and educational initiatives have been launched to address the problems of children and youth. Our nation still has no child health policy, and school health still has little priority. This is a rapidly changing scene, however, as will become evident in the chapters that follow.

3

▲▲▲

Support Services and Quality Education:
A Range of Possibilities

The contemporary vision of a full-service school did not emerge out of thin air; each component has been implemented in one school or another, and, in fact, the body of knowledge about successful programs is extensive. In almost every one of the nation's eighty-two thousand public schools (and in many private schools as well), one or more community agency is bringing some form of activity or service into the school.

In this chapter, we get down to specifics and review a number of existing programs grouped under broad categories of services that can be put together to make a full-service school (as in Exhibit 1.1). Particular emphasis is placed on support services, including health, mental health, family, recreation, and culture. However, we also address quality education, with a brief review of school-remediation and dropout-prevention programs and school-restructuring efforts. Finally, we turn to comprehensive one-stop multicomponent efforts illustrative of the concept of the full-service school. In general, we have employed two criteria in selecting examples: (1) one or more services is supplied in a school by an entity other than the school district; (2) funding for a program within a school is not derived primarily from the school district budget.

"School-based services" implies services *not* ordinarily offered by school systems but brought into schools by outside agencies. This definition does not hold in every case. In at least one community, Chelsea, Massachusetts, the entire school system is managed by a team placed in the schools by an outside agency, Boston University.[1] In other places, the entire school system is being "contracted out." The Baltimore Board of Education has arranged with a private industry, Education Alternatives, Inc., to administer nine of its public schools, expecting them to produce better educational outcomes for the same amount of money currently spent.[2] But these unusual attempts to solve the problems of education in disadvantaged communities go beyond the scope of this chapter, especially since the results to date have not confirmed the validity of turning school systems over to outside agencies. In a limited number of places, complex ancillary health and social services such as school-based clinics are supported and run directly by school systems. In many programs, school-employed teachers and other personnel are trained by outside agencies to administer programs in schools.

The second criterion, funding from outside of the regular school budget, is also somewhat ambiguous since some ancillary programs are supported by government grants directly to school districts, such as Chapter 1 (the Elementary and Secondary Education Act), the largest government program that seeks to reduce the inequities between advantaged and disadvantaged children. The Department of Education distributes more than $6 billion annually to school districts with needy populations for special programs.

A distinction has been made by others between school-based and school-linked services.[3] According to the Packard Foundation definition, school-linked services are provided through a collaboration among schools, health care providers, and social service agencies;

schools are among the central participants in the planning and governance; and services are provided at or are coordinated by personnel at the school or a site near the school. By this definition, some programs are placed near but not inside of school buildings, either by program design or because of space shortages within the school building. Most of the programs featured in this book are school-based, located at school sites. This chapter provides the evidence for the argument that significant programs of many types can be brought into schools at little or no added costs to the school system.

Support Services

Somewhere in the United States, it is possible to find an example of almost every category of human services located in a school. These programs serve not only students but everyone from infants to grandparents. The schools and agencies cited in this section were selected from hundreds of programs to provide a broad overview of the range of possibilities.

Health Services

We have observed that the responsibility for health services in schools has been left primarily to the school nurses. Only recently have additional arrangements for the provision of primary health care in schools been made through community agencies. School-based teams, dental clinics, and school-based clinics are among the most important emerging components of full-service schools.

School Nurses. Most school nurses are employed directly by school districts, but in a few states, such as Arkansas, the health department employs the nurses and places them in schools. Today, only about 15 percent of schools employ full-time nurses, a proportion that has dramatically shrunk following budget cuts during the 1980s.[4] Only thirteen states mandate school nursing. School nursing functions are limited by state laws (different in every state) to providing hearing, vision, and scoliosis screening; checking attendance; and keeping immunization and other health records. Most school nurses are prohibited from distributing prescription drugs, and some are not even allowed to hand out aspirin or other analgesics.

Increasingly, in the diminishing numbers of school systems that employ school nurses, the nurses are being integrated into broader programs as members of teams with psychologists and social workers. When a school-based clinic is initiated, the school nurse is often incorporated into the protocol as the central triage nurse, who assesses each client and determines what course of action should be taken by the other staff members. The University of Colorado Nursing School has instituted a program to retrain school nurses to become school nurse practitioners who can staff primary care clinics. Leaders in the nursing field believe that school nursing is in transition from "Band-Aids" to emphasis on preventive medicine, counseling, community outreach, and teaching. Still, in many disadvantaged communities, the school nurse remains the critical link between the school and the family.

School Team Model. Many schools organize their pupil personnel staff by teams, with many different configurations. Ideally, the school social worker, guidance counselor, nurse, and psychologist meet with the principal and selected teachers. The team reviews "cases" and works together to make sure that the needs of the students and their families are being met. One might think that school systems would be able to implement this kind of program without outside help given the trend toward the hiring of pupil personnel staff. David Tyack has shown that, despite the growing shift toward academic concerns in recent years, the proportion of school staff who are *not* teachers has grown significantly, from 30 percent in the 1950s to 48 percent in 1986.[5] He believes that schools are increasingly becoming "multipurpose agencies" in spite of turning away from the antipoverty fervor of the 1960s.

In actual practice, many school systems do not have the funds to employ pupil personnel staff. Budget cuts, particularly in disadvantaged communities, have made huge dents in these categories. If social workers and psychologists are employed by school systems, they are often shared between schools and cannot possibly work in teams because of the demands on their time. One solution to this problem in needy areas has been for outside agencies to put together teams and relocate them in schools.

In Catawba County, North Carolina, county government has assumed the responsibility for providing school services through a team. The Public Health Department contributes a nurse, Social Services provides a social worker, and a psychologist is supplied by the Department of Mental Health.[6] This team is placed in an office in a school and serves an elementary school, a middle school, and a high school. A second team has been organized to serve three elementary schools and one middle school. The lead team member is the psychologist; the team does intensive work with individual children, conducts home visits, follows up on attendance problems, refers students to the health department for medical care, and works closely with teachers singly and in groups.

The program is managed by the Public Health Department, which acts as the home base where records are kept, supervision is maintained, and a health clinic is located. This program was created jointly by the county manager and the school superintendent and is supported by county tax dollars. The success of this effort was attributed to starting with what the school system perceived as the problem—in this case, head lice. The first component was the implementation of a "no-nit" policy whereby health department staff screened and treated all students. After that, the team was free to work on other problems identified by the school staff, particularly teen pregnancy, truancy, and smoking.

School-Based Dental Clinics. As pointed out in Chapter Two, many schools had established dental clinics earlier in the century, but very few remain in existence today. Yet school-based health staff frequently report dental health needs as pressing; many disadvantaged youth have no access to a family dentist. A few school-based clinics have added dental services to their protocols. Typically, these sites have dental chairs where dentists from outside the school system can come in and see patients. The clinic in Pinkston High School, Dallas, incorporates a fully equipped dental suite and a full-time dentist on staff. When a new elementary school was built in Bridgeport, Connecticut, a large medical suite was included in the building plans, and one of the offices in the new clinic is equipped and used solely for dentistry. In what may be the most exemplary dental program in the nation, the Board of Health of the city of Beverly, Massachusetts, has maintained a school-based dental clinic for underprivileged children for seventy-six years. Each child is expected to pay 10 cents a visit. If the clinic exam reveals more complex needs (extractions, orthodontia), the student is referred to local dentists who complete the work free or at a reduced fee. The clinic also supports dental health education presented by a dental hygienist, who visits 135 classrooms annually. The clinic has a singing group called "The Merry Molar Singers" and a "Clean Tooth Club."

In a survey of eighty-seven school districts selected as models for comprehensive health programs conducted by the National School Boards Association in 1992, about half indicated some type of dental services.[7] A follow-up survey (with a 35 percent response rate) showed that most of the action was located in elementary schools. Some three-fourths of schools with dental services provided screening on site; about one-fourth also offered teeth cleaning, and one-tenth gave fluoride rinses or sealants for prevention of tooth decay. Actual treatment was provided in more than one-third of the schools with dental programs, and education for dental health was offered in two-thirds. Toothbrushes and fluoride toothpaste were distributed in several schools. Local dentists gave presentations or contributed their services at schools or accepted referrals with a low fee or none. In some communities, the Kiwanis Club was active in providing funds.

School-Based Health Centers. One response to the growing health needs of students has been the development of school-based health centers, most frequently in inner city high schools but increasingly in middle and elementary schools. A school-based health center is defined here as one or more rooms located within a school building or on the property of the school and designated as a place where students can go and receive primary health services. This center or clinic is more than a school nursing station; students are able to receive health services there not generally available in school, such as physical examinations, treatment for minor injuries and illnesses, screening for sexually transmitted diseases, pregnancy tests, and psychosocial counseling. Services are provided by nurse practitioners, health aides, outreach workers, social workers, and physicians. Most of these practitioners are employed by one or more local agencies: health departments, hospitals, medical schools, or social service agencies. Chapter Four presents a description of school-based health clinic organization and services.

Family Health Centers. A variant of school-based clinics proposed by Judith Igoe, a leader in school nursing, emphasizes the family and "empowers consumers by increasing ownership of their own health care."[8] These family health centers, endorsed by the American Nurses Association, would offer nurse practitioner–run "one-stop shopping," integrating health and social services. All family members living in the school neighborhood would be eligible, including senior citizens. Parents would be trained to assess the health of family members and to improve their access to the health care system.

Mental Health Services
Most middle and high schools and an increasing number of elementary schools employ guidance counselors. At last count, more than

eighty-nine thousand counselors were offering some forms of guidance, usually about educationally related matters such as curriculum choice and college applications.[9] However, the student/counselor ratio is so high that many students are shortchanged, particularly those in vocational tracks, and many counselors are not trained to deal with the complex psychosocial problems of today's students. In most schools, guidance counselors welcome collaboration with community health and mental health workers in addressing the more personal aspects of student development. Fewer schools employ social workers. Although their training facilitates more direct intervention into the lives of students and their families, their time must be divided between attending to disabled children and working with parents, teachers, community agencies, and deeply troubled students.

When school-based clinic providers are asked what the largest unmet need is among their clients, they most frequently mention mental health counseling. Students come in to the medical clinics with a litany of stress and depression, their typical adolescent problems exacerbated seriously by the deteriorating and unsafe social environment in which they live. In the words of one provider, "As soon as we open our doors, kids walk past the counselor's office, past the school nurse, past the principal, and come into our clinic to tell us that they have been sexually abused or that their parents are drug users." The fact that the clinic staff are outsiders and provide confidential services probably explains why students will bring their problems to the clinic rather than disclosing them to school staff. The demand for mental health counseling has led to the development of school clinics that have as their primary function the screening and treating for psychosocial problems. But mental health interventions in schools take many forms. In some communities, a mental health worker, either a psychologist or a social worker, is outstationed by a community agency in a school. Many universities have collaborative arrangements with schools for internship experiences in mental health counseling. Within a broader framework of training young people to enhance their social skills, many university-based social psychologists have been designing and implementing school-based curricula.

School-Based Mental Health Centers. A mental health center in a school transfers the functions of a community mental health center to a school building. In this model, a room or group of rooms in a school building is designated as a services center. This center is not usually labeled a "mental health" facility but is rather presented as a place where students can go for all kinds of support and remediation. Staff typically includes clinical psychologists and social workers. Depending on the range of additional services, other staff might be youth workers, tutors, and mentors. The goals of school-based mental health centers are to improve the social adjustment of students and to help them deal with personal and family crises.

A network of school-based mental health programs has been organized by the School Mental Health Project at the University of California, Los Angeles, a national clearinghouse that offers training, research, and technical assistance.[10] This project works in conjunction with the Los Angeles Unified School District's School Mental Health Center and is in the process of developing a guidebook based on that experience for practitioners who want to follow a mental health model. Project directors Howard Adelman and Linda Taylor believe that the major challenge for school-based mental health centers is to identify and collaborate with what is already going on in the school district. Many schools have programs focused on substance abuse and teen pregnancy prevention, crisis intervention (suicide), violence reduction, "self-esteem" enhancement, and other kinds of support groups. However, these efforts lack cohesiveness in theory and implementation, often stigmatize students by targeting them, and suffer from the common bureaucratic problem of poor coordination between programs. One of the most demanding roles for the mental health center is to establish working relationships with key school staff members.

An exemplary school-based mental health program was initiated in New Brunswick in 1988, funded by the New Jersey School-Based Youth

Services Program (see Appendix A).[11] It is operated in the high school and five elementary schools by the local Community Mental Health Center of the University of Medicine and Dentistry of New Jersey. Currently, the program has ten full-time core staff members, including eight clinicians (psychologists and social workers), one of whom serves as the director. The staff conduct individual, group, and family therapy and serve as consultants to school personnel and other agencies involved with adolescents. An activities/outreach worker plans and supervises recreational activities and outreach contacts at the high school. Specialized part-time staff include a pregnancy/parenting counselor, a substance abuse counselor, and consultants in suicide prevention, "social problems," and medical care.

The facility at New Brunswick High School is located in the old band room, fixed up to resemble a game room in a settlement house, with television, Ping Pong, and other active games, comfortable furniture, and books and tapes on loan. The center offers tutoring, mentoring, group activities, recreational outings, and educational trips. A number of "therapeutic" groups have been organized: social problem solving, substance abuse, Children of Alcoholics, and coping skills for the gifted and talented. Students are referred and provided with transportation to the local neighborhood health center for health services and treatment. During the past two years, one in four of the enrolled students have been involved in active mental health counseling with one of the clinicians. According to director Gail Reynolds, the demand for services is overwhelming, requiring immediate and time-consuming interventions with the family, the school, and other social agencies.

In a unique outreach effort, the Orange County (California) Health Care Agency has relocated all of its children's mental health clinics to school-based facilities and expends almost all of its $15 million budget for children's services in those programs. Orange County Mental Health Services combines traditional mental health screening and treatment services with case management and in-home supportive services in conjunction with other community agencies and the schools.[12] Treatment is provided to all types of cases, from behavioral problems referred by teachers and families to severely disturbed minors brought in by police, hospitals, and social service agencies. Schools have provided the county with twenty-three rent-free mental health offices and group therapy rooms in a variety of educational settings. Several special classrooms have been set up to provide individual and group therapy for the children and support for teachers, and family and parent therapy is provided within the school-based outpatient clinics.

Program staff include a service chief, five part-time psychiatrists, eight clinical social workers, eleven clinical psychologists, six interns, and a coordinator of volunteers. About 80 percent of the costs are reimbursed to the county by the state Mental Health Department. Each site is certified as a Medi-Cal provider. This collaboration between the school district, the county health agency, and other organizations has enabled the district to provide intensive psychological and social services to students and families far beyond those normally available and to pilot prevention models that cut down on the need for special education placements, intensive therapeutic treatments, and out-of-home placements.

Psychosocial Counseling Programs. The social workers and clinical psychologists employed by community agencies and assigned to schools generally focus on specific categorical issues such as substance abuse, teen pregnancy, and even school failure. These efforts generally augment pupil personnel services in school systems that want or need additional staff resources for dealing with psychosocial problems.

In Westchester County, New York, the Student Assistance Program, partially supported by state and federal grants, covers twenty-eight local school districts, with a focus on prevention of substance abuse. Typically, Student Assistance counselors are placed in schools at the invitation of the principal, are given an office, and work along with the school personnel as part of a team. They provide individual counseling to students referred to them by guidance counselors and teachers and organize group counseling sessions on subjects of particular importance in the school population, such as Children of Alcoholics, children of families experiencing divorce, and coping with stress and depression. Student Assistance workers train teachers and other school personnel to recognize the signs of stress and other problem behaviors among students.

Social Skills and Social Competency Training. Many school systems have been used as research laboratories for developing new curricula in the prevention of substance abuse, teen pregnancy, and conduct disorders. The "new wave" of prevention programs rely heavily on contemporary social psychologists' theories about resistance skills and assertiveness training. The process typically involves a university-based researcher who designs a prevention curriculum, field-tests within a school system, and conducts evaluations in a sample of classrooms or schools, either within one system or across systems. The testing of a curriculum is conducted under the auspices of the university, usually the psychology department, or a research organization such as the Rand Corporation, supported with a foundation or government grant, frequently from the National Institutes of Health. After the curriculum is tested, the researchers develop training materials and, rather than administering the curriculum themselves, work with the school personnel to train them to implement the program.

The Social Competency Promotion Program (SCPP) was developed by Roger Weisberg at the Yale University Department of Psychology, in extensive collaboration with the New Haven Public School System.[13] Using a detailed manual, SCPP staff train classroom teachers to provide intensive instruction on social problem-solving skills and to promote students' self-management capabilities. In addition, SCPP staff work in the school to develop school, parent, and community activities to support classroom social development instruction. After determining where the SCPP curriculum best fits—in health, science, or social studies or as a freestanding social development class—teachers are trained through meetings, a five-day intensive training session, the use of "master teachers" for on-site consultation, and the provision of detailed lesson plans. SCPP has been widely disseminated in twenty-five states and four countries.

Mentoring. In recent years, interest has developed in helping high-risk and disadvantaged youth by connecting them with an individual who can act as a role model, advocate, and counselor. This concept is being carried out in many different forms with mentors supplied to schools by universities (students and faculty), business groups, senior citizens, women's voluntary organizations, ethnic organizations, and fraternities.[14] Mark Freedman, an authority on the subject of mentoring, suggests that this approach would be more effective if it were more embedded in institutional arrangements and received greater support to insure consistency and quality.[15] For young people who need professional mental health guidance, mentoring is "good but not sufficient."

The Teaching-Learning Communities Mentors Program (T-LC) in Ann Arbor, Michigan, was initiated by Carol Tice with support from the National Education Association.[16] "Elders" are recruited from the community to act as tutors and mentors to junior high school students at risk of dropping out. A classroom has been set aside strictly for T-LC use as a kind of "oasis" for the students. The program stresses the arts, career awareness, personal goal setting, and school involvement.

A program in Washington, D.C., pairs African-American men, mostly professionals living in the suburbs, with youngsters aged eight to eleven who attend school in a disadvantaged area. The mentors work with the children during the summer prior to fourth grade and during the school year on Saturdays for tutoring and one-on-one conversations. A similar program in Providence is sponsored by the Urban League and includes after-school tutoring that uses college students as mentors. Other mentoring programs around the country use African-American women professionals, male fraternity members, businessmen, and athletes.

Family

Schools want to involve parents. Evidence is building to show that parents in disadvantaged communities will respond more readily to offers of tangible and needed services than to invitations to attend school events such as workshops on child psychology. Community agencies play an important role in developing responsive and creative targeted programs that enhance parent involvement.[17] As discussed previously, Edward Zigler created a framework for addressing the issue of parent participation in his Schools of the Twenty-First Century, calling for "comprehensive, integrated, community based systems of family support and child development services located in public school buildings".[18] Program components include full-day child care for preschool and school-age children, parent education and family support services, literacy training, training and support for family day-care providers, and teen pregnancy prevention services. Few school systems can afford to add these components without outside support from the public and private sectors.

Family Resource Centers (FRC). This has become a generic term for a whole array of programs that bring services together for parents and children. Some are located in school buildings, while others are community-based. A few states, including California, Connecticut, Kentucky, Florida, North Carolina, and Wisconsin, have passed legislation that appropriates funds for FRCs.[19] Kentucky's legislation mandates that every elementary school with more than 20 percent of its students eligible for free lunch must have a Family Service Center.

The Dr. Ramon Emeterio Betance School in Hartford, Connecticut, houses one of eight family resource centers, supported by the Connecticut Department of Human Resources and modeled after Zigler's concepts. The resource center operates a preschool program at the school site. Central staff manage a Families in Training program through which outreach workers routinely contact all families with newborn children and arrange to conduct home visits. An after-school program for elementary children uses school facilities and involves volunteers in leading various recreational activities. Adult education is offered in the evening, with courses in English and in high school equivalency (General Education Degree, or GED). The collaborating agency is La Casa de Puerto Rico, which trains neighborhood women to become home child-care providers and helps them obtain certification.

The family resource center in Gainesville, Florida, is located in seven portable units situated between an elementary school and a middle school. This program includes a health clinic; an experimental nursery; parent education, GED preparation, and literacy classes; case management; economic services (AFDC, Medicaid, Food Stamps); job training and computer education; a toy lending library; and family liaison services. The latter are provided by seven community workers, with the expectation that eventually the staff will grow to twenty-two outreach specialists, one in each elementary school in the county. Bebe Fearnside, the director, considers outreach the most important function of the resource center: going into homes, getting involved with families, teaching parenting skills, and offering connections to community agencies and the schools. As is typical of multiservice programs, the funding for this effort derives from many sources, including a state Full-Service Schools grant, Chapter 1, the College of Nursing and Medicine, Even Start, Head Start, Community College, Mental Health Services, the school board, state health grants, and Medicaid reimbursements. The state has awarded the program a grant of $2.5 million to build a new center with 2,500 square feet (currently they have 750 square feet).

Family Focus, a Chicago-based network of model family resource centers, has several programs located in schools. In Evanston, Illinois, the Family Focus program operates in three sites: an elementary school, a school for teen parents, and a storefront. Administered jointly by the school district and the community agency, each agency supplies a coordinator. The Chicago-based Family Resources Coalition acts as a clearinghouse for the development of family support programs that can deliver preventive, coordinated, community-based services. Some two thousand programs have been identified around the country with diverse components that provide the Three R's: resources, referrals, and relationships. Many of these family and child centers are located in school buildings.

Parenting Programs. A number of states have developed school-based parent education programs. The Missouri Parents as Teachers (PAT), most often cited as the model, provides home visits by trained parent educators to offer all families with children from birth to three years information and advice on child development, health monitoring and screening, and referral for special services.[20] Originated in one district with foundation support, the program is now funded entirely through the Missouri Public School System and so would not serve as an example of an "outside-supported school-based program." However, only after a privately supported demonstration project proved successful were the funds added to the education budget for the specific purpose of developmental screening and parent education.

A Parent Resource Center for families with children from birth to five years is operated by the Corning–Painted Post (New York) School District with support from the Corning Glass Works and the New York State Education Department. This drop-in center is open days, evenings, and weekends for a broad array of workshops, classes, and activities, parent education resources, toy lending, and referral. The center is also involved in training family day-care providers.

Parent education was not originally a function of school systems, and in most parts of the country it still isn't. The Family-School Collaboration Project of the Ackerman Institute of Family Therapy in New York City helps schools increase family participation and facilitates collaboration with school staff in support of children's education.[21] Project staff work with schools to create Family-School Forums, which bring together students, parents, and school staff to discuss problems, issues, and ideas. The staff create activities that provide opportunities for collaborative learning, planning, and problem-solving activities.

The League of Schools Reaching Out is a network of forty-two schools, identified by the Institute for Responsive Education, that seek ways to actively involve families and communities with supplemental funds derived from foundation grants.[22] Don Davies, the institute's director, is a pioneer in stimulating the concept of community schools. Although each of the league schools has a different configuration, half have Parent/Family Centers in schools, and 40 percent provide home visiting programs. Every school has at least six partnerships with community agencies, businesses, and cultural institutions to help coordinate services. Many have hired a specialized person, usually from the community, to function as a parent liaison or community coordinator. Some fifteen of these schools receive funding from the institute for special programs, including a parent center, home visiting, mentoring, and demonstrations of language learning techniques for young mothers and their infants during home visits. Nine of the schools are working with a facilitator hired by the institute to organize parent-teacher action research teams to study the impact of new programs.

Recreation and Cultural Enrichment. With increasing numbers of mothers in the labor force, more and more children are left to their own devices after school and during vacation time. Schools increasingly are becoming the locus for recreational and cultural enrichment programs that take place outside of school hours. Voluntary agencies such as Girls Inc., 4-H, Campfire, and other national organizations have expressed a growing interest in expanding their services to encompass the needs of high-risk children.[23]

After-School Centers. School buildings are being used as places for after-school events and academic remediation. In these programs, a community agency brings staff into the school after school hours, on weekends, and during the summer. School-based community centers known as Beacons are being operated in at least twenty New York City neighborhoods (with seventeen more about to be funded) with the support of the Department of Youth Services.[24] Foundations and corporations are providing supplemental funds for technical assistance, renovation, and documentation of the school-community partnerships. Each Beacon is different, reflecting the needs of the community, but they are all run by a community-based organization working collaboratively with the school board, principals, and a community advisory board to focus on new paths to neighborhood revitalization and to keep the school buildings open. New York City agencies are encouraged to co-locate services in these schools, resulting in various configurations that include employment, health, recreation, welfare, juvenile justice, and probation services. The Mosaic Community Center, operated in a local school by Bronx Community College, offers after-school activities and hot meals, an evening program of sports, women's gym nights, a course in effective parenting, training in building maintenance and construction trades geared to single mothers, and a weekend program that includes sports and films. The Mighty Mosaic Gazelles are an award-winning group of cheerleaders, who were formerly girl gang members.

The YWCA of Phoenix has developed an after-school program called GROW—Gaining Realization of Worth—that it offers in conjunction with selected elementary school districts and the Rotary Club.[25] Participants join teams, participate in recreational activities, and learn leadership skills from trained peer counselors. Thousands of programs bring the arts into schools during the regular school day. Theater groups, artists-in-residence, dance programs—all kinds of cultural enrichment are being offered within schools by various professionals. In some instances, one-shot performances are offered; in others, the artists spend a lot of time in schools as part of regular courses or in courses that they themselves teach.

Quality Education

It would be foolhardy to try to summarize what is going on in this country to upgrade the quality of education. Much ferment is being engendered by debates of educational goals and standards, with little assurance that these discussions will actually benefit disadvantaged children and their families. I have tried to select examples of those approaches most relevant to the development of full-service schools, interventions that would parallel the support services described above.

School Remediation and Dropout Prevention

Thousands of outside programs and projects attempt to help school systems deal with the problem of academic achievement. Thousands of alternative schools have been organized and are dependent on community agencies, businesses, and universities for enrichment, employment opportunities, and volunteers. Experience with alternative schools and community schools is being utilized in designing restructuring efforts. In some school systems, components of services are being brought in by community agencies specifically to address the problem of academic achievement and staying in school, efforts that do not go as far as restructuring but rely more on individual attention to high-risk youth.

Case Management. Cities in Schools (CIS) is a national nonprofit organization founded by William Milliken in Washington that since 1977 has promulgated a model for prevention of school dropout. Each local entity has its own version, but in general the program involves "brokering" community social service agencies in the provision of case management services within the school building. Local businesses are involved in arranging for mentoring and apprenticeship experiences.[26] CIS operates in more than 122 communities with 384 school sites to facilitate a process of collaboration to bring health, social, and employment services into schools to help high-risk youngsters.[27] In most programs, a case manager is assigned to each high-risk child. Communities vary in program design: some operate alternative schools; some offer special CIS life skills classes and other forms of remediation and tutoring. A wide array of partnerships have been established through the CIS processes, involving Boys Clubs of America, VISTA, United Way, and Junior League.

Several of the CIS programs have achieved national prominence. For example, Rich's Academy in Atlanta (one of six CIS schools in that community) is an alternative school created in partnership with a department store. CIS has joined with the Iacocca Institute and the Lehigh University College of Education in Pennsylvania to create the National Center for Partnership Development, designed to address the dropout problem by meeting the multiple needs of youth. The CIS strategy has been translated into formal curriculum and training materials and uses computer-based interactive multimedia sessions.

One CIS spin-off is the Pinal County (Arizona) Prevention Partnership, involving thirteen local middle and high schools in a collaborative effort between the Department of Human Services, the county school superintendent's office, and a nonprofit agency.[28] According to director Charles Teagarden, the strategy calls for "a school-based, integrated delivery system of networking service providers connecting at-risk youths through diligent case management to targeted prevention programs, then to job and career opportunities created by economic development, all monitored by a data system evaluation." More than one hundred different human service providers are brought into the schools to conduct these activities, or referrals are arranged. Family resource centers in eight of the schools allow parents to interact and work in support groups.

Incentive Programs. "I Have a Dream," Eugene Lang's promise to a sixth-grade East Harlem, New York, class of subsidized college study in the event of high school graduation, has "become one of the country's most celebrated private sector initiatives for disadvantaged youth."[29] In addition to the promise of subsidy and Lang's personal attention, the students receive support from a full-time social worker, services from Harlem's Youth Action Program, and volunteers who act as mentors. Most of the original participants graduated from high school and more than half enrolled in college. Nine new incentive projects have started in New York City and in at least twenty-two cities around the country. The impact of this kind of program may ultimately be measured by the influence of decision-maker million-aires who get drawn into the issues relating to the educational problems of high-risk youth. Several states have begun similar programs; New York offers "Liberty Partnerships," which promise high school students subsidy for college tuition upon graduation.

University-School Partnerships. Many examples of university-generated research conducted in schools have been cited. Some university education departments have established formal relationships with specific schools or school districts, using sites as laboratories for testing new curricula, methods of school reform and restructuring, and teacher training. Fordham University Graduate Schools of Education and Social Services created a joint Stay-in-School Partnership Project (SSPP) in five New York City elementary schools.[30] Selected schoolchildren and their families receive a comprehensive set of co-ordinated services from university social service staff (play therapy, counseling, advocacy, consultation, family problem-solving) and university educational personnel (one-to-one tutoring, individualized instruction, parental workshops). In addition, classroom teachers and building administrators receive in-service training on issues and practices related to at-risk prevention.

Business Partnerships. At one time, the Department of Education claimed that sixty thousand business-sponsored projects had been identified in schools, including Adopt-a-School, employee involvement in tutoring, gifts of equipment, and other forms of support. Virtually every report on new approaches to high-risk youth cites the Boston Compact as a reform that makes a difference. Through a series of arrangements between Boston's public schools and local government, business, labor, higher education, and community groups, collaborative efforts have been undertaken to improve school attendance, academic achievement, and post–high school opportunities.[31] Specific components of the partnerships include career counseling and job placement, sponsorship of teacher internship programs, grants for innovative teaching ideas, and participation in work-study programs. As the Compact has evolved, components have been added to get parents to sign a contract assuring that their children will attend school and do their homework, to provide more careful monitoring and tracking of students placed in jobs, and to create a written agreement between the schools and the teacher's union that assures more staff autonomy.[32]

This model is being replicated throughout the country. Youth Guidance, a nonprofit organization that collaborates with the Chicago Board of Education and is supported by the United Way, foundations, and private industries, offers direct support in schools, such as counseling and crisis intervention, teaching job skills, creative arts programs, and employment opportunity development.[33] Under Youth Guidance's auspices, the Hyatt Hotels Corporation built a kitchen in which to train students in culinary art skills in a three-year internship program.

Another dropout prevention program that involves business partnerships has been organized by WAVE (Work, Achievement, Values, Education), a private nonprofit corporation that provides teacher training for more than one hundred schools.[34] Using a special curriculum, WAVE students in grades nine through twelve are taught life skills, personal development, and work preparation. A recent Breaking Down the Barriers component brings business partners into the classroom to help students prepare for the school-to-work transition and to expose the volunteers to the reality of today's classrooms.

Teen Parent Programs. Not so many years ago, schools were permitted to expel students who were pregnant. After 1975, however, with the implementation of Title IX of the Education Amendments, publicly supported educational programs have been prohibited from discriminating on the basis of pregnancy status. Schools have been required to provide equal educational opportunities to pregnant teens and young parents, although not necessarily in the same building as the other students. In a number of communities, alternative schools for teen parents have been organized with funding from foundations and government grants. The model that has been used builds on concepts of comprehensive services, putting together a whole array of health, social services, educational remediation, child-care components, and a lot of individual attention. In observing these programs, it seems that these pregnancies might have been preventable if these comprehensive services had been available to the young people who ultimately became teen parents. Motherhood is the price of entry.

The New Vistas High School, located within Honeywell's corporate headquarters, is an alternative program of the Minneapolis public school system for pregnant teens and teen mothers.[35] The corporation provides the facility, funds for equipment and special projects, food, a staff liaison, volunteers, and mentors. The Minneapolis school system provides academic instruction and support services. Other corporations have donated computers and software. Health services are provided on site by the Minneapolis Children's Medical Center and the Health Department. A fully equipped day-care center, located next door, is staffed by the County Community Services, and a social worker is supported by the Big Brothers/Big Sisters organization.

Volunteer Community Service Programs. "On any given day, in communities all across the United States, young people are leaving school to clean up neighborhoods, visit nursing homes, educate children about drugs, serve at soup kitchens, register voters.... For these young people, and the teachers who encourage them, school is not just a place where one comes to learn, but also a place which provides important resources to those in need."[36] Community service was given a major boost in 1990 with the passage of the National and Community Service Act, an initiative designed to increase young people's bonding to the school and community. A large number of programs have been organized in middle and high schools to give young people an opportunity to do volunteer work in their neighborhoods at child-care agencies, hospitals, playgrounds, and senior citizen residences. In some cases, these efforts are arranged by community groups and local businesses. For example, many high schools have Key Clubs affiliated with the Kiwanis organization.

The Teen Outreach Project, started by the Junior League and cosponsored by the American Association of School Administrators, is now being replicated in seventy-five schools around the country.[37] Weekly community service assignments are carried out by students, typically in preschools or senior citizen homes. The students also participate in counseling sessions and small group discussions, using a specially developed curriculum emphasizing life planning and goal setting. In Los Angeles, twenty-two high schools participate in a Youth Community Services Program sponsored by the Constitutional Rights Foundation. Students are exposed to training at a two-day retreat followed up with weekly meetings at each school.[38] Professionals in the community serve as mentors for student projects in day-care and Head Start centers near their schools. Big Brothers/Big Sisters, a national mentoring organization, is testing a program that trains high school students to act as special older friends to elementary school students.

School Reorganization
Many of the examples discussed so far are aimed at categorical problems; they are single-component programs that attempt to prevent substance abuse, delinquency, teen pregnancy, or school dropout or multi-component programs that put together packages of health and social services. Yet many authorities believe that these separate programs only serve to "patch up" a few of a child's or a family's problems and that more massive changes in the way children are educated are needed for young people to succeed. Although this book is focused on the support services side of the equation, it is important to recognize the potential of exemplary quality education initiatives as well.

Several major authorities have emerged, each with a different view of what has to be done to change the environment in schools. None of these educational leaders is currently attached to a school system, but all of them are heavily involved in shaping school systems of the future through their academic centers. Henry Levin, of Stanford University, has proposed Accelerated Schools in response to the continuing failure of the schools to educate high-risk children. "The premises of the remediation approach are demonstrably false," according to Levin, "and the consequences are debilitating."[39] His group has initiated demonstration projects which are rich in curriculum content relevant to elementary school students' lives. The goal is to accelerate learning prior to sixth grade so that disadvantaged students catch up while they still can. Children are exposed to literature and problem solving and a range of cultural experiences. Rather than drill lessons, techniques such as cooperative learning, peer tutoring, and community outreach are incorporated. Parents, staff, and students enter into contractual relationships defining the obligations of each.

The School Development Program, a school-based management approach to making school a more productive environment for poor minority children, is an important example of how outside expertise can be utilized to influence the total school environment.[40] A "process," developed by James Comer from the Yale University Child Study Center, has been successfully implemented in several inner-city elementary schools in New Haven and is being replicated widely throughout the country in at least 165 schools. Around the country, school people report with great enthusiasm that their schools are being "Comerized." The program attempts to strengthen and redefine the relationships among principals, teachers, parents, and students. Representative management and governance is implemented through an elected School Advisory Council that includes the principal, teachers, teacher aides, and parents. A mental health team comprising the school psychologist and other support personnel is organized to provide direct services to children and to advise school staff and parents. An innovative Parent Participation Program calls for the employment of a parent in each classroom on a part-time basis. In addition to serving as representatives to the advisory council, parents are encouraged to volunteer as teacher aides and librarians, run newsletters, and organize social activities. A social skills curriculum has been developed that integrates the teaching of basic skills with teaching of "mainstream" (middle-class) arts and social skills. According to Comer, the strength of this project is its focus on the entire school rather than any one particular aspect, and its attention to institutional change rather than individual change. This is one of the few models that has successfully engaged parents in school programs.

Success for All is a demonstration program for elementary schools. Initiated by Robert Slavin and colleagues at the Center for Research on Elementary and Middle Schools, Johns Hopkins University, the program restructures the entire school to do "everything" necessary to insure that all students will be performing at grade level by the end of third grade.[41] Interventions include half-day preschool and full-day kindergarten, a family support team, an effective reading program, reading tutors, individual academic plans based on frequent assessments, a full-time program facilitator and coordinator, training and support for teachers, and a school advisory committee that meets weekly. The family support team works full-time in each school and consists of social workers, attendance workers, and a parent liaison worker. The team provides parenting education and support assistance for day-to-day problems such as nutrition, getting glasses, attendance, and problem behaviors. Family support teams are responsible for developing linkages with community resources. Success for All is currently being replicated in seven Baltimore schools and one in Philadelphia. One program has a public health nurse practitioner who provides on-site medical care; another school is connected with a family counseling agency that provides some school-based services. One Success for All school has worked with a community agency to have a food distribution center at the school, and another houses a clothes bank.

The Coalition of Essential Schools is a consortium of schools that have reorganized to incorporate the principles derived from the work of Theodore Sizer of Brown University.[42] From his experience studying American high schools, he has concluded that the most important task for schools is to teach students mastery of their schoolwork. Sizer believes that it is more important for children to learn a few important ideas "deeply" than to be exposed to fragmented and ineffectual teaching. In a model Coalition school, Central Park East in New York City, Principal Deborah Meier intensely exposes students in grades seven to ten to a classical curriculum in science and humanities. The last two years of high school are offered as an institute, with individual programs for each student, involving courses in other places, fieldwork, and projects. Teachers act as coaches and counselors for the students; each day begins with an advisory group of fifteen students where any subject may be brought up and shared with other students.

Comprehensive Multicomponent Programs

A number of school-based interventions that address an array of interrelated issues have been initiated. Based on the observation that - prevention approaches must be more holistic if they are to be successful, these programs are put together by an outside organization that provides a full-time coordinator and other services to the school to implement all the separate pieces of the package.

The Walbridge Caring Community is one of the most sophisticated models; it includes many components and many agencies. An initiative of the Missouri Department of Mental Health, this effort brings together the St. Louis city public schools and the Danforth Foundation in a collaborative effort with the state departments of health, social services, and education.[43] This program provides an array of intensive services to the children and families of the Walbridge Elementary School in a center that is also open to other community residents. Services include family counseling, case management, substance abuse counseling, student assistance, parenting education, before- and after-school activities, youth programs, health screening, and preemployment skills. The family counseling and case management component, directed at the most high-risk families, may involve a home therapist. Most of the funding for the intensive individual services (for fourteen positions) is provided by the state Department of Mental Health, while the Department of Social Services picks up the after-school program (five positions). Health services are provided by a school nurse, and the state Department of Health supports a home health visitor and a clerical assistant. Funds from the Danforth Foundation and the state offices jointly support the director. One of the unique qualities of this program is its use of an Afrocentric concept in developing self-help, community empowerment, and rites of passage ceremonies.

The New Futures initiative is a large-scale community-school collaborative effort that was launched by the Annie E. Casey Foundation in 1988.[44] Currently, five cities (Bridgeport, Dayton, Little Rock, Pittsburgh, and Savannah) operate programs with five- to seven-year grants ranging from $5.7 million to $12.9 million. In each city, the project is run by an "Oversight Collaborative," a nonprofit governing body representing various community sectors that assesses needs, sets priorities, and advocates for change in local institutions. To carry out their mandate to develop integrated systems for attending to the needs of high-risk children, the collaboratives have supported specific education, health, and employment programs. Typically, these interventions have focused on young people in two to four schools, mostly at the middle-school level. A management information system collects data on all enrolled students in each community, making it possible to track progress in changing behavioral outcomes.

Each city has a case management system operated by the nonprofit agency; the managers are located in schools for most of the day. All of the cities have been active in education reform efforts in the areas of school-based management, curriculum improvement, and increasing links to social and health services. In Savannah, the Youth Futures Authority works with the Board of Education to develop accelerated curricula for students who are behind grade. In Little Rock, the emphasis has been on restructuring, using interdisciplinary teams of teachers, flexible scheduling, and after-school enrichment programs.

Several of the cities are developing school-based health clinics and other health programs with the support of community health agencies. Employment activities include business/education partnerships, career counseling, life-planning curricula, and access to employment opportunities.

The School of the Future project is another large-scale foundation effort to help schools evolve into primary neighborhood institutions for promoting child and family development.[45] The Texas-based Hogg Foundation for Mental Health is supporting four major city efforts (Austin, Dallas, Houston, and San Antonio) with five year grants of $50,000 per year for using elementary and middle schools as the locus of delivery of services. An equal amount of funding has been set aside for evaluation and monitoring. The foundation is interested in creating and testing an intervention that combines "all of the above"—the Comer School Development Program, Zigler's Schools for the Twenty-First Century, school-based clinics, programs for community renewal, and family preservation. The model places a full-time project coordinator (a social worker) in a community to establish links and partnerships between the schools and health and human services providers and to involve parents and teachers in program activities. For example, at San Antonio's three school sites, family, group, and individual therapy was being provided by eleven graduate student interns, and ten graduate social worker students were providing crisis intervention, home visits, AFDC, and Food Stamp certifications and working with child protective services. Parent education, parent volunteer activities, after-school recreation, gang prevention programs, and other efforts were involving many local organizations.

San Diego's New Beginnings is frequently cited as the future model for integrated nonfragmented services. Located in an inner-city middle-school, this program grew out of a partnership formed by the city (police, parks, recreation) and county (health, social services, and probation) of San Diego, the school district, the community college, and the San Diego Housing Commission. These collaborators spent two years planning a school-based center to house a score of local agencies who were "expected to leave behind their parochial origins and become family service advocates."[46] Workers relocated from the participant agencies (family service advocates) serve all families with children aged five to twelve attending that school. Services include case management; preventive health care, screening, and immunizations; drug, alcohol, and mental health treatment; adult education and school tutoring; and other community services as needed, such as day care, translation, transportation, extended library and park hours. To link school and center staff, a task force was formed of administrative, clerical, and front-line workers to iron out the difficult process of changing roles and relationships. The New Beginnings model is being replicated in other school-communities with the mission of "a tearing down of barriers, a giving up of turf, and a new way of doing business."

Our search for comprehensive multicomponent school-based programs yielded two examples of schools on the way to becoming full-service. Their menus include most of the components of both quality education and support services (Exhibit 1.1). IS 218, a middle school in Washington Heights, New York, was recently opened through a partnership between the school system and the Children's Aid Society (CAS), a nonprofit organization.[47] With this unique arrangement, CAS has created a "settlement house" in a school. Hanshaw Middle School, Modesto, California, a model "community school," was created by the local school system and draws heavily on partnerships with community agencies. These two innovative schools are described in detail in Chapter Five.

Putting the Pieces Together

In this chapter, a number of interventions have been reviewed, roughly grouped under the subjects of support services and quality education, showing that at least as independent pieces of the action, certain program components can effectively achieve their objectives.

It is assumed that if pieces from both sides of the equation were put together, full-service schools would become a reality. And, in fact, a few unique schools have been identified that could make that claim.

I have attempted to accurately portray the current status of school-community agency interventions, but so much is going on that it defies orderly description. The examples discussed above don't tell the whole story. As stated previously, almost every school receives some form of outside assistance, and that adds up to millions of hours of additional subsidized and donated people-hours spent in schools. Virtually every category of professional and volunteer, from a vast array of public and private health and social agencies and businesses and industries, supported by every kind of local, state, and federal funding, can be found in today's schools. I emphasize the magnitude of this "outpouring" to bolster the argument that schools are eager to accept outside help as long as they are partners in the enterprise. Unfortunately, these separate and unique efforts in schools do not add up to enough power to substantially change the lives of the millions of children and families who live in troubled circumstances. Most of the exemplary interventions are still in the demonstration project phase. Many overlap with other programs, and few are integrated.

Ideally, a magic wand would be waved and the thousands of schools in needy areas would instantly acquire all of the components required to provide "full-service" to students and their families. Pragmatically, certain pieces of the action can move more rapidly than others. It is easier to bring a clinic into a school than to restructure an entire system. We leave that challenge to the educational experts and, in the remainder of this book, concentrate on the support services side of this equation. Nevertheless, we recognize that our social goals can never be met without a joint "revolution" in both the quality of schooling and the access of children and families to the supports they need.

In the next chapter, we focus on the provision of health and social services in school clinics, a substantial program component of full-service schools that has been widely replicated and can be described in an orderly way.

4

▲▲▲

School-Based Clinics:
A Look at Pioneer Programs

School-based health clinics are those programs organized under the auspices of medical practitioners, typically out-stationed from a health department, hospital, or community health center. As we shall observe, the earlier programs were heavily focused on pregnancy prevention, but as the model evolved, the focus has shifted to general medical care and psychosocial counseling, with pregnancy prevention moved to the back burner. The school-based clinics described in this chapter are primarily in high schools, with growing numbers in middle schools. Elementary school clinics are also proliferating, but that experience is less well documented. It is important to recall that the major impetuses for the development of school-based health and social services have been the rising incidence of the new morbidities among young people and the joining of the movement for school reform with the movement toward the improvement of adolescent health.

Background: The First Ten School-Based Clinics

My own introduction to school-based clinics came about quite serendipitously in 1983. While visiting the Mississippi Health Department on some family planning program business, I was asked by a state administrator if I wanted to see a health clinic in a high school that was partially supported with family planning funds. The clinic was located at the Lanier High School in Jackson, Mississippi, and operated by the Jackson/Hinds Community Health Center (CHC). This program was initiated in 1979 by a local physician, Aaron Shirley, founder and director of the CHC and still a major force in the development of health services in impoverished communities throughout Mississippi. He had attended Lanier High School himself and, at the invitation of the school principal, had come into the school building initially to provide sports physicals. He discovered a whole array of medical and social needs among the students and arranged for the grant for family planning services to augment the medical staff and services he brought in from his own health center. Today there are nine school clinics in Jackson run by the CHC.

This first sight of a nurse practitioner in a school conducting health screening, providing medications, and arranging for intensive counseling in a well-equipped office next to the principal's left a deep impression on me. Not only was this program providing medical services in school; it included a room set aside for sex education and individual counseling and a child-care center, in a mobile unit attached to the school, for the use of teen parents. Aaron Shirley and his staff knew the name of every baby in the child-care center. They demonstrated a strong commitment to pregnancy prevention with individual follow-up of every sexually active student who obtained contraceptives from the school clinic.

This experience was duly communicated to Sheldon Segal, program officer at the Rockefeller Foundation, who encouraged me to identify similar programs that were emerging and to assess their potential for

preventing adolescent pregnancy.[1] By the beginning of 1984, about
ten school-based clinic programs could be identified around the country (including—in addition to Jackson—Dallas and Houston in Texas;
St. Paul and Minneapolis in Minnesota; Muskegon and Ypsilanti
in Michigan; Kansas City, Missouri; Chicago, Illinois; and Gary,
Indiana).

A review of these early programs disclosed that the first school
clinic at the high school level had been organized in Dallas in 1970
by the federally funded Children and Youth Project of the University of Texas Health Science Center Pediatrics Department.[2] One of
the rationales for the West Dallas Youth Clinic was to try to overcome the barriers to family planning services the program designers
observed in their community: "A young woman would have to miss
a day of school to receive initial services. The family planning clinic
was a categorical facility where relatives and neighbors received services, which limited confidentiality. No services were available for
adolescent males. Staff turnover was high, making it difficult for the
adolescent to develop a relationship with the health provider."[3] This
pioneer clinic was (and still is) located in a prefabricated building adjacent to the area's only high school. Sex education, pregnancy testing, contraceptive services and counseling, adoption and abortion
referral, diagnosis and treatment of STDs, and follow-up counseling
were all included in this comprehensive program. An evaluation
published in the early 1980s showed a decline in the area teenage live
birth rate during the early years of the project. This success was attributed to the provision of family planning to adolescents in the
context of comprehensive health care in a school setting, with particular attention to follow-up of missed appointments.

At this time, the best-known school-based health clinic was located in St. Paul. Early reports of that program's success in reducing
childbearing caused a considerable stir[4] and stimulated those concerned with prevention of adolescent pregnancy to consider school-
based clinics as a potential new approach.[5] The program had been

founded in 1973 by Laura Edwards, an obstetrician who observed in her practice the problems resulting from the high rates of teenage childbearing. Edwards and her colleagues at the St. Paul Ramsey Medical Center received permission from the school board to offer prenatal and postpartum care, along with other reproductive health services, in an inner-city high school. However, utilization was minimal, and soon after the program's inception, the staff began to offer a wider variety of health services to broaden the clinic's appeal and to protect teenagers attending the clinic from being stigmatized. These new services included athletic, job, and college physicals, immunizations, and a weight-control program. After the program was expanded to include comprehensive health services and placed in three additional high schools, enrollment grew. In 1980, it was reported that birthrates had dropped significantly after the initiation of health services, including family planning, in four high school sites. However, this research did not include a control group and did not account for abortions (see Chapter Six).

When I visited the St. Paul program in 1983, I was impressed with the large number of students utilizing all the facilities and with the enthusiasm of the staff. A local researcher, Michael Baizerman of the University of Minnesota, made some interesting observations about why the program worked. He noted that the clinics were indeed accessible to the students and that they appeared to coexist with the school. Like other pupil personnel services, they were institutionalized and therefore invisible, so they did not "make waves" and were not threatening. While the staff was particularly proud of the professional attention the students were receiving, the students perceived that the clinic attendant, a local community resident, was the most important person for them because of her accessibility and caring.

A visit to Houston's school-based program revealed a different model, a freestanding Adolescent Health Center attached to an alternative high school that also served students who were bussed in from four middle schools and two high schools. The center was organized in 1981 by Donna Bryant, director of the Urban Affairs Corporation (UAC), which also operated child-care and senior-citizen centers in the deprived Fifth Ward of Houston. The program appeared to this observer as a "physician, social worker, and friend to a lot of very needy children." The clinic director, Sharon Lovick, was articulate in her support of this model as a prototype for school-based adolescent health care. Discussions with Lovick and Bryant resulted in the idea of bringing together the emerging school-based clinic programs to determine whether the concept did indeed have validity. The Ford Foundation awarded a grant that would allow the Center for Population Options (CPO) and the UAC to cohost a conference of school clinic administrators in Houston in the fall of 1984. CPO was a Washington-based program planning and advocacy organization with a strong interest in prevention of adolescent pregnancy. This first conference marked the emergence of school-based clinics as an incipient movement with potential as a specialized field of program development.

The common theme that emerged from these uncommon programs was that each was organized independently in response to a perceived need to provide adolescents with a comfortable and confidential health-care "home."[6] These program innovators, in very different community settings, each identified the school as the logical place to deliver services designed to meet the specific requirements of teenagers. An informal survey of nine of the ten programs revealed that all offered physical examinations as well as treatment for minor acute illnesses, accidents, and injuries. Each provided individual counseling about sexuality, gynecologic examinations, and follow-up examinations, for family planning patients. They either offered contraceptive prescriptions in the clinic or referred students to off-site birth control clinics. Only two of the programs dispensed contraceptives at school clinics. In addition, all performed lab tests, screened for STDs, provided nutrition education, and referred students with other problems to social service agencies. Most offered sex education to groups of students at the clinic and had programs for weight loss, drug and alcohol abuse treatment, dental services, immunization, and individual and family counseling. In several schools, classroom sex education or health education was provided through the program. Day care for children of students had been organized in three of the high schools.

With few exceptions, services were free. The service delivery patterns were surprisingly similar despite the diversity of the organizations, and this model of clinic services has persisted right up to the present—heavy use of screening procedures, identification of previously undetected diseases such as respiratory and heart problems, and extremely high demand for counseling and individual attention. Although the services were similar, the organization and operation of these first ten programs reflected the individuals who played a strong role in designing and inaugurating them. The full range of organizing agencies was represented—a hospital, a health department, a comprehensive health center, a voluntary youth agency, a family planning agency, a community development agency, and a school system.

Not everyone, of course, loved the idea of school-based clinics. Within a short period of time, the conservative element around the country discovered the emergence of "sex clinics" in the nation's high schools. As new programs began to be discussed, people from outside of school communities appeared at school board meetings, accusing school officials of corrupting American youth, encouraging promiscuity, and promoting abortion. The *National Right-to-Life News* covered the first conference in Houston and subsequently warned its readers that "the momentum behind the school-based clinic juggernaut may appear irreversible, but it isn't. A combination of grassroots resistance and an appeal to reason and common sense can be effective....Politicians have rejected the clinics and resistance is growing."[7] In only a few instances did these strident voices influence the votes of school board members, almost all of whom were convinced that the children in their communities needed access to health care.

These ten pioneer programs, building on the earlier work of Philip Porter and the Cambridge experience, were the models for the programs that followed them. The Support Center for School-Based Health Services was created by the Center for Population Options with Ford and Carnegie Corporation grants, and Sharon Lovick became its first director operating out of Houston. The "pioneers" were recruited onto technical assistance teams and worked with Lovick in responding to the growing demand from innovators around the country who were intrigued by the idea of school-based clinics.

Growth and Distribution of School-Based Clinics

Between 1984 and 1993, a large number of school-based clinics were organized in high schools and middle schools in almost every state, primarily in urban areas. In addition, many elementary schools have once again become sites for clinic services. My own best estimate is that at least five hundred clinics provide primary health care in or near school buildings, with additional sites proliferating rapidly. (See Chapter Seven for the count by state.) In addition to the sites that I have described as clinics, a number of other kinds of collaborative centers could be added to the count that are more focused on family services or after-school recreation. The function of many of the new centers, in Kentucky and Florida for example, is to centralize coordination, with an office in a school that facilitates referrals and outreach to a network of community agencies. California's Healthy Start program relies heavily on school-based case managers and parent programs, along with health services.

Whereas a major focus of many of the earlier programs was prevention of pregnancy, more recent entries address a wide range of goals, including dropout and substance abuse prevention, mental health, and health promotion. The growth of school-based clinics has resulted from a variety of forces: demand arising at the community level to help schools deal with the "new morbidities"; popularity of an innovative model for working with high-risk youth; responses to requests for proposals from foundations; and stimulation by state government initiatives. By 1986, the American Medical Association found that one-half of primary-care physicians approved of placing medical care clinics, including those that provided contraceptive information, in all high schools.[8] Many of the new programs have been initiated by specialists in adolescent medicine and by pediatricians who are eager to be involved in developing new delivery systems for children and youth.

Public acceptance of this new model of health delivery is much higher than might be expected. The 1992 Gallup Poll reported that 77 percent of respondents favored using public school buildings in their communities to provide health and social services to students, administered and coordinated by various government agencies.[9] Contrary to the "conventional wisdom" about how conservative the American public is, a majority of respondents (68 percent) approved of condom distribution in their local public schools, although one in four of them would require parental consent. A 1993 sample survey of North Carolina registered voters showed that 73 percent believe that health care centers offering prevention services should be located at high schools—with the strongest support from African-Americans and from eighteen- to thirty-four-year-olds and with no differences by gender, religion, or parental status. More than 60 percent favored providing birth control at the centers.[10]

Beginning in the late 1970s, the Robert Wood Johnson Foundation (RWJ) began funding multigrant national adolescent health programs, as well as single-site school-based projects, in Chicago, Kansas City, Flint (Michigan), and Houston. In 1986, convinced that school-based health services would improve adolescents' access to much needed care, RWJ initiated a grants program to establish school-based clinics to make health care more accessible to poor children and reduce the rates of teen pregnancy. The response to the Request for Proposals

(RFP) was extraordinary; the foundation received 179 letters of intent from one hundred cities around the country. As a result, twenty-four health clinics were organized in schools by teaching and community hospitals, county health departments, nonprofit agencies, and, in some cases, the school systems. However, school systems that received grants had to subcontract with community health providers, rather than directly hiring health professionals. According to Julia Lear, director of the RWJ initiative, "the primary reason for this approach was the belief that the way to strengthen health services provided in schools is to make those services an integral part of the community's health care delivery system.... [These] health care institutions are best able to arrange medical referrals, address infection control, arrange laboratory pick-ups, protect medical confidentiality, provide medical back-up when the health centers are closed, and respond to the myriad of issues that arise in the daily management of a health center."[11]

As of 1993, more than half of the states provided funds to stimulate the organization of school-based health programs at the local level, typically through competitive health department grants. In Chapter Eight, the role of states in supporting school-based services is discussed in detail. Certain communities have literally "taken off" in the direction of opening school-based clinics, usually because of an individual within the school system or the health system who moves proposals along. In Denver, David Kaplan, chief of adolescent medicine at the University of Colorado School of Medicine, has been a prime mover. In 1987, under the auspices of the Denver School-Based Clinics, a partnership of community agencies opened three clinics in high schools. The partners include the Denver Public Schools, Denver Health and Hospitals, and the University of Colorado Health Sciences Center and Children's Hospital. Based on the success of these initial efforts, the Denver School Health Coordinating Council was formed to encourage the co-location of community health and mental health resources in schools. In 1993, the Council received a five-year $672,500 federal Maternal and Child

Health special projects grant to provide services to a large community area with five elementary schools, one middle school, and a high school. Denver will shortly have fourteen school-based clinics, with a view toward further expansion as the need is documented.

For years, advocates in the state of Washington tried in vain to get the state to support school-based programs. Finally, building on the success of one privately funded high school demonstration site in Seattle, the voters passed a citywide Families and Education Levy, from which $268,000 could be expended annually for adolescent health centers. These funds, supplemented by general funds from the Seattle City Council, were sufficient to fund four more school clinics in the city. The expectation is that eventually all adolescents in Seattle schools will be provided with accessible and comprehensive health services. All the new clinics are operated under subcontracts with outside organizations (University Adolescent Medicine Division, School of Nursing, and Community Health Centers). A broadly representative Adolescent Health Care Workgroup was established to expand these programs and monitor their quality. The Seattle–King County Health Department coordinates these efforts and provides technical assistance to ongoing and future projects.

Baltimore has led the country in developing school-based clinics. In 1985, the Baltimore Department of Health, which has responsibility for providing health services in all of the city's 184 schools, moved to open clinics in a number of schools using Medicaid reimbursements as one of the sources of support. Today, the city supports ten clinics, four in middle schools, five in regular high schools, and one in an alternative school for pregnant and parenting students. (The latter achieved national notice when the department announced that students could obtain Norplant in the school clinic.) The Baltimore school-based clinics are comprehensive, include dental care, and have emergency twenty-four-hour backup arrangements with local health providers. All provide contraceptives, a policy that shifted from disapproval to approval following a survey of parents that showed that they wanted the school clinics to provide birth control to students with parental consent. Under the leadership of Bernice Rosenthal, the city administrator for Comprehensive School Health Services Program, the Baltimore schools have been certified as providers of managed care, and parents can arrange that their children's prime medical coverage be the responsibility of the school clinic. The health department, school system, and local health providers have all been active participants in a Comprehensive School Health Services Program Committee that meets regularly to address turf problems and develop new funding strategies. Although the city health department supplies the main funding ($2.4 million per year), the Baltimore school clinics also receive funds from eleven different sources, including Medicaid and state Maternal and Child Health grants.

Pittsburgh has taken the partnership route to school-based health services.[12] By the year 2000, it is expected that every school will be linked to a health provider through School Health Partnerships. Several years ago, this city appeared to be very resistant to the idea of school clinics. But after a new superintendent took over in 1992, the school system received funding from the Jewish Healthcare Foundation to work with the local nonprofit Health Education Center to plan for improved access to health care. A careful needs assessment reviewed by a Health Partnership Consortium found that more than a third of the students were high-risk and that many who needed medical care in the past year had been unable to obtain it. By mid 1993, the Pittsburgh School District had organized thirteen partnerships with major hospitals, health centers, and the Allegheny County Health Department, and eleven more were in the developmental stage. What is most unusual about this arrangement is that the health providers finance all of the programs out of their own budgets. When fully developed, on-site services will follow the typical school-based clinic model with physical exams, screening, attention to minor illnesses and injuries, and "human sexuality education in accordance with the school philosophy."

Throughout the 1980s, Boston child health advocates were unable to penetrate the notoriously conservative Boston School Committee's resistance to school-based health services. However, by 1993, the climate had so changed that the Health and Hospitals Department (HHD) was working collaboratively with the Boston school system to bring public health nurse practitioners into eight high schools, in addition to three other school clinics, one sponsored by the HHD, one by a hospital, and a third by a neighborhood health center. This impressive transformation resulted from the switch from an elected to a mayorally appointed school committee, a new superintendent, acceptance of school-based clinics around the state (see Appendix A), and new staff in the health department.

Organization and Funding

No single school-based clinic model has emerged during this developmental stage. According to the Center for Population Options (CPO), in 1991, 54 percent were sponsored by public health departments or community health clinics, 24 percent by hospitals or medical schools, 6 percent by community-based organizations, 7 percent directly by school districts, and the remainder by a variety of private, nonprofit agencies such as visiting nurses' associations and pediatric group practices.[13] A national survey of adolescent health services identified ninety-seven "comprehensive" school-based programs; most were administered by health service organizations, but more than one-fourth reported two or more "parent organizations"—usually the other partner was an educational agency.[14] Those school-based programs that were "noncomprehensive" were more likely to be run by schools and less likely to be run by health-related agencies.

School-based clinics are typically staffed by nurse practitioners, social workers, health educators, clinic aides, and other specialized personnel (nutritionists, psychologists). Physicians come in part-time for scheduled examinations and treatment and are available on call for consultations and emergencies. A nurse practitioner frequently acts as the clinic coordinator. If the school has a school nurse, her services are integrated with the clinic operations as much as possible. The RWJ-funded centers require that a pediatrician or family practitioner be on site for at least one half day per week.[15] Clinics staffed by academic medical centers and teaching hospitals use the school sites for training pediatric and family practice residents and physician assistants.

The past decade of experience has shown that it takes a long time to get a school-based clinic up and running—usually more than a year for planning the services, arranging for community involvement, writing a proposal, and working out arrangements and policies with the school. If a funding source has to be identified (if, for example, the proposal is not a response to a foundation or state initiative), the process can take several years. It took four to eight months for the RWJ projects, after they were funded, to "renovate health center space, hire staff, organize clinical services, negotiate relationships with the school staff, and market the services to the school faculty, staff, students and their parents."[16]

Because of the great variation of models and sizes, annual costs for school-based health centers range from $50,000 to $300,000 per year, and per-user costs range from $50 to $200. The expenditure figures do not usually represent the considerable amount of "matching," goods donated, and services rendered either by the school or the participating agencies. For example, rent is rarely included in grant funds, because the space is provided by schools. But renovations, which can be costly, may be included in the budget. To provide clinic services in schools, programs have to put together funding from a wide array of sources (see Appendix B on federal funding sources). About three-fourths of the funds for school-based services in 1991 came from public sources, including state health department grants (24 percent), state-administered federal Maternal and Child Health Block Grants

(17 percent), local governments (12 percent), Community Health Centers (7 percent), state human and social services budgets (6 percent), and Medicaid (5 percent). Very little financial support came directly from school budgets (8 percent). Foundation grants (18 percent), private insurance and patient fees, and other funds (3 percent) came from the private sector.[17] The situation in St. Paul reflects the complexity of the funding situation. Although the five school clinics (one more has been added recently) are still allied with the medical center, they are managed by a local nonprofit organization, Health Start, created to add flexibility to funding and policy options.[18] According to Donna Zimmerman, the director, Health Start is aggressive about recouping Medicaid and other third-party reimbursements. Other funds come from a local Children's Trust Fund, a federal Department of Corrections grant, Maternal and Child Health Block Grants, and national and local foundations. About 40 percent of St. Paul's enrollees have no health insurance, and 25 percent are eligible for medical assistance. The Denver School-Based Services Program relies on thirteen different sources, about two-thirds from foundations and nonprofit sources such as the United Way and one-third from public sources such as Maternal and Child Health and state health and education departments. Both Denver and St. Paul, along with all the other RWJ grantees, had to develop new strategies for funding when the foundation grants ended in 1993.

Parental Consent

Virtually all school-based clinics require some form of parental consent, but the range among procedures is quite broad.[19] Practitioners are interested in parental consent both to protect themselves from liability for damage and to involve parents in their children's health care. Some consent forms list all the services provided by the clinic, and the parent's signature indicates permission to receive the whole array. Others provide a checklist on which parents can indicate either which services they permit their children to receive or which services they do not want their children to receive. Under certain conditions, clinics can provide services without parental consent and without risk of liability, for example, in an emergency or when the student is a legally emancipated minor or an adult.[20]

In some states, the consent form lists all the services plus a notice that under state law, minors are authorized legally to give their own consent to certain services. The most common procedures for which minors can give consent include treatment of sexually transmitted or other contagious diseases, pregnancy-related care, family planning services, treatment of drug and alcohol problems, and outpatient mental health counseling. Although much of the work of clinics is covered by these minor's-consent services, the parental consent form is generally sought by clinics in order to avoid controversy.

One of the first tasks for the school-based clinic staff is to arrange for consent forms to be circulated to parents and, most important, to be signed and returned. Anyone who has worked in a school knows how difficult this assignment can be. The most successful attempts appear to be those that are collaborative efforts between the clinic and the school staff. Some schools require that parents bring their children and register them on the first day of school. At that time, the registrars hand the parents the clinic slip explaining what the services are and obtain the parents' signatures. This process is used in the elementary and middle schools, rarely at the high school level. In some schools, homeroom teachers are asked to distribute the forms at the beginning of the school year. In other schools, programs start with a mailing to every parent, including a brochure describing the clinic services and a tear-off consent form. Most clinics will treat any student for an emergency and many for a first visit, with the promise that the consent form will be returned the next day. In communities with large non-English-speaking populations, clinic staff produce materials, brochures, and consent forms in other languages, most often Spanish.

Given these problems in obtaining parental permission slips, it should not be surprising that the percentage of students for whom slips are on file varies widely among schools. Lear reported that after the first grant year, 34 percent of the students in the twenty-four schools had parental consent, but the individual schools ranged from 3 percent to 97 percent. In the second year, 59 percent had parental consent; in the third grant year, 71 percent.[21] More than 90 percent of parents who consented for their children did not limit the kinds of services their children could receive.

Services Provided by School-Based Clinics

The average clinic enrollment is around seven hundred students (within a wide range), with about two thousand visits per year.[22] In most schools, about 70 percent of the students register for the clinic. Most clinics provide general and sports physicals, diagnosis and treatment of minor injuries and illnesses, pregnancy tests, immunizations, laboratory tests, chronic health problem management, health education, extensive counseling, and referral. Over 90 percent prescribe medications.

A survey conducted by CPO in 1990 reported that 97 percent of high school and 73 percent of middle school clinics provided counseling on birth control methods.[23] About three-fourths of the high schools and half of the middle schools conducted gynecological examinations for birth control methods, followed up users, and provided referrals to other agencies for methods and examinations. However, only half wrote prescriptions for contraceptives, and only 21 percent actually dispensed them. Although the clinics say they are offering these "family planning" services, only 10 to 20 percent of the students report using the clinics for family planning. Not surprisingly, the clinics that offer the most comprehensive family planning services appear to be the most heavily utilized by the students for family planning. One study of six clinics found that at only two sites were more students using contraceptives than in comparison sites without clinics, but there were no differences in pregnancy rates or birthrates among sites.[24] Douglas Kirby concluded that the clinic could not have an effect on pill and condom use unless much higher priority were given to pregnancy or AIDS prevention throughout the program and the school and much greater attention given to follow-up of sexually active students to insure compliance with contraceptive methods. In Denver, where clinic staff aggressively track girls whom they refer to community agencies for birth control methods, 82 percent of the students referred complied with the protocol within a one-month period.[25]

A recent survey found thirty-six school systems that allowed condoms to be provided on site. For example, the Philadelphia school district has formed a collaborative relationship with the city's health department, the Family Planning Council of Southeast Pennsylvania, community health centers, and hospitals to operate health resource centers in nine high schools, where trained health educators provide students with education, referrals to health and community agencies, and condoms.[26] The Philadelphia Department of Health has provided $60,000 to purchase educational materials and 500,000 condoms for all of the centers.

Most school-based clinics can provide reliable statistics on clinic utilization. Program data from California show that clinic users are more likely to be females, African-American or Hispanic, and disadvantaged (eligible for free-lunch programs).[27] However, a large number of males do use the clinics, especially for physical examinations and treatment for accidents and injuries. Reports from clinic practitioners invariably mention personal counseling as the most sought-after service, reflecting the stressful lives of contemporary adolescents. In some clinics, 30 to 40 percent of the primary diagnoses are mental health–related.[28] In one year, the Balboa High School Teen Health Center in San Francisco found that 70 percent of the diagnoses indicated a need for further intervention for depression, anxiety, and family problems. The presence of a nonthreatening confidential advisor apparently opens up communication about such issues as physical and sexual abuse, parental drug use, and fears of violence.

Everyone who works in a school-based clinic has stories to tell about the needs of its clientele. Holley Galland, a sprightly family physician who inaugurated the RWJ program in Baton Rouge, Louisiana, described the results of administering preseason physicals to Westdale Middle School's basketball players: "In one afternoon of screening kids on the team, I picked up three asthmatics, none of whom were stabilized, all of whom I 'tuned up' and we had a winning season."[29]

Martha Arden, a pediatrician at the student health center at Franklin K. Lane High School in Queens, New York, reported, "We see quite a number of kids with emotional problems, and we find a high incidence of mental illness." One student referred to the hospital for a workup was found to have a multiple personality disorder. Another girl who showed up at the clinic with back pain had been beaten by her mother. Jose Cardenas, a psychologist at the Teen Health Center in San Fernando High School in California, discovered many students who had attempted suicide, were having difficulty with peer relationships, or were experiencing early pregnancy following sexual abuse. He set up therapy groups in English and Spanish. "This sort of thing happens much more frequently than we want to believe," he reported. "You learn about it only when you develop a relationship of trust with students you are caring for."[30]

A pediatric nurse practitioner from a rural school-based clinic in Pendleton County, West Virginia, recalls Richard, a fifteen-year-old who wandered into the school clinic with a foot problem. Five days earlier, he had run a nail through his sneaker on the farm. "He had a significant cellulitis and the classic red lines of blood poisoning running up his leg. I put him on a course of antibiotics, so he did not need to be hospitalized." In that community, most of the families are the working poor, not eligible for Medicaid but without personal health insurance, so going to the hospital creates a major financial problem for them. Richard's school-based clinic care was free.

Laura Secord was on duty at the opening of the Ensley High School Adolescent Health Center in Birmingham, Alabama. "I saw my first patient before we had knobs on our doors. She was 17 years old, with a severe kidney infection. She was also six months pregnant and had been starving herself in order to keep her pregnancy a se-cret. She was severely depressed. Her pregnancy was the result of sex-ual abuse by an older family friend."[31]

Students who use school clinics are articulate supporters of the model. Jennifer McCollough, a student from Forest City, Arkansas, told a Senate hearing, "If there had not been a clinic at our school, I would have been very embarrassed to go to the public health clinic. Most teenagers do not have the transportation to get there or they are just ashamed of the fact that they are either pregnant, or they are ill or they are poor and do not have insurance to go see a private physician."[32] Jay Bradford, a state legislator from Arkansas, told the same hearing why school-based services make good sense in his state. "On-site school based services offer drop-in appointments, some-thing which matches more closely with the lifestyle needs of com-pulsive active young people. Most clinics do not charge for services, so the lack of insurance coverage and the inability to pay is elimi-nated as a barrier. Lack of adequate transportation becomes a chief concern in addressing the health care needs of our rural citizens. Through school-based services, you already have the patient trans-ported to the services. Because the clinics are staffed by persons em-ployed by the State Health Department, rather than the school it-self, student attitudes toward the clinic personnel are different. If the clinic were staffed by the school district, the students would look upon the staff as part of the school, and someone that perhaps would not maintain the necessary confidentiality between the student and the providers. . . . You do not have to build a school-based clinic. The school district provides the housing for the clinic."[33]

Group Counseling and Health Promotion

Nurses, social workers, health educators, and clinic aides often get involved in classroom presentations and other activities in the areas of prevention of high-risk behaviors and promotion of health. In some schools, the school-based clinic has been given the responsibility for sex and HIV education; in others, the clinic staff is invited into classrooms or school assemblies for "one-shot" presentations. Clinic staff frequently participate in schoolwide events, especially those that include parents, by running workshops, coordinating "health fairs," and being available for individual consultations.

In Minneapolis, Minnesota, in addition to giving classroom presentations, school-based clinic staff conduct support groups, usually one hour per week over six to thirty weeks.[34] The most frequently offered group activities are sessions on prenatal care, adolescent development, pregnancy prevention, abuse, parenting, family therapy, social relationships, and grief and loss. Other clinics conduct groups that deal with depression, suicide prevention, support for gay and lesbian students, Children of Alcoholics and other substance-use issues, wellness, weight control and nutrition, and life planning. School clinic staff feel that they are in a good position to respond to crises in the school such as suicide and violence and to rapidly develop appropriate responses to these situations.

A "traditional" school-based health clinic in Albuquerque, New Mexico, evolved into a multidisciplinary project emphasizing prevention through classroom teaching.[35] Clinic staff provided by the medical school each adopted a class and worked with the teacher in the classroom on a special project. For example, a tenth-grade communication class worked on a presentation about AIDS for seventh-grade students. An English class did library research on drugs, invited guest speakers, made field trips to a nursery for newborns to learn about the effects of drugs during pregnancy, and developed a drug education curriculum.

The Columbia School of Public Health operates school-based clinics in four inner-city middle schools.[36] The programs have evolved over a seven-year period to respond to the particular needs of the students and faculty in each school. In addition to the provision of primary health services and psychosocial counseling, components include training in social skills and decision making; case management for students at risk of dropping out; career orientation, with role models, community service jobs, and the creation of videos and a newspaper; an academic skills program promoting higher-order thinking skills; parent advocates employed as facilitators and home visitors; training parents to be discussion group leaders on adolescent sexuality; and involvement with the school in implementing health education curricula. In one school, the Columbia staff worked in partnership with the school administration to design a major reformation of the school, helping to obtain a grant for technical assistance, organizing staff retreats, and serving as a "watchdog" to ensure that restructuring had occurred. As a result, the school has been reorganized into "houses" with management teams. One school-based clinic social worker is assigned to each house.

The Columbia program, building on seven years of clinical experience, recently initiated a new approach to pregnancy prevention. After observing the amount of individual attention students required to help them deal with sexuality issues, specially trained health educators were employed for what they call "in your face" sexuality education and counseling. Students who are identified by clinic staff or school personnel as at risk of unprotected sexual intercourse are referred to health educators. They are seen in groups at least once a week and individually when needed. The staff believe the intensity of the intervention is assisting young people to deal more realistically with the pressures to have sex and will eventually lower teen pregnancy rates in that community.

From Pioneers to Social Movement

A movement toward the development of school-based health centers has emerged during the past decade, reflecting a response to the overwhelming needs of today's students for health services. Fred Hechinger, a leading educational authority, concluded from his study of adolescent health that school-based health centers must be established for young people whose health would otherwise be jeopardized by the lack of access to services.[37] It is estimated that in aggregate some five hundred school-based clinics may now be serving at most half a million students per year, a minuscule proportion of the total number of enrollees in junior and senior high schools. Nevertheless, these "pioneer" programs prove that such efforts are both possible and feasible, and, in a sense, this cohort may be the "cutting edge" for the implementation of full-service schools, each individualized to the particular needs of the students, the school, the parents, and the community. In the next chapter, we will examine two fully realized models of full-service schools, and in Chapter Six, we review the pevidence from the emerging reports of whether school-based clinics are achieving their goals.

5

▲▲▲

Realizing the Vision:
Two Full-Service Schools

Most of the programs we have examined are "add-ons." An outside agency comes into a school and creates a new unit—a clinic or a center—that coexists with the educational system. Experience with some school-based programs has shown that as the health and social services program matures and becomes institutionalized, attention shifts to the reorganization of the educational side.[1] Yet it is very difficult to take an underfunded, overcrowded, inadequate institution and remake it into a fully functioning place. A major challenge for practitioners and advocates is the establishment of balance between the movement for support services and the development of quality education.

Across the United States, one can find exceptional schools, places that were designed from the start to respond to the needs of young people, exciting buildings that are the products of creative partnerships between school systems and community agencies. I have no idea how many of these exemplary schools there are. It is not even possible to define exactly when a school is "full-service" rather than "partial service" and where on the continuum of service components good schools emerge as the best. In my travels across the country, I visited two middle schools that stand out as models of how to put together both sides of the fundamental full-service equation: restructuring of education plus helping children and their families by providing health, mental health, and social services on sites. I selected these schools as examples because they serve similar populations yet have very different structural arrangements. Both of these schools, at opposite ends of the country, started from scratch with new principals and new facilities designed to enhance the educational experiences of the students. Both of the schools are located in poverty neighborhoods and enroll mostly students from disadvantaged Hispanic families. The first school, IS 218 in New York City, is an example of a "settlement house in a school," a prototype community-school initiated by a community social agency with funding from foundations. The second school, Hanshaw, in Modesto, California, is an example of school restructuring, a model promulgated by a school system that drew in an array of other agencies largely with public funding.

The Settlement House in the School

An excellent example of comprehensive school-based programming by a community organization can be found in IS 218, a middle school in Washington Heights, New York, recently opened through a partnership between the New York City school system and the Children's Aid Society (CAS), a nonprofit organization.[2] With this unique arrangement, CAS and school personnel have created a "settlement house" in a school. One of New York City's oldest and largest social agencies, CAS has a budget that exceeds $30 million and operates in twenty-six facilities such as community centers and mobile health stations, offering adoption services, foster care, counseling, housing for the homeless, recreation, medical and dental care, and jobs programs. According to Philip Coltoff, executive director, a program review conducted in 1988 suggested that the Washington Heights community was in need of additional services. When CAS began working with the local educational authorities to plan together, the idea of a community-school emerged. The vision was a school building open all days and evenings, weekends and summers, with a challenging educational program matched with after-school enrichment, health and social services, and community education.

A new School Construction Authority was in the process of planning for new buildings in New York City to replace the outmoded plants that house schools. As the plans began to develop, CAS obtained a grant from the Charles Hayden foundation for start-up costs related to the modification and equipping of the new school. CAS developed some specific qualifications for the architecture of this new kind of institution so that the building could be "zoned"; parts could be shut off for security and safety if access were wanted only to certain areas such as the gym or auditorium. Outdoor lighting was required for evening programs. Air conditioning was essential for summer use. The CAS architect, the Board of Education architects, and the School Construction Authority worked together in a unique collaboration to produce the new school.

While the school was being built, CAS worked to build bridges to the Dominican community, whose children would be enrolled in the school. Beginning in 1989, using private foundation funds, CAS staff initiated a number of activities to respond to the articulated needs of the area. Children from Washington Heights were registered for summer camp, a mobile van began to deliver medical and dental care, and a special program was started for disabled children. CAS worked with the Alianza Dominicana, a significant community organization, to obtain a grant and train staff for an after-school program as one of the New York City "Beacons" (schools that link with community-based agencies). These joint activities gave CAS credibility with the

Dominican community that was well established before the doors of the new school opened.

A working group was put together with staff from the school district office and CAS to plan how the actual institution would work, with an integrated educational program that would be carried out from 7:00 A.M. to 10:00 P.M. every school day. During the planning process, which lasted four years, the Board of Education had three different chancellors (and a fourth has just been appointed). At the outset, Coltoff obtained a long-term commitment to this partnership in the form of an official resolution from both the central board and the local district board.

In March of 1992, the doors opened at IS 218. Located in the heart of Washington Heights, this new building gleams—yellow brick with attractive gardens around the base, the elegant front entrance decorated with a huge mosaic of Hispanic themes. The school is called the Salome Urena Middle Academies (SUMA), after a Latino poet whose portrait hangs in the entryway. The building has been designed specifically to get rid of the institutional, prisonlike quality found in many of the neighborhood buildings and to incorporate an open plan with no straight halls and lots of curves, light, and color. As one enters the building, after passing inspection by the ubiquitous security guards, one finds a family resource center and a medical suite, accessible to the community. In this central lobby, student entrepreneurs from the CAS program have opened the SUMA school store, which sells student-made merchandise (jewelry, toys), books, papers, healthy snacks, T-shirts, and other items.

The school houses 1,200 students, who are enrolled in one of four academies, one on each of the upper floors: Math, Science, and Technology; Business; Expressive Arts; and Community Service. Each academy is a self-contained unit with five classes and five teamed teachers who act as advisors to the students in their units. Several times a week, advisory groups of fifteen students meet to talk about career plans, school, and family problems. The principal, Mark

Kavarsky, worked with the planning committee in refining the conceptual plans for the school. He had some decision-making power in the selection of teachers, encouraging team players who could also work independently and discouraging more traditional types. Under his leadership, the school faculty have been working with the CAS staff to create a "seamless program," tying together academics with all the other activities so that what goes on in the classroom is carried out throughout the day and after school and is also conveyed to the parents through the resource center. According to the staff, students remain in school because they want to, it is fun, and it has become "the thing to do" in this community. The fun continues into the summer, when IS 218 students can take lessons from the Alvin Ailey Dancers and receive mentoring from Teach for America teachers, along with the usual summer arts, sports, and courses.

The school opens at 7:00 A.M. with "zero period," featuring dance, Latin band, and recreation along with breakfast for about a hundred students who arrive at that hour. The after-school program operates from 3:00 to 6:00 P.M. weekdays and involves about five hundred students in a range of activities (with a small fee for enrollment). Unlike the brief period of tutoring often provided in traditional after-school programs, every activity at IS 218 is designed in collaboration with educators to maximize instructional components. A "Master Builders Program" involves students interested in math and architecture. Students from the Expressive Arts Academy continue in their talent areas after school, while Business Academy students work to form their own businesses, staff the school store, and prepare to involve their families in family businesses. From observations made during site visits, every classroom seems to reflect the teacher's desire to create an original and stimulating environment. Everywhere you look, in all the halls and in the classrooms, you can find art and science projects, maps, solar systems, flying cranes, motivating slogans, a constructive and exciting environment. Recently, the entire first floor was devoted to the celebration of the Dominican national holiday, culminating with a Saturday event that drew 1,400 people to the school for cultural activities and food. One activity that I found to be truly creative and relevant involved the local police precinct in Spanish classes. The students and their parents were the teachers, who, as a team, were working in the library with the police officers to instruct them in this language. In the evening, CAS extends many of the same programs to teenagers in the community and to parents of students in the school or other residents of the school zone. A family institute offers English as a Second Language (to four hundred registrants!), Spanish, aerobics, and entrepreneurial skills.

The family resource center, located at the entrance to the building, is open from 8:30 A.M. to 8:30 P.M. It offers help with immigration and citizenship, public assistance and employment, housing, crisis intervention, drug prevention, and adult education. This center is staffed by CAS social workers, paraprofessionals, parents, and other volunteers. Some twenty-five parent volunteers are part of a stipend program, learning to be dental assistants, secretaries, and receptionists. This group has designed and made a uniform, a navy suit with a white shirt and tie, which identifies them and gives them status in the school and community.

A clinic located next to the family resource center provides dental and medical services. A dentist and hygienists give examinations and routine care and refer for orthodontic services to community agencies. In the medical clinic, all sick children in the school are seen promptly by a pediatrician or a pediatric nurse practitioner. Additional vision and hearing screenings and immunization checks are held for all children. Students can be enrolled in this clinic by their parents to receive basic primary care. Medical backup for referrals and emergencies is provided by a nearby CAS community center that has a medical clinic. Negotiations are underway for the Visiting Nurses' Association to take over the operation of the medical component.

A mental health component is being initiated with a small staff of social workers. CAS is in the process of obtaining state licensing as a mental health outpatient clinic (CAS's community centers are already licensed). The full staff will eventually include a part-time psychiatrist and a part-time psychologist for testing and evaluation, a full-time graduate social worker as supervisor, several other social workers (depending on resources), a full-time preventive services (foster care) worker, several outreach workers, and various interns in social work, psychology, and nursing. The School-Based Support Team will include the above plus a pediatrician and a nurse practitioner from the health clinic. Referrals are expected from teachers, school guidance counselors, special-education personnel, and CAS staff, as well as through the family resource center. Space for this activity is spread between offices in the resource center and in the central CAS office on the second floor. Apparently, the health and mental health components will be physically separated. This aspect of the program is not yet as well developed as the educational and after-school components described above.

While this program is administered jointly in full partnership between the school system and CAS, the principal is responsible for everything that goes on in the school. He shares his responsibility with Richard Negron, CAS director of community schools, especially during the 3:00 to 10:00 P.M., weekend, school holiday, and summer hours. CAS staff also includes the director of the family resource center, the director of the after-school program, the director of the summer program, and several administrative assistants. In addition, about a dozen people work part-time, many of whom are SUMA teachers who staff the after-school program or work in the summer. A partnership as complex as this needs a mechanism for ensuring open communication at all times. The principal, the CAS community schools director, the CAS associate director, and the district superintendent of schools meet regularly to discuss problems and resolve any conflicts that might arise. To staff up for the opening of several other community schools in the area, CAS has also named a director of programming for Washington Heights who will participate in this cabinet.

Everyone who visits IS 218 comes away stimulated and enthusiastic. One foundation officer asked, "How do we get this in every school?" Adaptation of this approach is a very important issue. CAS has produced a manual detailing how to build a community school—"a revolutionary design in public education."[3] As Coltoff said at the outset, "this is not supposed to be a demonstration program, it must be solidly institutionalized in the system." To demonstrate that adding these services really makes a difference in outcomes, the Fordham University School of Social Work and School of Education have been retained to conduct a long-term evaluation. Early returns from the first several months suggest very high rates of school attendance and heavy utilization of every service that has been made available. During one visit, I asked a student how she liked her new school. "Oh," she said, "It's great, I really like it.... The food is much better here than my old school, they give you bigger portions." When asked if there was anything else different here, she replied, "They are respectful.... The people here treat you with respect." I was impressed that she used exactly the same phrase as the principal: "We treat the kids and their families with respect."

Currently, the community school costs CAS about $800,000 per year for the staffing of the family resource center, the health center, the social-work component, and the after-school program, an amount collected from a number of foundation grants and public programs. The school system contributes maintenance, school guards, and insurance, not an insignificant subsidy considering that the school doors must remain open most of the time. A local college also uses the school for continuing education and helps pay for after-hours guards and maintenance. The cost for central "downtown" CAS staff—for example, the associate director of the agency, who spends a great deal of his time in the schools—is not included in this figure. In addition to partnership roles, CAS provides grants management and general accounting services.

There are 1,200 children at IS 218, and their parents and siblings also participate in the program; the cost is less than $1,000 per student. When added to the educational expenditure per child in New York City of around $6,500, the total cost for this program still does not come near the amount spent in suburban schools.[4] Coltoff believes that a program like this could be operated for less, especially if other resources were used. In IS 218, half the students are eligible for Medicaid, and about one-fourth are actually enrolled. Many of the services rendered could be covered by services for people with disabilities, Medicaid, Chapter 1, and other sources of funds.

In summary, the idea of working with New York City schools to develop partnerships for integrating health and social services came about under positive circumstances. A strong citywide voluntary agency was able to garner the resources to invest in a new model. A local school district wanted help and was open to new ideas. Community-based organizations could be cultivated and could join in the advocacy for such an effort. All parties demonstrated an unusual amount of flexibility and commitment to change. The strategy involved the social agency in demonstrating its capabilities and establishing credibility in the neighborhood prior to the opening of the school. Two other factors contributed to the viability of this partnership: the school chancellor became its champion, and foundations were receptive to requests for support. But even after the chancellor's contract was not renewed, the school board indicated its continuing commitment. What is being created is essentially a new institution with education as its centerpiece. The school has become the center of community life and community activity, equally accessible and welcoming for the children and their parents. Warren Moses, associate director of CAS, recounts how this program has been designed with replicability in mind: "While the unique nature of the program allows CAS to develop and operate most components, some programs are offered by others as part of the collaboration with community-based agencies. Others considering replicating the program should consider the needs of their communities and adapt the model. Youth serving agencies, child welfare and mental health programs, colleges and universities, health care institutions, corporations, churches, public agencies, and the Board of Education all can and should participate in redefining the educational institutions in their communities. The community-school is for families, for children, for all, a center of lifelong learning for the community."[5]

Hanshaw Middle School, Modesto, California

Modesto is the county seat for Stanislaus County, a rapidly growing population center in northern California with increasing ethnic and economic diversity. Although the population is close to 175,000, the city maintains its rural flavor from its proximity to agricultural areas and its traditional value system, with churches on every corner. But suburban shopping malls have decimated the downtown, leaving many empty stores and marginal businesses. Modesto City Schools has become a large urban school district, serving 28,655 students in thirty-three schools. In former years, relationships between the school system and community agencies were very limited. In 1986, when James Enochs came on board as the new superintendent, he gave high priority to formalizing arrangements with local agencies for provision of services on school campuses. Efforts have been made to forge links between schools and agencies in a variety of areas, including mental health, physical health, juvenile justice, recreation, social services, and child welfare.[6] In the late 1980s, Stanislaus County formed an Interagency Children's Services Coordinating Council made up of the heads of the seven county government child-serving agencies, major nonprofit agencies, and school systems. The council's philosophy statement affirms its commitment to cooperative and collaborative service planning and delivery to provide the highest quality and most cost-effective services to children and youth in the county.

One of the goals of the revitalized school system in Modesto was to build several new schools in low-income areas that would be more responsive to the needs of the community. Hanshaw Middle School was created out of the vision of Chuck Vidal, the principal. Prior to opening the doors, Vidal went out into the community, door-to-door, and asked the residents what they wanted. The answer as interpreted by Vidal was a school where all the students would strive for a college education, a middle school that was designed to meet the developmental needs of the early teen years. Vidal knew a lot about this community, a poor Hispanic neighborhood where three-fourths of the students would be eligible to receive free or reduced-price meals and one-fourth are in families on welfare. One-third of the children are Limited English Proficient (LEP), and almost two-thirds speak a language other than English at home. Immigrants from Cambodia and Laos are recent arrivals here, and their children have language, health, and adjustment problems as well.

In 1991, Hanshaw unveiled its innovative $13 million campus in a neighborhood that "doesn't often see investments of this size and beauty."[7] The design of the school is inventive, a campus complex with six handsome white buildings arranged in a circle around a huge inner grassy quad that contains an outdoor amphitheater as well as picnic tables and other amenities. One building houses "exploratories" with arts and crafts rooms, laboratories, an auto shop, and home-economics facilities. A separate well-equipped gymnasium and multipurpose auditoriums are located close to a "state-of-the-art" band room and a chorus rehearsal room. Another building contains a library, a branch of the Stanislaus County library system. The school is adjacent to the Salvation Army Red Shield Recreation Center, a neighborhood-based agency for youth.

According to *Atlantic Magazine*, Hanshaw is "something entirely new and different; a new building, a new kind of teacher, a new educational concept, a new way of thinking about kids."[8] The school, with 870 students, is organized into seven student houses or communities. The teachers are "community leaders" and are responsible for their "citizens," the students. Each community has a theme and a connection to a branch of a California State University (Stanislaus, Sacramento, San Francisco, San Jose, Hayward, Sonoma, and Fresno.) Students visit the campuses of their adopted schools, and each university provides support to their student group and involves the Hanshaw students in relationships with the college students. Local businesses, including Gallo Winery, a local department store, an electric company, a newspaper, a medical center, and a radio network, are also involved in partnerships with the school-communities.

The educational content is as innovative as the environment. Hanshaw's thirty-nine teachers work long hours creating their own interdisciplinary curriculum integrating math, science, English, and history. Team teaching is encouraged, as is the use of cooperative learning techniques through which students teach each other, often in extended class periods. Vidal recruited the teachers himself, looking particularly for those with disadvantaged backgrounds who would understand Hanshaw's students. Like a "corporate raider," he said, "I've stolen the best." The school climate is designed to encourage flexibility, personal responsibility, and collaboration. Students sit around tables rather than in rows. Every room has a computer linked into a network. Technological subjects such as robotics, hydroponics, and desktop publishing are included on a list of exploratory classes for students. A schoolwide closed-circuit television system has been installed to allow teachers and students to broadcast lessons. The dress code is seriously enforced—students are encouraged to wear T-shirts with the names of their sponsoring universities, not sports figures and rock stars. The motto "Always do your personal best" is prominently featured. Cultural differences are respected. The

announcements on the intercom are repeated in Spanish, recogniz-
ing the importance of students who have not yet mastered English.

Vidal and the Modesto city school system did not stop with academic and environmental initiatives. To fulfill their commitment to
improving the academic performance of all students, they acknowledged that this goal could only be met for high-risk students if their
health and social needs received proper attention. As in other
schools in the Modesto system, partnership agreements were worked
out with various agencies to bring practitioners into Hanshaw, including a mental health clinician, a part-time student assistance
counselor, and a DARE (police) officer, and the school system supplied a part-time psychologist, a school nurse, three migrant education supportive services aides (one Laotian, one Hispanic, and one
Cambodian), and a supervisor. Within a year of opening the doors,
Hanshaw had a lot of activity going on, but services were still fragmented and not well coordinated.

Impressed with the Modesto "spirit," in 1991 the Stuart Foundation
provided a grant to the Modesto City Schools to develop a case management approach to the delivery of social services. As part of the
planning process, a needs assessment was conducted that revealed
some of the problems confronting this community: many local physicians and dentists didn't accept Medi-Cal; parents had a lot of problems with violence, conflict, and alcoholism; Hispanic families, in
particular, needed an Alcoholics Anonymous program in Spanish,
help with referrals to services, more medical care, and help with communication with the school on educational matters; and parents, in
general, wanted educational programs, such as parenting courses, high
school equivalency classes, and computer instruction. Around the same
time, the county health department expressed concern about the
lack of accessibility to health care services and the inability of the
public health system to keep up with the increase in the number of
low-income families in the county. They cited factors such as education, language, and transportation as major barriers. According to the

Department of Mental Health, use of alcohol was a major problem in this county, one that should be addressed through school-based services including staff training and prevention and treatment services. The work conducted under the grant from the Stuart Foundation put the Modesto City Schools into an excellent position to respond to a Request for Proposals (RFP) circulated by the California Department of Education for Healthy Start grants.

In 1991, the California legislature passed the Healthy Start Support Services for Children Act to establish innovative, comprehensive, school-based or school-linked health, social, and academic support services throughout the state. (See Appendix A for more details on state programs.) School systems had to submit evidence of working collaborative partnerships with health, mental health, social services, drug and alcohol, probation, and other public and nonprofit agencies. The legislation required that all grants be matched by a consortium with a local contribution of one dollar for every three dollars awarded by the state (a 25 percent match). In response to the RFP, a Healthy Start steering committee was appointed by the Interagency Council. The steering committee was composed of representatives of potential participating agencies, who worked with school staff, parents, and community members over a six-month period to design a coordinated school-based interagency service network.[9] Top agency heads were involved, directors and executive directors, along with school superintendent Enochs and dynamic leadership from the school system—Sharon Rohrke, assistant superintendent, and Patricia Logan, supervisor of pupil services.

In June of 1992, Modesto City Schools, as the lead agency for a Healthy Start consortium, was notified that it had been awarded two of the forty operational grants in the entire state. "This is the highlight of my career as it relates to pupil services," Rohrke told school board members on the night they voted to accept the Healthy Start grant, "What we're asking tonight is that you open your mind to new ways of serving children and their families. We need to look at new ways to serve children with desperate needs."[10] Not everyone agreed with the school board. The proposals drew opposition from several local parents concerned about the appropriateness of school-based services and referrals. A local representative from the Traditional Values Coalition asserted that the district was following a trend toward abortion referral and condom distribution in schools: "These types of programs don't work, they're expensive, and they undermine parental authority." Other parents testified on the success of programs that were already in place, such as mental health treatment and health screenings. Hanshaw received almost $400,000 from the state and reported a commitment of in-kind contributions from community agencies of $822,986 to round out a three-year budget of over $1.2 million, or $400,000 per year. The other recipient school was Robertson Road Elementary School, the feeder school for Hanshaw.

What does the Healthy Start initiative bring to the Hanshaw school? The Healthy Start operational grant mainly funds the implementation of an interagency case management team and an on-site resource center to house primary health and dental care. This project is governed by the Interagency Children's Services Coordinating Council through the Hanshaw Healthy Start Committee, which is composed equally of parents (50 percent) and school and agency staffs (50 percent). Most of the state funds are being used for personnel, including a project coordinator, a neighborhood services worker, and a youth development worker. The coordinator makes sure that the case management team functions efficiently and also staffs the Hanshaw Healthy Start committee. The neighborhood service worker facilitates the linkages between school and service providers, while the youth development worker is charged with increasing youth peer programs and cross-age tutoring with students in elementary school and links students to the adjacent Salvation Army Red Shield Center and other community youth-serving programs. The heart of the initiative is the provision of integrated case management to the Hanshaw families who are the highest users of multiple-agency services. Workers from the participant agencies meet routinely to share information about students and their families, and one worker is assigned the responsibility to follow up on a specific student and family. This new way of conducting "business" builds on those service components that were already in the school and adds some new ones.

The Hanshaw project is designed to integrate services by co-locating them at the same site. By the fall of 1993, the various components of the Healthy Start initiative will be united in a new resource center, a portable building providing two thousand square feet of space in the middle of the campus, adjacent to the school cafeteria and next door to the Red Shield Center. The facility will house three medical examining rooms and two dental stations; an office for the case management team; offices for the project coordinator, neighborhood development worker, probation officer, and other staff; and a waiting room for families and children.

A close look at the Hanshaw project shows how public and private agencies can become partners to schools. The Stanislaus County Department of Mental Health currently has school consultation contracts with four school districts in the county, as well as Head Start. Prior to the Healthy Start initiative, the department already had a full-time mental health clinician at Hanshaw. Under the new arrangement, the clinician continues to work at the site but is now a key member of the case management–family advocate team. Department staff also participate on the Healthy Start steering committee and contribute time for staff training on conflict resolution and working with drug-addicted families. The county Department of Social Services (DSS) is providing a liaison person to help with the development of the case management model at Hanshaw. The Public Assistance Division is committed to restructuring eligibility procedures to provide better linkages to the Hanshaw Middle School community in terms of AFDC, Food Stamps, and Medi-Cal. DSS staff are involved in training school staff in regard to public assistance services and child and sexual abuse issues.

The Center for Human Services, a nonprofit social services agency, has been providing prevention and intervention programs in Stanislaus County since 1970. In addition to community-based facilities such as a runaway and homeless youth shelter, the center contracts to provide student assistance programs in sixty-three K–12 school sites. Under the Healthy Start initiative, Hanshaw Middle School continues to receive services three days per week from a bilingual, bicultural counselor who provides counseling, information, referral, and consultation with the school staff. The Merced Family Health Center is a nonprofit, federally funded migrant and community health center. On-site prevention and primary medical care will be provided by a team of a physician or physician's assistant and a medical aide five days a week when the center is opened. A health education team from West Modesto Clinic is available to provide education on topics such as tobacco use/abuse, HIV, and parenting. Stanislaus Medical Center is owned and operated by the county and is the major provider of Medi-Cal care, emergency services, and outpatient care to low-income families. At Hanshaw, the Stanislaus Medical Center will coordinate dental evaluations and treatment plans with West Modesto Dental Services. The medical center will act as the referral and backup site for students and family members in need of further medical care.

The Stanislaus County Department of Public Health is making a bilingual community health worker available to provide education and outreach in regard to the Child Health and Disability Prevention program (CHDP). (This is a California initiative to provide comprehensive health assessments to Medi-Cal–eligible children and children from low-income families.) Eventually, the department expects to extend its contribution to in-home case management, family interventions, and working with pregnant and parenting adolescents. The county probation department is the juvenile authority that deals with youth who are arrested or cited by law enforcement for law violations. Modesto City Schools funds two probation officers: one provides supervision for middle school students who have previously exhibited problems in school in addition to delinquency; the other works with children who have been identified as high-risk or gang-involved. Under the Healthy Start initiative, the chief probation officer has committed a part-time probation officer to Hanshaw to participate in the case management team and provide in-service training for school administration and staff on delinquency prevention, gangs, and out-of-control children.

The Modesto City Schools was the prime initiator of the Healthy Start proposal, building on collaborative arrangements that already existed with most of the participating agencies. In the grant application, the school system officially contributed time of the assistant superintendent for administrative and pupil services (Rohrke) and the supervisor of pupil services (Logan). Logan is expected to spend at least thirty hours per month (and obviously spends a great deal more time) coordinating agency partnerships, facilitating program implementation, acting as liaison between the school district and everybody else, and continuing as an active member of the steering committee. The principal of Hanshaw, Chuck Vidal, is also expected to spend at least twenty hours per month on the Healthy Start project. He is responsible for supervising all school and project staff who participate in the Healthy Start program and for maintaining the new center when it opens.

The more than $800,000 contributed by participating agencies as "match" and "in-kind" does not necessarily mean that the agency lays out cash for its donation; rather, it lends various staff members for limited periods of time and covers that expenditure out of its regular funds. In the long run, the state of California believes that most of the services provided at Hanshaw (and other collaborative programs) can be financed through Medi-Cal. It is expected that Modesto City Schools will take steps toward obtaining Medi-Cal certification under a new provider category for school-based Medi-Cal–eligible services at the school sites. Under this arrangement,

Hanshaw would be certified as a Medi-Cal school provider, and Medi-Cal would be the primary source for funding dental, primary health, and mental health services.

In summary, the Healthy Start initiative in Hanshaw Middle School expects to make accessible a range of support services to enhance the innovative educational environment that has been created for middle school children. On-site services include mental health treatment, substance abuse prevention and treatment, family support and parenting education, health and dental screening and assessment, child welfare services, academic support and tutoring, and information and referral. Healthy Start makes referrals to off-site locations that can provide dental treatment, health services, extensive mental health treatment, housing and temporary shelter, and food and clothing.

Hanshaw Middle School, with its Healthy Start initiative, is a unique example of a school-system-initiated full-service community-school. The Modesto City Schools and Hanshaw principal Vidal were prime movers in building the partnerships essential to restructuring education with access to health and social services. One of the important factors in their success has been the careful involvement of all the significant players, the assurance of the commitment of the top echelons of decision makers in the constituent agencies. Another significant accomplishment has been the involvement of the community, with home visits early on to determine what kind of school the people wanted for their children, invitations to participate in planning, and, ultimately, services that parents really wanted. Responsiveness to the cultural diversity of the neighborhood is evident. The fact that all of this activity is taking place in a new campus-style facility greatly enhances the innovative spirit. Everything is new—the school, the principal, the faculty, the curriculum, and, finally, the integrated services system.

One area that is less clear to the outside observer is the governance of the Healthy Start initiative. The project started out with the rhetoric of "collaborative" shared decision making among peer agencies, but it has evolved into partnership agreements with the school system as the lead agency. Originally, a decision was made to place the fiscal responsibility for the resource center outside the school system to bypass complex union negotiations and make it possible to hire staff with different qualifications and personnel practices than in the school system. However, the community-based agency that had been designated would have needed to receive additional indirect costs from the state grant to absorb the outlays for hiring and supervising staff and managing local grants. At that point, it was determined that the school district could take on the management responsibility at a lower cost, so Modesto City Schools ended up as the fiscal agent for the entire Healthy Start grant. It should be noted that the central office of the school system furnishes strong staff support in the personae of Rohrke and Logan, who are deeply committed to the success of the school and contribute significant amounts of time and energy to this project.

Since a major requirement for outside-funded demonstration projects is to be replicable, a process evaluation of this initiative will clarify the governance issues for other schools that wish to emulate the innovative work being done at Hanshaw. The assumption is that if all these services are provided and the educational system is maintained, then the outcomes for the students and their families will be greatly improved. We won't know for some time whether that assumption is correct. In response to the state's mandates, there are extensive plans for evaluation. In the short run, daily attendance is close to 98 percent, about as high as a school can go, and test scores are beginning to go up. In the future, program planners will look for such changes in child and family behaviors as improved academic performance, reductions in family violence and child abuse, improved health, and reduced poverty. Changes in the social service system will be measured by increased access to services for families and reduced cost to the system (fewer out-of-home placements).

Community change will be measured by increases in neighborhood safety (lower crime occurrence), participation by businesses, health services, and recreation and youth development activities in the neighborhood. These expected outcomes are ambitious, to say the least, and it is unlikely that some of the more complex factors such as poverty can be affected. But one cannot help admiring the optimism of these Modesto innovators and hoping that they are right. As one student put it, almost exactly echoing her counterpart in New York, "Everybody treats you here with respect."

One of the most remarkable qualities of this school is the attention to detail in the constant altering of the school environment to improve the morale of the students. Every Thursday, the morning announcements are followed by a rendering of the school song, "I Am But a Small Voice," which concludes, "Come, young citizens of the world, we are one, we are one. . . . Peace, give us peace, prosperity, and love for all mankind. I have but a small dream to smile upon the sun, be free to dance and sing, be free to sing my song to everyone."

Are These Full-Service Schools?

SUMA and Hanshaw have many factors in common. At both ends of the country, the movement to create these model schools is being driven by dedicated reformers who are trying to prove that schools can be "user-friendly." These innovators are trying to create environments that teach and delight, raise expectations and meet expectations. Those interested in replication can learn from their experiences. Both of these schools started with a vision, one the dream of a settlement house worker, the other that of a seasoned educator. These events took place in school systems that were open to change, with previous positive experiences with partnerships with community agencies. Foundations played major roles in giving these visionaries adequate funding for making community needs assessments and taking adequate time to plan carefully. Community involvement received very high priority in both places, with continual consultation among Hispanic families and great sensitivity to cultural diversity. Before the doors opened, credibility and acceptance were well established in the neighborhoods.

Both principals had the necessary skills and imagination to restructure their schools by developing smaller units that allowed for individual attention. Few bureaucratic obstacles between conception and implementation were created by higher authorities. Teachers in each school were given maximum responsibility for developing and implementing new curricula and adopting effective teaching methods. The two academic programs evidence sophisticated understanding of the developmental needs of middle school children, with carefully structured environments to maintain discipline and promote compliance with rules and regulations, along with very respectful treatment of individual differences. All of these positive forces are greatly enhanced by the fact that they are coming together in new buildings—bright, clean, well-designed structures that stand in marked contrast to shabby neighborhoods. Both of these programs have received a remarkable amount of media attention, not only in the press but also with extensive television coverage.

On the full-service side of the ledger, the community-school concept was embraced in each project, although the building blocks differed somewhat. IS 218 started with the settlement house concept (a community center that was also a school) and then went out and found the appropriate educator. Hanshaw started out as an educational enterprise but rapidly moved to the full-service concept when the Healthy Start grant made it possible to integrate services provided by an array of community agencies and to organize a case management system. The school system is clearly the lead agency in Modesto, responsible for both the fiscal arrangements and the direct supervision of personnel. IS 218 is more of a two-agency collaborative, with joint direction shared between the school principal and the CAS director of the community-schools. In both of these programs, governance issues are complicated, with many levels of advisory groups and multiple sources of public and private funding. The concept of "ownership" is important in developing full-service programs. CAS, the settlement house, "owns" IS 218, while Modesto City Schools "owns" Hanshaw.

It would be naive to believe that these programs will be so effective that all the students will emerge ready to cope with lives in difficult environments and troubled families. In fact, we do not know what will happen to these students when they go to high schools that lack individual attention and creativity. We do not know whether these schools can maintain the enthusiasm and dedication of the staff. Will the teachers suffer from the same burnout as other inner city teachers and workers after a few years? What would happen if either principal left—would the staff keep going? Will the full-service components be dropped under other school administrations that do not believe that case management, parent training, after-school arts, health services, and all those other benefits belong in schools? Of course, a major issue is the assurance of adequate funding on a long-term basis. Both programs have been careful to assure long-term commitments from the school systems and community agencies, and both have taken steps to become certified as Medicaid providers to obtain reimbursements for services.

Can the full-service model work as well in an old building? Certainly it is a great benefit to be able to design a facility that can house all the requisite components. But, as we have seen in other programs, space can be renovated if the school "buys in" to the concept and the funds are available. The spirit and dedication of the innovators may be more meaningful than bricks and mortar.

These two schools have excellent full-service potential. Neither is fully realized yet, but both appear to be committed to bringing in whatever the students need to make it. Families are already receiving crucial services—crisis interventions, help with food and housing, parenting skills, job skills, and English as a Second Language. Eventually, in both sites, primary medical and dental care will be available every day. At IS 218, children are being exposed to arts and commerce and all that a multicultural city like New York has to offer. At Hanshaw, children are being exposed to scientific exploration, university life, and the expectation of achievement. Many, many agencies are being drawn into these community-schools to provide whatever they can. The extra cost per enrolled student for full service averages $500 to $1,000 per year, bringing the total expenditure per child in disadvantaged, underfunded school districts closer to the amount spent in more privileged areas.

6

▲▲▲

Evaluating the Potential of
School-Based Services

When a new program concept begins to take hold, the first question asked is "Does it work?" Do school-based health and social service programs really make a difference in the lives of students and their families? The descriptions of the comprehensive school-based programs in Chapters Three to Five should provide compelling evidence that many children and families are gaining access to quality services and are getting attention from caring people. It is not hard to imagine that these interventions have substantial effects. In this chapter, various indicators of certain impacts of school-based programs are presented. But we must start off with a strong caveat: the state of the art of program evaluation leaves much to be desired. The difficulties of evaluating multicomponent programs have been well documented. Deanna Gomby and Carol Larsen place evaluation of school-linked service efforts on a "frontier that is both lively and less than fully explored."[1] Of the sixteen exemplary school-linked initiatives cited in their report, only three had yet generated evaluation findings related to outcomes.

In my view, school-based health and social service programs have been put to a more rigorous test than many other social programs, with the expectation that they can rapidly alter behavior and produce strong benefits. This test has rarely been applied to other interventions. For example, it has been well documented that many substance abuse prevention interventions do not have any effect, yet they continue to be implemented.[2] Few delinquency prevention interventions have been shown to work, and some authorities have even urged that traditional efforts be abandoned.[3]

One could present a textbook of reasons why evaluation of social programs is so difficult. We leave the details to other sources and only mention a few particular problems.[4] The disadvantaged children and families for whom these services are designed are "moving targets." It is not unusual for half of the students who start the school year to have left before the end of the year. We might expect that phenomenon among high school students because of dropout, but younger children in elementary and middle schools shift rapidly from one place to another along with their highly mobile families. The problem of tracking students for long-term follow-up is weighty, not only methodologically. The cost of quality evaluation can often equal the cost of the intervention!

Reported Effects of School-Based Services

We will review the available data starting with the thorniest issues—sexuality and pregnancy. School-based clinics have been criticized for both promoting promiscuity and failing to prevent pregnancy. At this stage, school-based clinics can generate only limited evidence to prove that these programs are effective at pregnancy prevention, although they show enormous promise as centers for integrating services such as counseling and general health screening that may have indirect impact on sexuality behaviors.[5] No evidence has been found that the presence of a school-based clinic increases the rate of sexual activity among the students. The original Dallas and St. Paul results showing declining birthrates in target schools are more than a decade old. Since that time, the effect of school-based clinics on the reduction in birthrates has been reported by programs in Muskegon, Michigan; Jackson, Mississippi; Palm Beach and Quincy, Florida; Baltimore, Maryland; rural Colorado; and a scattering of other places, but these claims have not been supported with rigorous documentation. A recent retrospective study of schoolwide birthrates in St. Paul, using a newly developed methodology, showed fluctuating birthrates not significantly lower in the years following the opening of any of the five clinics than in the years preceding it.[6] However, the measures were applied to all students, not just users of the clinic for family planning services, and the population in the schools changed significantly over the years to higher-risk groups.

One demonstration program in Baltimore combined sexuality and contraceptive education and individual and group counseling in schools with family planning services in a nearby clinic site (a school-linked program).[7] At the end of the three-year demonstration period, pregnancies among students in the experimental schools decreased 26 percent, while a substantial increase occurred in the control schools (from 32 to 51 percent). Laurie Zabin, the prime researcher, attributed the success of the program to the quality of individual attention that the students received from the staff at the school and the clinic.

Controlled studies that encompass changes in pregnancy rates are difficult to conduct in every setting; pregnant girls may drop out of school and be hard to track, or they may stay in school and have abortions that are unknown to the staff. One problem with school-based clinics is the small number of users of the family planning services component (10 to 20 percent), which reduces the effect in aggregate statistics.[8] Research on the question of the effect of clinics on the incidence of sexual activity among the students has not shown that the rates increase after the clinic opens. A two-year follow-up survey in Kansas City revealed almost no change in reported sexual behavior.[9] Following the three-year school-clinic demonstration project in Baltimore, Zabin found a postponement of first intercourse that averaged seven months among program participants.[10]

A survey of students in a school that is part of the Houston school-based clinic program showed that school clinic attendance was an important determinant of the frequency of contraceptive use.[11] Clinic users were more than twice as likely to use contraception every time they had sex as those who had not been to the clinic, and they were less than half as likely never to use contraception. Among students who were already sexually active, clinic patients in Kansas City showed higher rates of contraceptive use than nonpatients, and registered a striking increase in use of condoms among males. In Baltimore, Zabin found that male and younger female students in the experimental schools were much more likely to use birth control than those in the control schools. And in St. Paul, female contraceptive users had an extremely high rate of continuation; 91 percent were still using the method (mostly the pill) after a year and 78 percent after two years of use.[12] (Freestanding family planning clinics report a twelve-month program dropout rate of close to 50 percent.)[13]

A program in four inner-city middle schools operated by the Columbia University School of Public Health in New York City developed a monitoring system to track changes through annual surveys of students who used the school-based clinics.[14] Preliminary findings suggest that among students identified as sexually active, contact with the program appeared to be related to increased use of contraception, less positive attitudes toward pregnancy, and fewer pregnancies. During the school year, 58 percent were seen at least once by a social worker, 55 percent by a medical provider, and 33 percent by both. Among sexually active students who had intercourse within thirty days of the survey (and were therefore at high risk of pregnancy), 67 percent who made one or more visits to the social worker reported using birth control, as compared to only 31 percent of those who did not see a social worker. Among those who made medical visits, there were no significant differences.

Although the numbers are small in this age group, contact with the clinic among sexually active adolescents appeared to be related to a reduction in pregnancy. None of the sexually active females who had seen a social worker had been pregnant, compared to 9 percent of those who had not seen a social worker. None of the sexually active females who had seen a medical provider reported a pregnancy on the follow-up survey, compared to 9 percent of those who had not. Fewer effects were shown for male students.

Changes in attitudes about pregnancy were significantly related to both medical and social service visits among the girls but not among the boys. One of the interventions, Life Planning Groups, designed to increase the use of birth control and reduce pregnancy, was evaluated using pre- and posttests and a randomly assigned control group. The students who participated in the Life Planning Groups showed a significant increase in knowledge and positive attitudes toward the use of birth control. However, postprogram behavioral measures on contraceptive use did not differ significantly between experimental and control groups. During the school year, 15 percent of seventh-graders and 16 percent of eighth-graders became sexually active for the first time. Analysis of clinic attendance showed that the initiation of sexual intercourse was unrelated to contact with the school-based clinic, confirming findings from research in other clinics.[15]

Because of the controversy surrounding the provision of birth control services in school-based clinics, much of the evaluation has centered on that subject. Yet as these programs have evolved, their stated goals have included many other outcomes in addition to pregnancy prevention, such as improvement in attendance, reduction in truancy, lower dropout rates, and reduction in substance abuse and delinquency. It was reported by Senator Brock Adams of Washington at a Senate hearing that a school clinic in Seattle's Rainier Beach

High School "prevented 40 students from dropping out of school and significantly reduced the number of youth sent home from school."[16] In the San Fernando (California) High School, school-based clinic users were half (9 percent) as likely to drop out of school as nonusers (18 percent).[17]

Most school-based clinics can produce utilization statistics, and although these kinds of reports cannot substitute for outcome evaluation, they are nonetheless useful for their implications about effects. The sheer volume of services provided by clinics is one type of evidence of effectiveness. In Dallas, 85 percent of the student body is enrolled in the program.[18] One of the impacts reported from Dallas has been a lower rate of hospitalization for youngsters from the target area. Almost all programs report utilization rates of 75 percent or higher, and many believe that the use of emergency rooms has been reduced substantially. In Quincy, Florida, the use of emergency rooms as the most recent source of care among male students dropped from 35 percent to 18 percent two years after the school clinic opened.[19] Decreases in the use of emergency rooms by students in schools with clinics were also reported in San Francisco (from 12 percent to 4 percent over two years) and San Jose (from 9 percent to 4 percent). At the same time, significant increases were shown in the percentage of students who said they had access to health services when needed, presumably through the school-based clinics.[20]

Clinics appear to be treating needy clients. One large program found that 38 percent of the users had no other source of medical care and that two-thirds were not covered by either Medicaid or private insurance.[21] The school-based clinic in San Fernando, California, specifically targets students with little or no access to health care— 93 percent of its clinic enrollees report no other source of medical care and no health insurance.[22] A unique finding was the high level of use of mental health services in school-based clinics among students with HMO (health maintenance organization) and private insurance. According to the researchers (Claire Brindis and colleagues), the extensive use of the school clinic by students with other health care options "implies that the clinic is able to provide mental health services in a manner that is more acceptable to the adolescents, and that the integration of this service with a comprehensive array of health services may help diminish the stigma often associated with this kind of service. . . . [It] may also reflect the relative unavailability. . . of these services as provided through HMO or private insurance coverage."[23]

Edward Tetelman, an official of the New Jersey Department of Human Resources and a staunch advocate of school-based programs, presented some strongly suggestive raw data about several New Jersey School-Based Youth Services Centers.[24] In the Pinelands program, substantial decreases were shown in suspensions, dropouts, pregnancies, and suicidal ideation, while in Hackensack the number of fistfights was cut in half. In 1989, the Michigan Adolescent Health Services Program conducted a survey of five hundred users of teen health centers.[25] More than 21 percent of the respondents indicated that they would not have received health care if the center did not exist. The main reasons given were lack of transportation and no family physician. Some 38 percent reported learning of new health problems during the visit, including cancer symptoms, penicillin allergy, ear trouble, and high cholesterol, and 65 percent indicated that their behavior had changed as a result of their contact with the teen health centers.

In the late 1980s, the Kansas City program reported a substantial drop in substance use among clinic clients during a two-year period.[26] This program places high priority on teaching healthy life-styles and discouraging risk-taking behaviors through group and individual counseling. Kansas City also reported changes in mental health outcomes, including reductions in hopelessness, suicidal ideation, and low self-esteem. At Lincoln High School in Denver, when a student commits a drug offense, he or she can enter into a treatment contract for seven sessions at the school-based clinic as an alternative to suspension. This component has resulted in an 80 percent reduction in suspensions.[27] The Quincy, Florida, school-based clinic reported that about one student a week comes in saying that he or she is either contemplating or has attempted suicide.[28] Students who report higher rates of high-risk behaviors such as substance abuse and early initiation of sexual intercourse appear to be more likely to use school-based clinics than other students. A study of students in four schools in Oregon showed a consistent and significant relationship between increasing numbers of clinic visits and increasing numbers of high-risk health behaviors.[29] Only one-third of those students who reported no high-risk behaviors used the clinics, as compared to more than two-thirds of the highest-risk students. Frequent users (three or more times) of school wellness centers in Delaware were more likely than nonusers to report having engaged in high-risk behaviors such as repeated suicide attempts, substance abuse, unprotected sexual activity, and eating-related purging.[30]

Almost three-fourths of New York City students who used school-based clinics thought that the clinic had improved their health, and more than one-third stated that the clinic had improved their school attendance. Most (91 percent) stated that the clinic had improved their ability to get health care when they needed it, and 88 percent stated that the clinic had improved their knowledge of and ability to take care of their bodies.[31]

A recent study of a clinic located in an alternative school and run by a health department is a unique example of an evaluation that focuses entirely on school performance.[32] Students who used the clinic were twice as likely to stay in school and nearly twice as likely to graduate or be promoted than were nonregistered students. The more visits that the student made to the clinic, the higher the graduation or promotion rates. The researchers found this relationship "particularly striking" among black males and attributed these successful outcomes to the trust and support provided by the clinic staff to help students bond with and function better in the school. Although it is difficult to locate evaluations that look specifically at the effect of the provision of medical services on long-term outcomes, some success stories are emerging from an array of other kinds of school-based interventions. Several of the Success for All elementary schools in Baltimore that include family support teams (social worker, school nurse, facilitator) and integrated human services (on-site health clinics run by the health department or services from family counseling or a mental health agency) showed significant improvements in attendance and reduced the numbers of students retained (left back) to close to zero.[33] A strong school-based case management program in Fresno, California, conducted in conjunction with the county Department of Social Services, showed a 40 percent reduction in unexcused absences, a decrease of 70 percent in referrals for misbehavior, and a substantial increase in parental involvement.[34] A year-round skills development joint effort between the Job Training and Partnership Act and the Maryland school districts produced a dropout rate among participants that was half the rate among nonparticipants, as well as increased school achievement.[35] A school-based clinic in Washington, D.C., reported dramatically lower dropout rates for teen mothers under their care, with almost every known pregnant student coming in for prenatal care.[36] These high-risk mothers had greatly improved birth outcomes and very low rates of infant mortality. The clinics in Baltimore, Denver, and Jackson also report very high rates of initiation of prenatal care in the first trimester among pregnant students.[37]

One study documented the importance of providing services on school property (school-based) rather than nearby (school-linked). A health center was removed from school grounds in Quincy, Florida, during the tenure of a conservative governor who refused to allow public funds to be used for school-based clinics.[38] The level of service activity declined immediately, with a drop of 30 percent during the year, particularly among males and younger students. Students using the clinic for first aid showed the largest decline (66 per-

cent). According to the staff, the implementation of more complicated, less private procedures for obtaining permission to visit the
center during the school day tended to reinforce the negative effect
of the relocation. Students had to go through the central office to
leave the campus and walk across the street to the clinic. Almost the
first act of a new governor (Lawton Chiles) in 1990 was to inform
county officials of his intent to return the center to the school
grounds. A new building on the campus was dedicated in early 1991,
and utilization immediately climbed back to its previous level.

The recent focus on immunization suggests another important
role for school-based clinics: the ability to rapidly respond to epidemics and crises in the health system. The New York State Department of Health recently created a pilot immunization project to be
carried out by three state-funded elementary school health centers in
New York City.[39] Brochures were developed to advertise the campaign, and outreach efforts were undertaken to encourage parents to
bring their children in for shots. Many immunizations were provided
not only to school children but also to their younger siblings, at low
cost. However, the highest-risk families failed to respond, causing the
providers to recommend a better-orchestrated annual immunization
campaign, more appropriate educational materials, and central coordination and support.

Many states have initiated school-based service programs that require evaluation, but few states have issued reports so far. When the
state of Florida created the Supplemental School Health Services Program (including full-service schools), the legislation mandated evaluation to study the effectiveness of the program in meeting its objectives, pregnancy prevention and the promotion of student health.[40]
The first-year report produced by the Florida State University was
based on student surveys and site visits in twelve counties. Each of the
grantees had a designated health room in the school, and the evaluation found heavy utilization rates, primarily for physical complaints,
physical examinations, and minor injuries. One important effect was

the high percentage of students who were returned to class after being seen in the health room. Only 10 percent of elementary students and 18 percent of high school students were unable to return—much lower rates than in routine school nursing practices. The evaluation also stated that school-reported pregnancy rates had declined in 56 percent of the schools with programs; 14 percent reported no change, and 31 percent had an increase. "The most dramatic shift occurred at Glades Central High School in Palm Beach where the pregnancy rate dropped almost 73 percent. This project is also the only one where students can obtain prescriptions for contraceptives at the school and where there is a family practice physician available three days a week."[41] The researchers found greater decreases in pregnancy rates in middle schools than high schools and in schools in their second year of participation than those in their first year. It was acknowledged, however, that the pregnancy data were, at best, estimates and difficult to validate.

Student surveys in Florida schools with school-based services showed that students who engaged in high-risk behaviors were more likely to visit the health room than the other students and that the incidence of high-risk behaviors was reduced among students in project schools. Students reported high levels of satisfaction with the program, as did school administrators and parents. "Principals seemed very accommodating [of school-based health services staff] because their presence relieved other staff from dealing with students with various health needs: calling parents for pick up, delivering first aid, and at least in one site, delivering a baby in the school parking lot."

The limitations of published evaluations of the impact of school-based services programs on health and educational outcomes are undeniable. However, monitoring of utilization has contributed important insights into our understanding of who uses clinics and for what purposes. More than one hundred school-based clinics are currently using a data system devised by David Kaplan of the University of Colorado, all of the previous RWJ grantees were required to keep computerized records for each client, and a number of programs are being tracked by Claire Brindis of the University of California. The RWJ programs are currently being evaluated by an independent contractor (Mathtech), and a substantial evaluation of the California Healthy Start initiative is to be conducted by SRI, also an independent contractor. With support from the Casey Foundation, Kentucky has developed a comprehensive data collection system that will be used for management information and outcome analysis, as well as to develop a profile of children and families who use the family resource and youth services centers. Florida's Full-Service School initiative includes evaluation procedures.

Summary of Evaluation Findings

Based on the data currently available about school-based clinics and full-service schools and the program reports referred to in other parts of this book, we can affirm with some confidence that these new programs have significant potential. The following summary statements can be made:

1. Programs are located in the communities and schools with the greatest needs.
2. School clinics are being utilized most by the highest-risk students who report the greatest number of problems.
3. Many of the school health clinic users have no other source of routine medical care and no health insurance. Use of emergency rooms has declined in areas with school clinics.
4. Students are being taught how to gain access to the medical care system through relationships with clinic staff and community health agencies.
5. Because minor illnesses such as headaches, menstrual cramps, and accidents on school property can be treated in school, absences and excuses to go home have decreased.

6. In centers with mental health personnel, substantial numbers of students and their families are gaining access to psychosocial counseling that was not available to them within the community. The demand is overwhelming.

7. Scattered evidence suggests that school-based clinics have had an impact on delaying the initiation of intercourse, upgrading the quality of contraceptive use, and lowering pregnancy rates, but only in programs that offer comprehensive family planning services.

8. Programs are just beginning to produce data on other effects. Clinic users have been shown to have lower substance use, better school attendance, and lower dropout rates.

9. School-based clinics have the potential capacity to respond to emergencies—for example, to conduct immunization campaigns and do TB screening.

10. In addition to offering individual counseling, clinic staff have an impact on students' behavior through health education and health promotion in classrooms and through group counseling covering a range of youth problems such as substance use, family relations, sexuality, nutrition, and peer relationships.

11. Utilization figures show that the characteristics of students who use the centers generally mirror those of the school population, with slightly higher usage by females, younger students, and African-Americans.

12. Students, parents, teachers, and school personnel report a high level of satisfaction with school clinics and centers and particularly appreciate their accessibility, convenience, and caring attitude.

Research Needed

The emergence of these diverse school-based programs creates a rich territory for researchers interested in tracking complex models. It will not be easy to sort out impacts or to be able to attribute any particular effect to a specific program component in a comprehensive program. To gain a more consistent fix on outcomes and to track the long-term effects of these efforts, researchers should clearly give evaluation high priority. It should be reiterated, however, that the emerging field of "full-service schools" should not be put on the defensive because it has not proven its worthiness. No other social endeavor has been so criticized so early in its evolution.

Research questions that might be considered include the following:

- Long-term effects of use of school-based health and social services on school retention, attendance, achievement, pregnancy and birthrates, and involvement with drugs.
- Cost-effectiveness of providing health and social services in schools compared to other means of providing services to children and adolescents, such as private physicians' offices, community health centers, health maintenance organizations, and hospital outpatient and emergency departments.
- Cost-benefit of providing preventive and health promotion services in schools compared to not providing those services anywhere.
- Operational management of school-based centers: most efficient staffing mix; appropriate roles of pediatricians, nurse practitioners, social workers, physician assistants, health educators, aides, and other personnel; and most efficient scheduling and arrangements between the backup referral agency and the school center.
- Comparison of administrative "lead agencies": efficiency and effectiveness of programs operated directly by school systems compared to those operated by outside agencies such as hospitals, community health centers, and public health departments.
- Inclusion of questions about utilization of school-based health and social services in national surveys—the National Health Interview, Youth Risk Behavior Survey, and other such instruments.

One component that is essential for turning a loosely defined group of programs into a specific field of endeavor is a uniform data base. The system developed by David Kaplan, *School Health Care—Online!!!*, was designed as a management information tool for school-based clinics. Currently, this software program is designed to collect data on individual physical and mental health, health screening, risk behaviors, epidemiology, administration, billing, and program outcomes.[42] The computer system is set up to produce over a hundred preprogrammed reports, including "tickler" files listing referrals and follow-up information and statistical reports on users, immunizations, case management, and health screening.

In the near future, we will have access to more reports about the effectiveness of school-based health services and family resource centers. Until a rich evaluation literature is compiled, decision makers will have to rely on these scattered returns as they make policies that will produce quality full-service schools.

7

▲▲▲

Putting the Pieces Together:
Organizational and Service Delivery Issues

As we move into the twenty-first century, the concept of integrating human services and "wrapping them around" children and their families is finding many advocates. Much of this innovation has come about through a "bubbling-up" process stimulated by local activists and practitioners. This phenomenon has been described as an explosion of decentralized experimentation unguided by outcome evaluation or cost-benefit studies. The school building has emerged as *the place*, the one piece of real estate in declining communities that is publicly owned, centrally located, and consistently used, at least by children. Once a center is located in a school, it acts like a magnet drawing in other services. Some would maintain that the school system is the one central institution in the community with enough viability and strength to organize comprehensive delivery systems. Others believe that school systems should be partners in the development of communitywide efforts but not given the entire responsibility for "systems reform."

Much of the rhetoric surrounding the emergence of school-based services focuses on the need for systems change, "the revision of the ways that institutions think, behave, and use their resources to affect fundamentally the types, quality, and degree of service delivery to children and families."[1] Molly Coye, the California commissioner of health, portrayed her state's Healthy Start program as one component in a growing movement to "revolutionize" government by building a comprehensive system to promote child growth and development from ages zero to eighteen.[2] We have examined one example from California that lends support to this optimistic scenario: the Hanshaw School (Chapter Five) exemplifies a revolutionary conceptualization of how schools can organize systems to respond to the needs of children and families. In reality, few programs in California or anywhere else have moved beyond rhetoric to reach this level of sophistication. In previous chapters we reviewed many school-based programs that fall along a continuum of complexity, from an organization or business that brings one targeted service into a school (tutoring) to cooperative-partnerships, whereby programs are co-located in a school to increase the number of services available on site (a school-based clinic) to collaboratives, in which school systems and community agencies redefine their responsibilities, share decision making, and jointly develop a new institution (a fully realized community-school). My observation of this scene is that the programs currently being developed sit in the middle of the continuum; most are cooperative relationships, partnerships, but not true collaboratives that radically change the governance of institutions. William Morrill, another observer, has commented that "the force of rhetoric and limited demonstrations have not proved to be powerful enough to bring about significant systems change."[3]

In this chapter, I will address a number of issues that have been raised by practitioners, program developers, critics, researchers, the media, and the growing group of experts associated with service integration concepts. I have focused primarily on administrative questions and observations made during visits to programs around the country. For those interested in more details about "systems reforms" (the major restructuring of educational, health, and social services institutions), other source materials are recommended.[4]

I start this discussion with what I call the "it" problem. What is the school-based model that is being promoted on these pages? I then turn to an overview of the many organizational problems that have arisen in the pursuit of collaborative school and community agency programs. Finally, I examine two important issues: controversy surrounding school-based services and the relationship of school restructuring efforts to the movement for full-service schools.

What's the Model?

At a meeting in Washington on integration of youth services, a highly placed representative of the Department of Education commented that he had "trouble grabbing on to what this thing is." You readers may share this problem. The primary model put forward in this book is the school-based health and social services center: space set aside in a school building where services are brought in by outside community agencies in conjunction with school personnel. But, as a result of diverse state and foundation initiatives, new entities are proliferating under a panoply of labels: school-based clinic, school-based youth service program, youth center, family resource center, parent center, community-school, and full-service school.

In the spirit of innovation—and in the absence of national standards or models—states have developed different variations of school-based services programs. Appendix A presents an overview of twelve significant state efforts, no two alike. In general, the approaches fall into three categories:

1. School-based health clinics that deliver primary health care, psychosocial counseling, and health education, operated by health departments, hospitals, or community health centers.

2. School-based youth service or family service centers that offer health, mental health, and family counseling, drug and alcohol counseling, recreation, employment services, parenting education, and/or child care on site and/or through linkages with other community agencies.

3. Youth or family service centers that provide coordination with and referral to community agencies.

I have portrayed the full-service school as an ideal, a label adopted from the Florida legislation: "A full-service school integrates education, medical, social and/or human services that are beneficial to meeting the needs of children and youth and their families on school grounds or in locations which are easily accessible. A full-service school provides the types of prevention, treatment, and support services children and families need to succeed... services that are high-quality and comprehensive and are built on interagency partnerships which have evolved from cooperative ventures to intensive collaborative arrangements among state and local and public and private entities."[5]

The concept of the full-service school is like a big tent into which all the other models fit. However, few programs operate at such a high level of integration and "intensive collaboration," even in Florida. The exceptional schools described in Chapter Five are on the way to becoming fully developed "one-stop" systems. They are located in buildings especially designed to incorporate the concept of integrated services—facilities that can offer a seamless experience for the students, parents, and the staff. School and community agency personnel have common and shared goals and participate in joint decision making.

To achieve the ideal of the full-service school, certain building blocks are necessary. In my particular vision (Exhibit 1.1), the movement must encompass both quality education and support services. In this book, we concentrate primarily on the proven components of support services that are responsive to the needs of the school and the community. At this stage of development, "it" is the school-based health and social service center, one of the better defined components, a building block of full-service schools that is ready to be replicated. The specifications and the barriers are similar whether the main focus of the center is child, youth, or family.

School-Based, School-Linked, and Community-Based

To promote more rational planning for service systems of the future, we need to sort out three related concepts of service delivery. As we have seen, school-based services are those delivered directly in school buildings. The use of the term "school-linked" has come to mean integrated services provided in a building near a school, with an administrative structure that links the school system to the provider agencies. Community-based services are those administered by community agencies, but they also serve as referral points for school practitioners whether they are employed by the school system or the school-based services center.

One might ask, If the purpose of school-based centers is to give people access to health and social services, wouldn't it be more cost-effective to arrange for outreach and transportation to community agencies than to set up a whole new system in schools? School-based practitioners maintain that few community agencies are organized to provide primary health care to young people and attend to their complex psychosocial needs. Since the stated purpose of school-based programs is to give the students and their families maximum access to the services they need "where they are," it seems more efficient to integrate services into the school environment to achieve the "seamless" effect.

However, school-based programs are clearly reluctant to fully integrate pregnancy prevention services, whether they are family resource centers, teen parent programs, or clinics in middle and high schools. Centers located off of school property have a much easier time providing quality birth control services that include not only counseling, physical examinations, and screening and treatment for sexually transmitted diseases but also provision of contraceptive methods and referral for abortion counseling and services, if requested. In some communities, provision of substance abuse treatment and mental health services in school buildings is also controversial. Most of the school-linked programs were organized to bypass the barriers schools put up to comprehensive care and do not differ markedly from community-based programs. In some communities, young people and their families need access to both school-based centers and community-based programs such as family planning clinics, STD clinics, and substance abuse treatment programs so that they can choose the kind of provider that best fits their needs. School-based centers will never be so comprehensive that they obviate the need for all referrals, so in that sense, all programs require linkages to different community agencies. In regard to family planning, recent experience suggests that the barriers to provision of birth control in schools are lowering in response to the threat of AIDS. The concept of school-linked services as an alternative to school-based services may become obsolete in the future.

Many young people have already dropped out of school and must rely on community-based agencies for their health and social services. The Door in New York City is often cited as the model for a freestanding community-based agency that offers a large number of services to hundreds of young people, many of whom have dropped out of school. In recent years, the connection to the educational system was made when the Door became accredited as an alternative school by the New York City Board of Education. Increasing numbers of communities are finding ways to develop creative working partnerships between grass-roots organizations and school systems. But many school-based programs have not yet resolved the problem of serving dropouts or other nonstudents.

Organizational Issues

It is important to examine the specific roles of schools and community agencies in moving toward the development of full-service schools. The identification of the appropriate "lead agency" can shape the entire endeavor. Collaborative plans are difficult to achieve because of the differing characteristics of the agencies involved.

Lead Agency

If the school is to be the place, what has been learned about the positioning of the school system in the governance and organization of noneducational service delivery? Clearly, no one model has emerged as the way to build more comprehensive service systems. The decade of experience with school-based health and social service centers has been better documented than other models. While the number of centers has grown from ten to about five hundred, the proportion that are administered by school systems has remained lower than 10 percent. This rate is probably increasing because of state policies to fund youth and family centers programs through local education agencies, but even in those states, many of the school systems are choosing to subcontract with community agencies for direct services. In Kentucky, all grants for family resource and youth centers are awarded directly to school systems, but these are relatively small programs that focus primarily on placing a coordinator in a school to facilitate referrals to community agencies.

No research studies have been identified that compare the effectiveness of school-based programs according to type of lead agency. One study of adolescent health services found that school-based programs with services provided by outside health agencies were more comprehensive (offered more services with greater accessibility) than those operated by educational agencies.[6] A review by Harriet Fox and colleagues of school-based health services in fourteen communities attributed the development of outside-run school-based clinics to several conditions: willingness of community-based providers to support a health services program in a school; a shortage of primary care resources in the community; reluctance of private physicians to serve Medicaid and uninsured children; advocacy by parents and students for making health services more convenient; and the belief that this arrangement would be the most cost-effective.[7] Fox concluded from this study that sponsorship by a community agency rather than a school system had the advantages of establishing eligibility for additional types of public and private funding and facilitating access to third-party reimbursements, particularly Medicaid. Having outside sponsorship also eliminated the need for medical liability insurance, facilitated referrals back to the sponsoring agency, assured entry into community service networks, and, in some cases, placed the user into an existing patient tracking system. Fox asserts that outside-administered school health clinics may be more acceptable to school administrators and board members who prefer to concentrate on academic matters.

Observers believe that few school systems are in a position to take on the entire responsibility for health, mental health, and social services for children and families. The state of Connecticut has advised potential grant applicants that "school systems can manage a school-based clinic but this is usually not the optimum choice, due to lack of expertise operating health care systems, liability and conflict of interest. Research has shown [sic] that school-based clinics function best as independent facilities on school premises."[8] Terrance Keenan, RWJ executive, told a Senate Children's Caucus that although schools should serve as the locus of health care, it was better not to impose the responsibility for the organization, delivery, and financing of care on the schools. Rather, he preferred that this responsibility be assumed by traditional health service institutions such as hospitals and health departments. The designers of the first school clinics, among whom RWJ had a strong influence, worked hard to insure that the clinics remained fiscally and administratively separate from schools to maintain confidentiality and generate students' trust in clinic staff. Edward Tetelman of the New Jersey School-Based Youth Services Program summed up his argument in favor of utilizing nonprofit agencies as managers: "These organizations generally have social and support services as their main focus and are able to make rapid changes as necessary. Schools often have other priorities, are often unable to make rapid adjustments to programs, and at times have gotten mired in political disputes unrelated to the program."[9]

One of the strongest arguments for relying on community agencies to provide health services in the schools is that they bring their own liability insurance with them. Schools are therefore relieved of a fiscal responsibility that looms large enough to act as a barrier for most school systems. Thus far, no clinic has incurred liability, and only one lawsuit has ever been filed against a school-based clinic.[10] A group of ministers, objecting to the distribution of contraceptives by the DuSable High School clinic in Chicago, alleged that the clinic's activities amounted to genocide. The case was dismissed by the court.

The phrase lead agency has been used to identify the organization that has the fiscal and legal responsibility for the program. I believe that programs can be broader if an agency other than the school acts as the lead or a new entity is created that is responsible for the collaborative process. As we have seen, the typical school-based center is operated by a nonschool entity—a public health, community health, public welfare, or community mental health agency or a nongovernmental agency such as a voluntary hospital, school of public health, voluntary youth-serving agency, or even a Private Industry Council. In a few communities, a new nonprofit agency or commission has been organized to provide services in schools—for example, the New Futures programs and some of the Cities in Schools. The original St. Paul program evolved from a hospital-based effort to a newly constituted freestanding agency, Health Start. A local youth bureau, the Urban League, or United Way could also serve as the lead agency. School systems that directly operate school-based health centers have been advised to incorporate the services program as a non-profit with written agreements with major employees and contractors.

In addition to a lead agency, comprehensive programs that provide health or social services require a "backup" agency. If the school-based program is oriented toward health services, then a hospital or health center must be available for emergency services, referrals to medical specialists, and twenty-four-hour call when the school center is closed. For social services, a local agency must be identified for treatment, follow-up, and other kinds of social referrals.

Having made the claim that outside agencies are probably better situated to run school-based services than are school systems, it must be acknowledged that community agencies may not always be ideal. Each kind of public and voluntary agency lives within its own bureaucratic culture. Local public health departments can easily get bogged down in paperwork and regulations. Many suffer from acute funding shortages brought on by massive local and state budget cuts. Public health personnel may experience difficulty arranging for medical backup with hospital-based physicians. Some voluntary hospitals are notoriously bad at responding to community needs and unwilling to commit any of their own resources to collaborative projects that don't include substantial gains to the hospital treasury. The success of a community agency's involvement in partnerships too often reflects individual commitment rather than agency commitment. Some one person in the agency really wants to make a difference in the school and the community and works very hard (always overtime) to garner the resources to get a program going. Schools legitimately express concern about what will happen to the services after the "Florence Nightingale" leaves the agency. How will continuity be insured in a program not fully controlled by the school?

Collaboration

The theory goes that educational authorities and representatives of health and social service systems sit down at the table together and devise collaborative programs. The practice is a little different. One of my favorite definitions of collaboration is "an unnatural act between nonconsenting adults." It is important to understand the difficulty in creating new institutions and in convincing entrenched bureaucrats to change their ways and share authority and decision making. Program developers should beware of raising expectations and devising overly ambitious constructs that topple from the weight of unrealistic structures.

The "buzzword" of the early 1990s is *collaboration*. The stream of documents emerging from various study groups that give advice on how agencies can better work together is impressive. The general theme of this literature is that putting together programs that involve even a minimum of two governing bodies—a school system and a community agency—is no simple matter. The experience gained from a decade of developing school-based health clinics is similar to that emanating from the family resource center movement. One experienced practitioner warned that "the policy generating machines at each level and within each level have independent time lines, political interests, multiple and changing special interest groups, and few incentives to spend the time and energy to coordinate their efforts. Policies compete, overlap, and often conflict."[11]

Collaborative efforts have a much higher probability of success if the participants start out with a common vision of what the program will look like when fully implemented. It is not sufficient for people to come together to talk about collaboration if they have no idea what the potential models might be. I have observed a number of efforts that would be greatly enhanced if both the school people and the community agencies were more exposed to the good program models around the country (which is, of course, one of my reasons for writing this book).

Right from the start, top-level administrators have to be involved. These "stakeholders" have to sign on to the collaborative effort and put aside their separate agency agendas. The Annie Casey Founda-

tion New Futures experience is well documented. Some of the earlier approaches foundered because of insufficient "buy-in" from local
schools and teachers.[12] What top-down program developers thought
was going to be a "piece of cake" turned into a complicated and difficult challenge of getting the players together to change the youth-
service system. Whatever emerges—a partnership, a cooperative effort, or a collaborative—must be graced with a legal contract or a
memorandum of agreement that creates a formal structure and clar-
ifies roles and responsibilities in great detail. A strong leader, someone with passion for the welfare of children and the skills of a trained
facilitator, is helpful in these deliberations. Those who have been
down this path before strongly advise all parties to avoid confusion
over goals, structure, and money. Open communication is essential.

Role of the School Board

All of these programs where the lead agency is not the school depend
entirely on the school's willingness to be a participant in the cooperative effort. The school board must allow "it" to happen, signing
whatever contractual arrangements are devised. School systems are so
overburdened with demands for academic improvement that they
particularly welcome prepackaged and easily implemented initiatives.
In some communities, school board members have been the initiators
of the clinic programs. In Los Angeles, where the members are elected,
a Republican and a Democrat who were often adversaries jointly sponsored the board statement in favor of clinic services. School boards
generally determine overall policies, particularly in regard to the provision of birth control on the premises. As programs become more
comprehensive, school boards must be prepared to deal with difficult
issues such as conflicting personnel practices and union contracts;
complying with regulations for dealing with AIDS, STDs, TB, and
other diseases; framing policies about substance abuse and mental
health treatment on site; and approving procedures for working with
dysfunctional families. In the typical program, the school contribution

that the board must approve includes space, maintenance, safety and security, and most important, the principal's leadership.

Role of Community Agencies

Many different kinds of agencies are entering into schools with various formal and informal arrangements. Just as school systems have boards, so do community agencies. Health and social welfare departments do not act independently. They may be units of city or county government or largely controlled by state agencies. Hospitals are extremely complex and often arcane bureaucracies with many layers of authority—administrative, medical, fiscal—that must be involved in decision making. Community health centers are required to have community boards that approve policies. Not all provider agencies are eager to enter into fiscal arrangements with schools or any other agencies. Practitioners who work for these health and social service agencies often experience frustration and stress when trying to obtain all the necessary approvals and commitments from what can be many layers of bureaucrats.

Among community-based "grass-roots" consumer groups, concern has been expressed about using school sites as the exclusive base for developing family programs. Community activists fear that schools will be insensitive to the true needs of the local people and lack the flexibility to be responsive. One criticism frequently voiced about establishment agencies is the absence of staff who are culturally and ethnically representative of the clients. Welfare departments, hospitals, and other local agencies may have "bad vibes" for community people.

Grass-roots groups can become the most enthusiastic supporters for full-service schools if the planning process is truly inclusive and responsive. At the same time, community provider agencies can be assisted to overcome their own organizational barriers through this same process. Ideally, the full-service school concept would be embedded in the planning and development of "full-service communities," places where all service systems including the schools were organized to be comprehensive, unfragmented, and client-sensitive.

Service Delivery Issues

Arrangements at the program level can be critical to the success of the effort. When community agencies bring their services into school buildings, an array of issues arise, such as "turf," quality of care, staffing, and parent involvement. Current experience with expanding programs around the country provides a useful perspective to examine these questions.

Role of the Principal

When it comes to policies that relate to the use of a school building, the school principal has a great deal of power. His or her power emanates from the superintendent's office, but most of the decisions appear to be at the building level. In general, the school administrator acts as interpreter between the school staff and the outside staff, controls the traffic flow, facilitates the use of the services, and is in charge of whatever happens under the school roof. The principal has to set out policies for the release of students from the classroom and work with the clinic staff to schedule appointments at appropriate times. Although teachers are supposed to abide by those rules, they may be reluctant to release students from formal classroom activities to go to clinics for medical services or counseling, particularly students who have difficulty making up the time lost from academic pursuits. Some teachers who have been in the system for a long time feel that the schools should not be the place for the provision of services and that these outsiders only intrude on the smooth running of the institution. Teachers worry that some students use the clinics to "hang out" and get out of classes. They believe that the children's families, not the school, should be charged with the responsibility for health and mental health care.

The principal and the school-based services program coordinator work to promote harmony in the school. Clinic staff may assist teachers with health and sex education classes, thereby freeing them up for other duties. Some clinics offer occupational health consultations to the school staff, with screening procedures such as blood pressure and cholesterol checks and throat cultures. In one school clinic, I saw a kidney dialysis machine for the use of a teacher.

School-based clinic personnel are beginning to take on some of the medical and psychosocial services required under the Education for All Handicapped Children Act (Public Law 94-124). The law requires that schools provide the least restrictive environment possible to large numbers of students with physical and mental disabilities. In some schools, nonmedical personnel including teachers have been performing tasks such as suctioning mucous from the airways of children, inserting catheters into bladders, administering insulin and other injections or medications, or inserting feeding tubes. The American Federation of Teachers has recommended that nurses and trained health care aides rather than teachers be given the primary responsibility for providing health care services to medically fragile children.[13]

Principals may create school services teams that include clinic practitioners, school personnel, special education staff, and pupils. These teams meet frequently, review specific "cases" among the students and their families, and make decisions about who will do what. Clinic staff know that their services are well integrated when the principal claims ownership of the program. When I asked a principal how a public health clinic in his school was doing, he said, "The clinic has become an integral part of our school." This principal has facilitated the expansion of the clinic from three rooms to eight, and he checks in with the clinic staff daily to ask about how various students are being cared for. Although the cost of the program does not come out of his school budget, the program belongs to him.

Whenever one visits a school center, the principal is marched out by the practitioner to testify to the importance of the program. He or she invariably says, "I don't know how we got along without this center." Most principals were involved in the planning of the effort and support the concept. A major problem arises when the principal leaves the school or the superintendent leaves the system. Turnover rates are extremely high; each time a new decision maker comes on the scene, the practitioners and the teachers have to start all over again with building relationships and insuring program continuity.

Turf

One anonymous expert who has worked at developing collaborative projects portrays school bureaucracies as the biggest barrier to reforming systems. Another expert who has represented school systems in negotiations for full-service projects portrays community-based professionals as rigid, arrogant, and difficult to work with. Both parties would concede that it is like having your mother-in-law come and stay in your house—you have to work through all the dynamics. The concern that is voiced most frequently in both domains is the place of existing pupil personnel services in the delivery of externally organized comprehensive services. School nurses often feel displaced by school clinics. In one school, to gain entry to the clinic it was necessary to walk through the school nursing office, where the school nurse distanced herself from the clinic by displaying an openly hostile attitude. Sometimes the situation is mediated by maintaining separate offices and functions for the school nurse (primarily attendance-related) and the clinic nurse practitioner (health care and counseling).

This is not ideal, of course, and certainly does not fulfill the goal of organizing unfragmented services. The most favorable resolution places the school nurse in an important role in the new program. In Bridgeport, Connecticut, where a new school was designed specifically to include the public health department's school-based clinic services, the school nurse (covered by the school budget) was used as the central coordinator of the clinic. Her office was placed in the middle of the facility, and she performed triage, seeing each student and either tending to needs for preliminary screening or arranging for medical, mental health, and dental visits on site with the public health personnel.

The more comprehensive the program, the more likely that existing school personnel might feel undermined by the new effort. School-employed guidance counselors, social workers, and psychologists also feel bypassed when their counterparts are brought into schools by outside organizations. One social worker questioned whether the counselors and outreach workers on center staffs have the training necessary to identify deep-seated problems among the students and their families. She suggested that only professional school social workers could adequately perform this service and that if schools needed more psychosocial services, a much better strategy would be to finance larger school staffs. One of the most difficult jobs is that of a coordinator in a services center that focuses on referral (as in Kentucky). A new person is dropped into the school from the outside and expected to build a cohesive team with diverse school personnel while establishing relationships with outside community service organizations that must provide the actual services.

School discipline policies and practices are potential sources of turf problems. When a clinic opens in a school, the school is exposed to close observation by personnel who are sensitive to the effects of repressive environments on the health and well-being of youth. A student waiting in a clinic told me that he got a stomachache every time he went to math class. He was an interested student who had been placed in a Spanish-language class (which he did not require) where the teacher did not know math. Clinic staff hear many stories like that and many much worse, involving abuse and excessive control or just poor practice. If the clinic staff run to the principal and complain, the teachers and counselors feel undermined. If they do nothing, the clinic staff feel they are not being responsive to the students. Programs that anticipate these turf problems give high priority to the establishment of formal procedures and policies that govern how students are treated within the school. Frequent joint staff meetings and multidisciplinary teams are important components of communication.

The most troublesome conflict that I have encountered was between school personnel and the directors of a community-based program that brings comprehensive services into an inner-city middle school. As the services program people were awaiting the visit of a major sports figure and the mayor, they observed that a school guard had handcuffed a student to the fence in front of the school. The principal claimed that he approved of the action because the "kid was out of control" and, in any case, the school guards were employed by the superintendent's office, not by the local school. A phone call to the district office resulted in the immediate dismissal of the guard. However, in the days that followed, school personnel made their feelings clear that "a good guard had been sacrificed in order to keep a bad kid around." This extreme example demonstrates how school and community agency staff can have very different perceptions about appropriate methods of discipline within the school community.

Given this situation, with two sets of pupil personnel workers reporting to different entities, the probability is high that personnel practices will differ. In general, public health nurses are paid more than school nurses, and community mental health practitioners earn more than school psychologists and social workers. Nonunion community aides and preschool workers are at the lowest end of the salary scale. Staff of comprehensive school-based programs are expected to work long hours, including weekends and holidays and in summer.

Space Allocation

Though the idea of having a clinic or a center in a school may be very attractive, not all schools have adequate space for such a venture. The sense of hopelessness conveyed by a program tucked away next to the boiler room is hard to overcome even by the most caring staff. I visited a comprehensive teen-moms program located in the basement of an inner-city school that had the effect of hiding away these young women, conveying a strong message that they weren't worthy of anything better. In fact, the young mothers were allowed to smoke while holding their babies during a discussion period about how to say "no" to their boyfriends.

Some schools are so run-down and overcrowded that it is difficult to renovate any space to provide services that are confidential and professional. A child welfare researcher from South Africa I took to visit a drab, regimented, and depressing school was dismayed by what she saw. At the time, the clinic space had been carved out of a small narrow locker room (the kids called it the Submarine). Although cheerfully decorated and well equipped, it was jam-packed with waiting students. Within a year, the principal, who had been a reluctant partner at the outset, made available an adjoining classroom to be renovated for medical and social services, and the school interior was painted and repaired. All kinds of settings are being used for school-based programs—prefabs and trailers attached to school buildings, former sewing rooms, food service classrooms, old storerooms, and in one school, three former math classrooms. According to RWJ, essentials for a center include a waiting area, at least two examination rooms and a private counseling room, a small lab, a bathroom, and secure files and cabinets.[14] It has been observed that as space is extended with additional rooms, more and more students and their families use the facility, so the demands are never met.

Safety and security are large issues in contemporary society. Many city schools employ school guards, and visitors have to identify themselves and sign in. When I went with a group to visit a center in Detroit, we were greeted at the door by a uniformed junior ROTC student who marched us up to the program area. In addition to security, arrangements have to be made between the school personnel and the center staff for maintenance, cleanliness, and hours of access. Increasingly, school-based programs are designed to be open from early in the morning until evening, on weekends, and during summers.

This is quite a change for the school system that is accustomed to shutting down the building in the midafternoon. Paying guards and maintenance people can be a costly add-on for new programs, especially in schools that are less than enthusiastic about allowing the building to be used by community agencies.

Parental Involvement

The first question typically asked about school-based services is "Where do the parents fit in?" Schools report disappointing experiences in trying to involve parents in their children's education. Parents have had negative experiences in trying to deal with schools and teachers. It is quite well established that parents in low-income communities can be attracted to schools, but only if the efforts are well designed and sensitive to the social environment in which many disadvantaged families live. In fact, in some communities, the new school-based services have led the way because they offer parents services they understand, need, and cannot otherwise afford, namely, free medical care for their children and, often, family counseling, parent education, advocacy, and referral.

When it comes to family involvement, it is important to distinguish between elementary school and high school. The parents of young children are much more accessible, and the services that they are offered in the emerging family resource centers (described in Chapter Three) engender little controversy. These programs start with the needs of the parents for help with raising their children and supporting their families. Programs located primarily in high schools and middle schools start with the needs of adolescents, and one of those needs may be gaining independence from family ties. The confidentiality offered by school-based clinics is the quality that most students mention in surveys of user satisfaction. Parents are consulted only if the student agrees, unless mandated by law.

School-based clinics, as we learned in Chapter Four, have had little difficulty obtaining parental permission for clinical services. It has been pointed out that the schools where parental consent is the most readily secured are those in which the principal and the teachers collaborate with the clinic staff. Most school-based services programs either are mandated or voluntarily decide to have an advisory council. It has been shown that these councils can play a very important role in helping the program become accepted in the community and maintained over time. As one practitioner reported, "Parents are the best defense against the 'crazies.'" When the DuSable High School clinic was organized in Chicago, a local paper announced its presence with the headline "PILL GOES TO SCHOOL." Protesters picketed the school, and the school board got very nervous. However, the people in the local community, led by parents of children from that school, effectively organized a supportive campaign, and the program was preserved in its entirety.

Some programs find creative ways to hire parents to conduct outreach in the community. In Los Angeles, when no funds were available for community aides, vouchers for food markets and free child care were used to reward people for their services. In South Beach (Miami), Florida, parents have been organized as advocates for students and their families. They have an office in the school and work with local health, social service, legal, and housing authorities in addition to assisting the school with cultural events. The Vaughn Family Center, also in Los Angeles, is operated by a commission made up of parents and providers who share decision making regarding the hiring of the director and which services are provided in this school-based program.

A proposal for developing a health clinic in a high school in Oahu, Hawaii, documented how parents feel about these services: "The parents of our communities love their teenagers and want to see the best for them, but too much is left up to the school and too little actually is able to be done with the limited resources available. The idea of a health services center is generally heralded as a great idea by parents. The North Shore is so service-poor and most parents

work, forcing them to either use their own sick leave time to trans-
port teenagers, or worse, having to allow their teens' health to go un-
attended.... Parents understand all too well the need for services
their adolescents require in this era of complicated mental and physical health."[15]

Quality of Care

Certain issues transcend location and are significant whether comprehensive health and social service programs are placed in schools or
in community sites. We know that young people have specific needs
that can best be met by practitioners who understand youth development and can deal with the problems inherent in treating the "new
morbidities," the consequences of sex, drugs, violence, and stress.

The issue of quality of care in integrated health and social service
programs is not often discussed or documented. From observations in
schools and community agencies, one could conclude that the range
of service provision is very broad, with very different levels of input.
One facility may have a "full-service clinic," with an adequate number of well-trained, qualified, personnel, while another may be limp-
ing along with a part-time coordinator and an occasional visit from
a nurse practitioner or mental health professional. Clearly, these are
not the same models and will never have equivalent effects. At the
outset, every program going into schools or community agencies
should have a set of medical and social service guidelines that spell
out specific protocols for the treatment of different presenting problems and cover issues such as parental consent, informed consent,
minors' consent, release of clinic records, and reporting requirements
for child abuse and sexually transmitted and contagious diseases.
Policies regarding AIDS and HIV testing, counseling, and treatment
should be documented. The arrangements for backup services for
emergency care and referrals must be clearly specified. Provisions
should be spelled out for outreach and follow-up, two essential components to assure compliance with prescribed regimens. These guide-

lines can be used for training as well as for communicating with the school staff, parents, and the community about the practices within the clinic.

Robert Haggerty, a distinguished professor of pediatrics, cites two major weakness in school-based health clinics. He is concerned about the absence of services nights and weekends, "which means that the youth involved have discontinuity of care when they have to go to an emergency room during those off-hours. The other missing feature is the complete lack of integration with the rest of the health care system. Such physicians frequently do not have admitting privileges, do not have close working relations with specialty referral clinics and laboratories, and in my view they should if these clinics are to live up to their promises."[16] Rebecca Stone, summarizing experience with the Ounce of Prevention Program in Chicago, urged that "a real support initiative for school-based clinics has got to move away from supporting start-up and toward helping school-based clinics grapple with the emerging issues of service delivery... handling violence, drug addiction, the rise in adolescent HIV and STDs, the role of nurse practitioners and the shortage of them, and the impact of Norplant."[17]

Not all school-based centers have long waiting lines; those that are underutilized may not be attractive to students because of staff attitudes, limited services, limited outreach, or other reasons that should be identified. Students report that the quality of "trust" is the most important attribute of those they rely on for help. They require constant assurance that their need for confidentiality is respected. Guidelines must pay particular attention to assuring the confidentiality of records. One of the most difficult turf issues revolves around keeping everyone informed about the progress of individual students and families without violating the confidential relationships that are the hallmark of effective services. Clinic guidelines generally maintain that client records cannot be revealed without client permission, even to a parent or to school staff. School records, on the other hand, can be shared with parents and may be shared with clinic staff if the school staff deems it necessary.

Certain exceptions to confidentiality regulations may be found in state statutes regarding the reporting of child abuse. Clinic staff would generally be required to report suspicions of child abuse or neglect to the designated child protective agencies. The law is less clear on the reporting of suicidal ideation to the child's parents, but many legal authorities believe that contacting parents would be the most appropriate action to take.[18]

Staffing

If the popularity of school-based services continues to grow, expansion may be limited by an acute shortage of personnel. If the proposal to open up sixteen thousand school centers in communities with high-risk families were to be taken seriously, where would the staff for these programs come from? A typical clinic might employ a full-time nurse practitioner, social worker, receptionist, and community aide and have the services of a part-time pediatrician, psychologist, health educator, nutritionist, or substance abuse counselor. The primary category of staff currently coordinating school-based clinics is the nurse practitioner (NP), and programs already report great difficulty recruiting them. In 1991, nursing schools had the capacity for graduating 1,600 NPs a year (of whom only three hundred are pediatric NPs.)[19] The competition for NPs is intense, not only from community health centers and family planning programs but also from private physicians, who are adding NPs to their office staffs and group practices. The same situation exists for social workers, who are in great demand to provide the mental health component in clinics.

Several of the statewide initiatives (Florida, Kentucky) are based on the theory that most services in schools can be provided by people already employed by a community agency. One report of "stakeholders'" views of full-service schools in Florida strongly stated that committed full-time staff were necessary for developing a program.[20]

As they pointed out, "we can't just add on to a person's responsibility and expect it to work."

One approach to the staffing problem may be to train school nurses to become school nurse practitioners (SNPs). Every state has different regulations and certification procedures, but in general this can be accomplished with about a year of supplementary in-service training. However, training capacity is severely limited; only eight programs in the U.S. graduate eighty SNPs annually. Although there are about 1.7 million registered nurses in this country, the demand for their services is growing rapidly, and many RNs are interested only in part-time employment or in specialized hospital-based services. Efforts will have to be made to interest nursing schools to focus more on training NPs.

Physician assistants (PAs) are also being recruited to work in school-based clinics. There are about sixty thousand certified PAs in the country, and possibly their training could be more focused on adolescent health services. Both pediatric and family medicine residents are being trained in school clinics. It is important that they understand how these programs work so that they can be participants when they enter either private or public practice. Physicians are essential for medical backup, training, and specialized care. Many of the leading multisite school-based programs are directed by pediatricians trained in adolescent medicine.

In response to the growing interest in integrated youth programming, consideration is being given to a new category of personnel—someone with cross-disciplinary training who can manage and coordinate multicomponent, multiagency programs. This type of center director has to be able to bridge the fields of adolescent health, psychosocial development, and education. He or she has to know how to manage multiple funding sources, be accountable to various kinds of health and educational agencies, relate to a wide range of professional and nonprofessional staff, and respond well to crises. Several university centers have already been organized to produce new kinds of staff. Hal Lawson of

Miami University (Ohio) has called for the creation of human service professionals, practitioners who are trained to focus on children's needs across disciplines. [21] Rick Brandon of the University of Washington and Sid Gardner of California State University at Fullerton also have initiated significant new cross-disciplinary training programs.

One of the most pivotal questions to be addressed is, who takes the initiative to create a school-based program? Some of the most interesting programs are started by individuals—either within the school or outside—who have a burning desire to make changes. They are often charismatic enough to convince the various establishments, either school or community gatekeepers, to allow them to move ahead and implement their programs. Today's enlightened principal and superintendent are standing by the schoolhouse door, inviting outside agencies and even individuals to come in to help act as surrogate parents to an increasingly deprived population of poor youth. A task force from the National Health Policy Forum made the observation that "leaders of innovative programs tend to conceptualize what they want to achieve, to pick their ways through mazes of public and often private support, to build networks of people who share their vision, and to be able to market their ideas to others."[22]

I visited a group in Kauai, Hawaii, in the early stages of program planning, who were plowing through the health department bureaucracy to get approval for staff positions and the school bureaucracy for space allocation. The project director, Mimi Snyder, was undaunted. She told me that she expects to devote the rest of her working days to ensuring that a clinic opens in every school in Hawaii. A hurricane hit soon after, but within a few months the Kauai clinic was open. The school-based clinic movement, because it is new and challenging, involves many dedicated people like Snyder. One program manager found that rather than necessarily having educational credentials in a specific field, staff had to be smart, flexible, culturally sensitive, creative, highly organized, very dedicated, willing to work hard and tolerate stress, and genuinely care about people.

Controversy

It is true—not everyone loves the idea of integrated comprehensive school-based services for families and children. Not only are school "sex clinics" marked as undesirable for adolescents; opposition has been organized against bringing any kind of services into school buildings, even at elementary schools. When the Kentucky Youth and Family Centers were first proposed, the Eagle Forum put out brochures referring to the program proponents as "child snatchers." The phrase "one-stop shopping" has been questioned by those who fear that it will lead to another version of the "shopping mall" high school, with too many diverse offerings and too little substance. Some people believe that the purview of schools should be limited to educational interventions only, that teaching basic cognitive skills should be the primary and sole function of schools. It has been theorized by some that if schools were adequate and if children bonded to their educational experience at very early ages, they would be able to "make it" without additional interventions.

State initiatives that offer grants to communities that develop collaborative projects have provoked some negative responses from the local practitioners. At a planning conference, one group of representatives from a remote rural area expressed concern about "Big Brother." They did not want the state to be telling them how to organize services in their community. They feared that a school-based collaborative project that placed social services with health and child protective services might "inflict help" on people who didn't want it. Concern was expressed that "one-stop" services might make families more dependent rather than empowering them to act for themselves. In some communities, objections have been raised to the provision of mental health services and substance abuse counseling in the schools because they are too "personal."

Of course, the spectre of the "sex clinic" always arises at early stages in the development of school-based services of any variety.

This is ironic in light of the fact that many states prohibit the provision of contraception on school sites. Even in states with no restrictions, most school clinics do not provide comprehensive family planning services to students, and students do not routinely utilize the school clinics for this purpose. It may be that the expectation of controversy has a cooling effect on service provision. In the few clinics that have more assertive efforts to provide sexuality education and counseling and offer contraceptives, the utilization rates are much higher. Articulate state officials can make a big difference. When Joycelyn Elders was director of health in Arkansas (she is currently Surgeon General of the United States), she strongly supported the concept of school-based services, always emphasizing that the decision about how to provide family planning was strictly up to the local school and community. Several local school boards voted to provide contraception when given the option.

Susan Hunt tracked the history of decision making about school-based clinics in Boston from total rejection to acceptance and concluded, "What should be noted about the politics of school-based clinics . . . is that despite community controversy over these life style issues, almost all attempts to implement a clinic in a community succeeded eventually—even [in] the most traditional areas of the country."[23] She attributes success to the ability of policy makers to address issues such as birth control in a comprehensive, sensitive, and courageous way and to their willingness to make compromises (as in the case of Boston) to forgo the provision of family planning on site. Currently, the Boston School Committee and the City Department of Health and Hospitals are considering a division of labor whereby the school provides abstinence education to the students and the health department is allowed to distribute condoms through their nurse practitioners who are stationed in most of the city high schools.

One of the most dramatic episodes in the modern history of school-based services occurred in Miami.[24] Following an offer of an RWJ-funded clinic, the Dade County School Board voted to initiate one in a Miami high school. Board members received bomb threats. "We had our escape route all worked out. The police barricaded the doors, and police dogs sniffed out our meeting room for explosives." Janet McAliley, school board vice president, learned from this experience that local leaders can overcome such threats if their goals are to "protect the health and well-being of the student, reflect the will of the community, and preserve parents' rights to consent to a child's health care."[25] In this community, two-thirds of the public supported the health center. According to McAliley, "For all the noise they made, the members of the opposition were just a noisy minority; their power was out of proportion to their number." But it took more than two years to open the center because the governor (Robert Martinez) refused to allow the Department of Human Resources to receive the grant. A new sponsor was found in Miami's Public Health Trust, which includes Jackson Memorial Hospital.

Even for programs that have longer track records, the controversy over reproductive health services—whether real or imaginary— never seems to completely disappear. Existing state support for school-based clinics has been threatened when groups try to make the delivery of family planning services into a major issue. For instance, a couple of years after New Jersey instituted its School-Based Youth Services Program, a bill was introduced that would have outlawed school-based centers entirely or limited services to those that had no relationship to reproductive health care. Even for teen parents, practitioners would not have been allowed to offer counseling on preventing a second pregnancy. Those who supported the bill (largely Right-to-Life groups) alleged that school-based clinics were encouraging sexuality. They also asserted that the teen pregnancy rate had risen because of school clinics. But an overwhelming defense was mounted by teachers, students, health organizations, the PTA, and religious groups, testifying about the importance of the New Jersey program. They made it clear that parental consent was required for reproductive services and that contraception could not be distributed by the centers. The legislation never made it out of committee, but it was clear that many people in the state were poorly informed about the program. It reconfirmed the importance of frequent program updates to state policy makers.

School Restructuring and Full-Service Schools

Much of the rhetoric (including my own) supporting comprehensive care for children and youth links the goals of school success with the drive toward changes in health behaviors. The argument states that in order to benefit from improved educational settings, young people and their families need access to an array of health and social services. It appears that the two objectives (improving schools and assuring access) overlap, yet the movements that propel them are rarely generated simultaneously. School reformers are occupied with school organization, site-based management, curriculum design, and testing, while health reformers are interested in health assessments, screening, psychosocial counseling, and referral for treatment. Both movements are concerned with parent involvement and community participation.

Although the rhetoric of restructuring encompasses building collaboration between schools and the community, most restructuring concentrates primarily on enhancing student experiences through new teaching methods and changing teachers' professional lives via staff development.[26] Much less attention is being paid to changes in school management than would be assumed from the literature, and real or perceived political barriers stand in the way of community interactions.

Michael Sedlak and Stephen Schlossman, leading historians of school movements, have colorfully portrayed the views of those opposed to bringing additional services into schools, who feel that "the schools have been victimized...by the ambitions and fuzzy-headedness of educators who envision the school as repository for an endless stream of services justified in the name of child welfare and community uplift. Since the Great Society era, the schools' intellectual mission has been diluted by the incorporation of numerous social service and curricular innovations that sap limited economic resources."[27] Those who follow that line of reasoning are clearly more interested in test scores than in immunization rates.

One window on changing perceptions of what should take place in schools has been provided by the experience of the "New American Schools," a privately funded initiative to bring about "fundamental institutional change in American Schooling."[28] A striking feature of the nine award-winning designs is what they have in common, what *Education Week* labeled the "new conventional wisdom": individual attention by advisors, multiage classrooms, and small groupings; teaching methods such as cooperative learning and hands-on project-oriented activities; use of computer technology; and longer school days and school years.[29] Most important, nearly every proposal addressed the need for increasing coordination between education, health, and social services. Different plans call for a community health team of teachers, parents, psychologists, social workers, and nurses; contracts to bring in the whole array of ancillary services; learning centers to integrate and link services from thirty different agencies; and family development centers with a family support team to integrate services. The most far-reaching proposal, presented by the National Alliance for Restructuring Education, focuses on schools that are willing to "break the mold" and "reinvent systems." The plan calls for the creation of integrated, comprehensive services, beginning with prenatal care and including family support services, child care and preschool education, before- and after-school care, recreation, and links between schools and home.

One design, "The Modern Red Schoolhouse," a creation of William Bennett, frequent critic of school-based services, proposes that "the school address the needs of at-risk students by providing an academic support system that has as its guiding principle that the school should do what it can do best—and other agencies in the community should do likewise. Character building will be the school's unique contribution to help its at-risk youth."

We do not know which of these design teams will actually produce models that are then widely replicated. But it does appear that comprehensive models are being promoted by many of the leaders in the educational reform movement.

8

▲▲▲

Who Will Pay?
Local, State, and Federal Perspectives

The concept of full-service schools can never "go to scale" and expand to meet the growing demand without the infusion of new funds. School-based health and social service programs, including family resource centers and youth service centers, cost between $100,000 and $300,000 a year depending on the size of the school and the comprehensiveness of the program. The amount of new money required depends on which goods and services are actually paid for and which are contributed either by the school or the participating agencies. One principle has been firmly established: all programs require new funds, at least for the initial staffing, starting with a full-time coordinator. I heard one highly placed government official claim that "too much money up front is a bad thing." In his view, all that was required was to get the human services systems to change the way they operate. The idea that comprehensive programs can be created only with "reconfigured funds," by moving existing funding from one program to another, has not been demonstrated in any place identified to date. If new funds are not available, it is not possible to initiate such programs.

The most urgent question raised by advocates of full-service schools is how to finance them after the demonstration grants run out. In the case of foundations, the funding period is typically three to five years—they support demonstration projects, not public services. Governors and legislators go in and out of office and programs follow, making uncertain the longevity of state grants as well. In any case, state administrators are eager for old programs to find long-term financing so that the state funds can be moved to initiate new programs. No state has committed the amount of funds necessary to develop and maintain a system of school-based service centers for families and children in every community that needs one. The last group of RWJ grantees were warned to prepare for the end of their six-year programs. "The time for reckoning is here. The existing pool of financial resources must be aggressively attacked."[1]

This chapter starts with the view from the local providers regarding alternative sources of funding. Then we turn to an examination of how certain states, the mainstay of support, have created innovative new school-based service programs. Appendix A presents details on twelve states with substantial programs. Up until recently, little action has taken place in the federal government to further the concept of full-service schools. However, a number of legislative initiatives have been proposed, including new health reform approaches that would either create a new comprehensive school-based services program or expand the capacity of categorical agencies to respond to the demand for services. Appendix B presents further details on federal funding sources.

Local Funding Options

Variations in the design of full-service schools and school-based clinics reflect the range of different sources of funding. In some cases, local practitioners have worked with school personnel to design a school-based program and then pursued financing from local or national foundations or local health departments. In other situations, foundations or state agencies have stimulated the development of programs by issuing requests for proposals from local consortia. As the field matures, older programs often rely on many sources of funding—public and private, local and state—to add components to their service mix. Most school-based centers must learn to deal with multiple financing arrangements, be able to capture reimbursements from third-party insurance and Medicaid, and be fully accountable to foundations and state agencies for expenditures. Moving into the era of managed care places even more hurdles for managers to overcome in order to ensure that school-based clinics will be certified as providers for students under health reform.

Categorical Funding

One approach to funding comprehensive programs has been to put together the pieces from categorical sources, federal programs with funds dedicated to a specific problem. Astute program developers know how to build a package, combining basic health services (Maternal and Child Health Block Grant), case management for high-risk youth (Child Protective Services), substance abuse prevention (Drug-Free Schools), and after-school remediation and cultural enrichment (Chapter 1). Experience has shown that the program does not have to be fragmented, even if the funding is, but this takes a lot of "know-how" on the part of the managers. The problem with this kind of funding is that each categorical program has its own eligibility, regulations, reporting requirements, and fiscal years. As Frank Farrow and Tom Joe of the Center for the Study of Social Policy point out, "By the time the funding stream reaches a community, the stream consists of a confusing and inaccessible array of funding 'opportunities' that very few people understand."[2] One experienced practitioner warned providers not to "chase dollars" just because they were available but, rather, to start with a comprehensive design of services and try to fund the most important services from the outset.

Fee for Services

Some of the earlier school-based health clinics expected to charge students an annual fee. The concept was that students would learn to value health care more if they had to pay for it. The results have generally been negative. Providers find that it is not worth the hassle required to collect the money; even though the amounts are small, students perceive this expenditure as a barrier.

Almost all services delivered in school-based programs are free. However, this does not necessarily apply to referrals. Problems arise when the clinic practitioner or center coordinator refers a patient to another provider who may not have the financial support for treating patients without cost, for example, if eye glasses or hearing aids are needed, or expensive X rays, or even birth control pills. These costs can constitute a barrier. Some clinicians report that they make their own private arrangements with their backup institutions so that students can see selected practitioners at the participating hospital or health center without charge. In some communities, service clubs such as Kiwanis or Lions contribute funds specifically for eye glasses or dental treatment for needy children.

Medicaid

It is possible to initiate school-based services with Medicaid funds. In Baltimore, the school-based health services program in 1985 grew out of the Maryland Medical Assistance Policy Administration's interest in targeted outreach and case management services for Medicaid eligible children. As a result, the Baltimore Health Department, through its Bureau of School Health, organized seven high school clinics. No other city has done this as effectively. All across the country, program administrators are looking toward Medicaid as the financial savior. Yet only 5 percent of current expenditures for school-based clinics is derived from Medicaid reimbursements. The proportion of students who are Medicaid eligible varies markedly, from about 15 to 33 percent of all enrollees, but very few programs are able to bill Medicaid for school health care because of site-based problems with determining eligibility and state-level problems with bureaucratic obstacles.

Many clinics have difficulty determining whether the students they serve qualify for Medicaid; teens rarely have their own Medicaid card, and many fear that their confidentiality will be violated if they use the family's card. Other low-income students come from families that appear to qualify for Medicaid but need help with application forms. Families move in and out of eligibility for Medicaid frequently, and if they are disenrolled, their coverage ceases.

A significant barrier is created when clinics do not meet state requirements for certified Medicaid providers, such as having a physician on staff at all times. Those that do qualify as Medicaid providers often find the billing procedures burdensome. However, many school-based clinics use their backup affiliation for accounting purposes, and most hospitals, health departments, and community health centers are already certified providers with the capacity to perform Medicaid billing. Medicaid payment rates are frequently lower than the actual cost of service. For example, in California, a visit of fifteen to twenty minutes that cost a clinic $40 was reimbursed at only $18.24.[3]

The use of Medicaid reimbursements to finance school-based programs can be significantly increased. Medicaid-eligibility and other outreach workers can be placed on-site or in the community to work with students in filling out application forms. Systems are being developed so that adolescents can obtain their own Medicaid cards. Some state Medicaid programs are assisting school clinics to become certified Medicaid providers to meet federal requirements for increased EPSDT screenings for adolescents. Efforts are underway to certify entire schools in low-income areas as Medicaid eligible, clearing the way for charging health and social services to Medicaid for all students in those schools.

However, several developments may limit the potential for increased Medicaid financing of school-based health programs. Given the trend toward cutting back on Medicaid expenditures, it is possible that states will eventually put a "cap" on the amount that can be spent in the state, and the school-based centers will be the first to be decertified as providers. Medicaid programs are adopting "capitation" approaches to provider reimbursement. Under this system, the state pays a specific amount per Medicaid enrollee in advance to a health plan to cover a total package of health services. The health plans, such as HMOs or other group practices, then provide the care through staff or contracted providers.

Managed Care

In every discussion about the reform of health care, "managed care" seems to be the leading contender. In this system, families are assigned to one provider, typically an HMO, a community health center, another group medical practice, or a private physician, and, as with the Medicaid arrangements described above, the provider receives an annual preestablished "capitation" amount to cover all necessary services. Under managed care, it could be required that entire families, including the children, use the same provider. Yet children and youth may not receive such needed services as mental health counseling, substance abuse treatment, and family planning from their managed care provider. School-based center models may not fit into the regulations governing managed care because they provide extensive individual and group counseling, with repeated visits by high-risk students. This new system could create significant problems for school-based health services because they could no longer collect payments from Medicaid or health insurance systems for student services. The assumption could be made that the health system was being billed twice for the student, once through the family managed-care plan and once through whatever Medicaid reimbursement the school clinic received for its services.

It is possible that school-based services can be exempt from these provisions or that the school could be certified as the care provider for specific children in families. Managed-care systems are already operating in thirty-two states with options for Medicaid recipients. In St. Paul, local managed care providers have subcontracted with Health Start, the nonprofit coordinating agency, so that students can get their care at the five school-based health centers.[4] The DHHS Inspector General's Office is conducting a study on how school-based clinics and managed-care providers coordinate health care to children.[5] The design of the research as stated by DHHS is significant in that it implies that school clinics are established public health service entities similar to family planning clinics or community health centers. Advocates for school-based health services should be encouraged by the inclusion of school clinics in plans for restructuring the health system. I will review the proposed health reform legislation further along in this chapter when I examine the federal role in supporting full-service schools.

States Move Forward to Support School-Based Services

Beginning in 1980, it was apparent that very little new support could be expected from the federal government for innovative services. Over the years, the federal government gave states more authority to provide a range of human services but cut back on the funds required to meet growing health and social needs. During this period, many state governments embraced the concept of comprehensive integrated programs. (Appendix A describes twelve state approaches to supporting school-based services.) New initiatives sprang up all over the country with state governments and state administrators using state grants to initiate school-based health and social services in various forms. The main approaches used were reviewed in the previous chapter.

As described earlier, the first batch of school-based clinics came about because of individual efforts. Several enterprising state administrators came to the first Conference on School-Based Clinics in 1984 to learn more about the model and then went home to develop state-level efforts to fund local schools and community agencies. The simplest mechanism was for the state Department of Health to decide to use a portion of its federal Maternal and Child Health (MCH) Block Grant for school-based services. Several states adopted laws or officially supported the development of school-based clinics through policy statements or direct funding.[6] By 1986, in thirty-five states, legislative initiatives had passed through committees and appropriations had been placed in state budgets. Detractors also introduced bills to limit the use of state funds, particularly in regard to the provision of family planning.

Several, but not all, of these initiatives were quite successful. New York's legislature was the first to authorize state general revenues— $1.8 million in the early 1980s—to be used as start-up funds for communities around the state to open school-based clinics. In New Jersey, a special $6 million line item was added to the human resources budget to create the School-Based Youth Services Program in 1987. New state appropriations also have been approved as part of a special governor's or legislative children's initiative, as in California's Healthy Start program or Kentucky's education reform package. However, most state programs start out with small sums of money allocated to just a few pilot programs.

Not all attempts to obtain official state support are productive. In Minnesota, bills supporting school-based clinics have died repeatedly in the committee stage, never making it to the full legislature for a vote. Though St. Paul, Minnesota, is considered to be the birthplace of modern school-based clinics and has served as the model for many programs throughout the country, the Minnesota Right-to-Life group successfully kept the state from officially supporting clinics. Although the state government acknowledges twenty school-based clinics, all of them are located in St. Paul or Minneapolis and all operate without any direct support from the state. These clinics receive *indirect* state support from the state's federal MCH Block Grant by way of funds distributed to local health departments, which decide to allocate funds to the programs.

Current Status of School-Based Services in States

One can observe extreme differences between states, both in the degree to which they are willing to subsidize school-based services and in the types of programs that they promote at the local level. The situation is changing so rapidly that it is almost impossible to present an accurate count of the number of sites across the country where health and social services are delivered in school settings. For example, as this book goes to press, state MCH dollars are being used in Texas for the first time, to fund four school-based health programs. The initial call for proposals made half a million dollars available to new grantees. Advocates expect more than $5 million to be authorized for school-based health programs in 1994, a significant increase in a state where existing clinics previously had almost no state support.

Models differ significantly, and it is difficult to distinguish between school-based and school-linked clinics or between centers that provide services on site and those that coordinate and refer. We do know that by mid 1993, school-based service programs were located in the majority of states. Table 8.1 shows the distribution of school-based clinic sites by state for 1985 (32), 1988 (137) and 1993 (574). The 1993 figure includes school-linked as well as school-based clinics and represents a maximum estimate based on three different sources: surveys of providers by the Support Center for School-Based Clinics; a survey of adolescent health coordinators in state health departments conducted by the author; and a telephone survey of state authorities in early 1993 by Christel Brellochs and Kate Fothergill, School Health Project of the Columbia University School of Public Health.

The latter group found 481 school-based or school-linked programs with primary health care, social support, and mental health services.[7] Less than 10 percent were school-linked, designed to provide family planning services near but not on school sites. Brellochs found 37 programs she described as school-based integration initiatives

Table 8.1. Distribution of School-Based Clinics by State, 1985, 1988, 1992–93.

State	1985	1988	1992–93
Alabama	0	1	2
Alaska	0	0	0
Arizona	0	3	1
Arkansas	0	0	26
California	0	7	20
Colorado	0	5	10
Connecticut	3	5	31
Delaware	0	1	6
D.C.	0	0	1
Florida	0	1	7
Georgia	0	0	38
Hawaii	0	0	3
Idaho	0	0	0
Illinois	1	5	6
Indiana	1	2	6
Iowa	0	0	8
Kansas	0	0	2
Kentucky	0	0	20
Louisiana	0	3	5
Maine	0	2	6
Maryland	0	7	11
Massachusetts	0	2	16
Michigan	4	8	22
Minnesota	8	10	19
Mississippi	5	6	9
Missouri	3	4	3
Montana	0	2	0
Nebraska	0	0	0
Nevada	0	0	1
New Hampshire	0	0	3

Table 8.1. Distribution of School-Based Clinics by State,
1985, 1988, 1992–93, Cont'd.

State	1985	1988	1992–93
New Jersey	0	19	34
New Mexico	0	9	29
New York	5	14	140
North Carolina	0	3	14
North Dakota	0	0	0
Ohio	0	1	1
Oklahoma	0	0	0
Oregon	0	8	18
Pennsylvania	0	1	8
Rhode Island	0	0	6
South Carolina	0	1	4
South Dakota	0	0	0
Tennessee	0	3	3
Texas	2	2	19
Utah	0	0	0
Vermont	0	0	0
Virginia	0	1	3
Washington	0	1	6
West Virginia	0	0	3
Wisconsin	0	1	1
Wyoming	0	0	0
Puerto Rico	0	0	3
Total	32	137	574

Source: 1985 and 1988: W. Wesson, Support Center for School-Based Clinics. 1992–93: Information supplied by D. Hauser, Support Center for School-Based Clinics, for 1992 and updated by two surveys of state health departments in 1993 by Kate Fothergill, School Health Project, Center for Population and Family Health, Columbia University, and by author. 1992–93 figures include school-linked clinics.

that offered additional programs such as recreation and job training and served families and other community members. Based on my own estimates and discussions with many state respondents, it seems a safe assumption that at least 500 school-based health and social service programs are currently functioning in the United States. This does not include family resource centers and youth centers without health services.

Only in ten states were no school-based clinics identified, mainly mountain states with small widely dispersed populations. By 1993, at least fifteen states had more than 10 school-based clinics in operation. New York topped the list with 140 sites; many of these were elementary school programs, and 86 of them were located in New York City. In California, Florida, and Kentucky, school-based service program development was moving so rapidly in early 1993 that it was hard to keep track of the sites that were in the planning stage and those that had begun operations. As we will see, each of these states has initiated large-scale programs to promote integrated service systems in schools. California has so far funded 140 systems for planning or operations, Florida has already supported 134 full-service school grants and 192 school health grants, and Kentucky has more than 400 youth and family resource centers in place. (Table 8.1 includes only those sites reported by those states to be school-based clinics.)

Building Support for State Programs

Because nearly every state program had to withstand resistance from opponents, program proponents had to obtain high-level support from community leaders and top decision makers at the outset. One of the most effective strategies for gaining their support was constituent advocacy efforts, aimed at getting elected state officials to back the program. In Michigan, the Adolescent Health Services program was launched after a governor's task force composed of public and private representatives developed a proposal for teen health centers throughout the state that was later translated into authorizing legislation. Connecticut's successful implementation of school-based clinics reflects the strong leadership by the staff of the Department of Health, bolstered by unusually well-organized advocates. Everyone said "it" could never happen in Louisiana. Yet school-based clinic advocates were key to the passage of the Adolescent School

Health Initiative, which called on the Office of Public Health to "facilitate and encourage development of comprehensive health centers in public and middle schools."[8]

Program advocates attribute some of their success to building "ownership" among state officials, making sure that as many elected officials as possible received credit and visibility for supporting programs that could make a difference back home. In New Jersey, for example, the School-Based Youth Services Program was planned expressly so that each county would receive a grant. In some states, the initiation of a program was due more to the efforts of one prominent individual who made the critical difference. In Arkansas, for example, when Joycelyn Elders was the director of the health department, she undertook a personal crusade to visit rural communities and convince them that the welfare of their children depended on allowing the health department to provide services to children in the schools. Governor Chiles of Florida has been credited with successfully promoting the large-scale promulgation of full-service schools. "He looks forward to a time when we keep schools open to ten o'clock every night, have them going twelve months a year, make them places where poor families can pick up food stamps and their food from the WIC program and where they can sign up for job training."[9]

Even if such advocacy efforts were not required for a program's initial development, advocates believe that they are essential to the program's ongoing maintenance. In New York State, school-based clinic providers only recently organized a Coalition of School-Based Clinics to advocate for continued state support and to develop program standards. In Delaware, advocates reported that a ground swell of support helped to maintain funding for the state's school-based wellness centers during a fiscal crunch.[10] A reduction in Oregon's state 1992 budget caused by passage of a tax limitation amendment placed in jeopardy nearly all of the $1.4 million in state funds allocated to the state's eighteen school-based clinics.[11] Groups of parents and students organized phone and letter-writing campaigns, local program representatives held press conferences and lobbied before legislative committees, and advocates of all stripes, including representatives of the religious community, met individually with key legislators. As a result, the program received $750,000 to fund eleven school-based clinics through June of 1993—a drastic budget cut— but at least it kept the doors open. At the same time, Multnomah County Health Department restored full funding of $1.3 million to the seven clinics in the Portland area.

In most states, the SBC program was launched through the Request for Proposals (RFP) process, whereby the state issues a formal "invitation" to potential grantees to apply for funds. Most of these grant applications require evidence of collaborative arrangements. The RFP process in itself stimulates a lot of thinking about comprehensive programming and partnerships, clearly opening up communication between schools and community agencies, often for the first time.

In many states, the greatest obstacle to introducing or expanding school-based service programs has been opposition from those who claim that such programs are only providing contraceptives and abortions or promoting sexual activity among teenagers. Such opposition can be difficult to overcome, especially when it emanates from the governor or powerful interest groups. In Wisconsin, advocates were able to obtain a $2 million appropriation for school-based clinics in 1987, only to have it vetoed by Governor Tommie Thompson. During the 1980s, legislative proposals to fund school-based clinics in Indiana and Colorado were defeated. Some states chose to dodge the issue by prohibiting state grantees from providing family planning services, distributing contraceptives, or referring for abortion on school premises. Other states leave it up to local advisory groups or school boards to decide which services are offered in their school-based clinics, including reproductive health and dispensing of contraceptives. Arkansas adopted the latter policy and ensured that no school would be penalized if it chose not to offer family planning services. One state

switched from one policy to the other; Connecticut originally restricted grantees from distributing contraceptives but later allowed
local programs to make this decision for themselves. Since the
change, at least four communities in Connecticut decided to distribute birth control at school-based clinics with parental consent.

Using State Funds to Stimulate Local Programs

State governments have played increasingly significant roles in promoting school-based services in local communities by providing seed
funds or ongoing operational funds to local programs. The U.S. Office of Technology Assessment reported that the percentage of
school-based health centers' budgets that derived from state sources
increased from 16 percent in 1986 to 28 percent in 1989.[12] By 1991,
this proportion reached 47 percent. Using my own estimate of five
hundred clinics, and an average budget of about $100,000, roughly
$50 million is currently being spent on school-based health clinics.
A recent survey reported a total state expenditure for school-based
clinics at $25.6 million nationally, of which $8.7 million came from
state MCH Block Grants and $16.9 million was derived from other
state and local sources.[13] Some twenty-one states reported using
MCH funds for supporting school health services. It should be kept
in mind that MCH funds are actually federal dollars, but states make
decisions about how to use them. An additional $50 million in state
funds is being spent on large initiatives in three states—California,
Florida, and Kentucky—bringing the total amount up to about $100
million on comprehensive school-based services of all kinds.

One problem with state funding strategies has been "reconfiguration," the transfer of existing program resources from a community
site to a school site. For example, if a nurse practitioner is relocated
from the local health department to the school-based clinic, it doesn't
cost anything. But if health department funds are not replaced, the
services the nurse practitioner previously provided may be elimi-
nated. To maintain services at the community level, the health de-

partment has to receive new dollars, but this does not always happen. States also use creative financing strategies to redirect discretionary categorical funds towards school-based service programs, including community mental health, Drug-Free Schools, teen pregnancy prevention, AIDS prevention, and Chapter 1 school remediation programs (see Appendix B). By combining these funds, school-based programs are able to make an impact on several different problems that often had common sources.

By 1992, the amount of state funds allocated to school-based services in the fifteen states with more than ten reported sites ranged from $20 million in California to under $1 million in Georgia and New Mexico.[14] The totals are small compared to the number of schools in each state, and only a few schools or agencies actually receive funds. Many state grants for school-based centers were minimal, less than $100,000 per site; the New Jersey program operated at a higher level, about $250,000 per site. In states like Kentucky, grants often serve as seed money for start-up costs—just enough to hire a full-time coordinator/director and to subcontract with some key community agencies for priority services. But each local center has to then find resources from other funding sources and community agencies to operate more than a skeletal service package. The low level of state funds allocated to school-based programs did not necessarily signify lack of commitment by the state to the programs. The economic recession between 1989 and 1993 made it very difficult for many states to allocate as much as they might have liked during this difficult period. Kentucky's commitment is to support youth or family resource centers in all 1,100 eligible schools (those with more than 20 percent of students eligible for free lunch). By 1994, it is expected that more than 500 sites will be covered, with the expenditure of about $25 million in 1993–94. To cover all schools by 1996, as planned, will require about $82 million ($75,000 average per site), a lot of money in such a poor state.

Similarly, the California legislature appropriated $20 million in 1992 to a new Healthy Start initiative for development of school-based health, mental health, social, and academic support services. Given the enormous size of the school-age population—nearly 6 million—this amount was almost negligible. But in light of the state's severe budget shortfalls, even this amount was deemed an important start. Unfortunately, the appropriation was reduced to $13 million in 1993 as the fiscal crisis deepened in California. The recession and states' resulting budget problems also put a freeze on attempts by some states to launch more modest efforts. For example, in 1991 Hawaii legislators finally appropriated $170,000 to the Health Department to support three pilot school-based health centers. But after the programs were initiated, with six more sites in the planning stage, no more funds were authorized for after 1993. The state is trying to "map" other resources to use for the centers, including Medicaid and other health insurance schemes. Although advocates in the state of Washington could not obtain state funds for school-based clinics, they were able to convince Seattle voters to pass a special tax in 1990 to support the development of school-based clinics across the city.

Finally, a few states dramatically increased the amount of money allocated to school-based service programs. As local programs demonstrated success and gained critical community or political backing, some state officials and advocates requested and actually received higher funding levels from the state legislature. For example, Florida provided almost no financial support to the few school-based clinics in the state before 1990. In spite of their popularity in the sponsoring communities, it took the 1990 election of Governor Lawton Chiles, noted for his support of children's health services, for the state to make almost $10 million available through the Department of Education to school districts for "Full-Service" school health and social services in fiscal year 1992. A complementary program in the Florida Department of Health and Rehabilitative Services provides another $9 million in "Supplemental School Health Services Grants" to more than a hundred schools (few are actually clinics). In addition, $13 million has been made available to school districts for the creation of new facilities or the renovation of old ones for school-based health, mental health, and family resource centers.

Training, Technical Assistance, and Evaluation

States provide more than money to local school-based service programs. In most states, an office in state government provides critically important training and technical assistance to local programs. Adolescent health care coordinators have been designated in thirty-three state health departments. In other states, the state government works closely with a private organization that provides training and technical assistance to grant recipients. For example, in California, a consortium of foundations has funded a nonprofit agency to monitor, evaluate, and provide technical assistance to communities and schools. And in Iowa, the Child and Family Policy Center received a grant from a private foundation to assist state grantees with service integration issues and to conduct evaluations of the programs.

State offices or organizations often concentrate much of their technical assistance on helping local programs negotiate contracts or make other arrangements to enable outside agencies to enter into schools. To address these problems, the director of New York's School Health Program, Michelle Cravitz, spends a great deal of time in the field working with school and community groups, especially because the rapid turnover among school principals requires continuous reorientation to the program. In New Mexico, Karen Gaylord, adolescent health coordinator, travels the back roads helping schools and community agencies in very rural areas to find practitioners to work in school-based clinics and suggesting solutions to difficult transportation problems. Florida's unique Full-Service Schools initiative is headed by Lynn Groves, director of the Office of Interagency Affairs in the Department of Education. She administers the grants program, oversees evaluation contracts, conducts training sessions for providers, and acts as liaison to the Department of Health and Rehabilitative Services and to other departments, the legislature, and the governor.

Training and technical assistance by state agencies also focuses on how to find other sources of funding. As we have seen, Medicaid is increasingly viewed as a potential funding source, but this does not happen without extensive work at both state and local levels. Few states look to education funds as a source for school-based services. Edward Tetelman, assistant commissioner of human services in New Jersey, warned program developers not to expect financial support from state or local education authorities, because their financial conditions are tenuous and most are hard-pressed to provide any new money for services other than educational remediation. He believes it is sufficient for school systems to cooperate in nonfinancial roles.

Most state programs have established basic qualifications for applicant schools or agencies receiving state funds, to provide some consistency in the approaches and encourage local programs to adopt policies that have proven beneficial. For example, state guidelines often compel clinics to meet state licensing requirements or standards of care, to ensure that clinics provide high-quality care. Nearly every state's guidelines require programs to establish local advisory boards in order to ensure community involvement, which state officials believe to be fundamental to the programs' success. State direction has also helped local programs define useful roles for advisory boards and assisted them in sorting out policy, governing, and administrative roles.

States have also played important roles in program evaluation. Michigan has maintained an exemplary data system that tracks service utilization in each of its funded programs. The legislation in Florida and Kentucky requires evaluation. And in California, a major study of the Healthy Start initiative, with support from a consortium of foundations, will monitor and evaluate systems change, as well as program services and outcomes.

State Agency Management

States have placed management responsibility for school-based services with different state departments. Although there are a limited number of choices—usually the departments of education, health, or human services—the choice often reflects the preferred approach at the local level. For example, in a state such as Connecticut that focuses on school-based or school-linked health clinics, the health department has been given program responsibility. In states that are promoting a broader range of health and social services in school settings, such as New Jersey and Kentucky, the umbrella human resources department has lead responsibility for administering grants to school-based youth service centers, even though in Kentucky all grants are made directly to local education agencies.

Regardless of which agency has chief responsibility, the lead agency works closely with other state agencies, since multiple funding sources are often required and lines of authority have to be carefully delineated. For partnerships between human service and education agencies at the local level to work, multiple state agencies have to collaborate to simplify application forms and develop consistent eligibility criteria. Thus, though a state may give authority to one agency, it also requires consultation by others.

For example, in Florida, the Department of Education is responsible for allocating funds to local schools, with advice from the Department of Health and Rehabilitative Services on health and social service delivery issues. Likewise, in California, the new Healthy Start grants reside in the domain of the Department of Education, although all the other departments are involved in a partnership to oversee the results. And in Virginia, the Departments of Education and Medical Assistance Services (Medicaid) were responsible for jointly issuing requests for proposals to plan and implement new clinics, because Medicaid was seen as a primary source of revenue for them.

Several major foundation initiatives will pick up on the momentum created by the states to further the development of comprehensive school-based services. The Robert Wood Johnson Foundation will fund several states to create a state-level office for school-based services and model clinics in two local sites with a particular emphasis on funding. The Pew Charitable Trust has recently launched the Children's Initiative in several states to reshape service delivery systems to improve child health and family functioning and to reduce barriers to school performance. States will initially concentrate on developing family centers for families with children up to six years of age, with a goal of creating a reformed service system for the whole state with the capacity to serve families and all children up to the age of eighteen. The Carnegie Corporation is supporting states in an initiative to help middle schools link students to comprehensive health and social services as one component of middle school reorganization.

Throughout the country, states, foundations, advocates, and individual practitioners are creating new institutional arrangements that focus on both the improvement of academic performance and the assurance that children are healthy. The strategy for achieving these goals involves changing both educational and human service systems in fundamental ways. The ultimate goal of these programs is to create a "seamless" school in which health, mental health, social, and recreational services are completely integrated with education programs (as in Exhibit 1.1). Now eyes are turning toward Washington in hope that the time has come for the federal government to play a role in this "revolution."

The prospects for an expanded federal role in the development of new forms of school-based services appear to be positive. During his 1992 election campaign, President Clinton cited the savings in lives and dollars from preventive and primary care as the major reason for including such services in a core benefits package of a national health plan. He also recognized that in order to increase access to such services, it was important to create "more primary clinics and providers—including school-based clinics where needed."[15] If this proposal survives and is included in the health care reform package that ultimately is enacted by Congress, then states can expect to get a significant boost in their efforts to expand school-based services initiatives, and they can finally look toward a real partnership with the federal government in reaching this goal. Another indication of the current administration's understanding of the link between educational restructuring and support services can be found in President Clinton's educational reform package. It requires state education agencies to demonstrate how they will coordinate access to social services, health care, nutrition, and child care.[16]

The Federal Role in Promoting Full-Service Schools

Where was the federal government as the movement to expand school-based services spread across the country? Although repeated attempts were made in the past to develop a federal funding mechanism for comprehensive school-based services, no major program moved forward through the federal bureaucracy to provide support. However, many categorical federal funding programs were tapped. In fact, at least one-third of all funds being used by school-based health clinics are derived from federal sources such as the Maternal and Child Health Block Grants, Community Health Centers, and Medicaid.[17] But, to make effective use of these federal funds, local program managers had to piece together grants from separate categorical service programs, along with funds from other public and private sources. Furthermore, local program officials had little direction or leadership from federal agencies on how to make it all work when each categorical program had different eligibility criteria, varying reporting requirements, and conflicting rules.

Beginning in the early 1990s, several new initiatives were directed toward joining the forces of educational systems with community health and social services programs. As the Clinton administration took over, a number of different legislative proposals were being introduced, but it was not clear which ones would be supported by the new team or what the "grand plan" was for furthering the development of full-service schools. This description of the federal scene is being written at a time of change, when new cabinet members, a different Congress, and the early stages of health care reform legislation have come to Washington.

Despite all these changes, the categorical funding resources in Washington from which all current health and social services receive support are still significant (and, in my view, always will be). These sources are described in Appendix B. Most of the relevant programs reside in the Department of Health and Human Services (DHHS), but they are also spread out among other agencies such as Education, Justice, Labor, and Agriculture. No matter what happens with health reform, it is important for those interested in creating innovative service systems to understand the many sources of dollars and how they may be obtained and utilized.

While federal dollars are the primary source of support for human service programs of all sorts, other activities go on in Washington that are relevant to this discussion. In the public arena, the federal agencies have the power to waive regulations and change policies, while Congress has the power to draft new legislation and appropriate new funds. In the private sector, many national organizations are working on issues related to integrating services and building more effective collaborative institutions at every level. And, of course, the support of the president and his administration can make a major difference in the success of a program.

Initiatives Leading to Full-Service Schools

Human services planners have long been concerned about the need for better service integration, for cutting through bureaucratic red tape to create less fragmented programs. They observed the great difficulties encountered by school-based practitioners, who were frequently stymied by grant programs' conflicting eligibility criteria and restrictions on services provided. The growing family resource center movement encountered similar frustrations in trying to develop family-centered programs that pulled together health and welfare services, along with parent education and child care. A new initiative was developed by the office of the Assistant Secretary for Planning and Evaluation in DHHS that supported a National Center for Service Integration to provide technical assistance to the rapidly growing demand for the creation of collaborative institutions. Six national organizations were included in a consortium, funded to develop a clearinghouse on organizations and programs, provide examples of programs using different service integration models, conduct studies on barriers to service integration, and convene work groups and conferences.[18]

Around the same time that the integration initiative was launched, the Department of Health and Human Services and the Department of Education jointly convened the Interagency Committee on School Health, bringing together top-level representatives of federal health and educational agencies to communicate with one another. This group is charged with identifying and overcoming barriers to meeting the needs of children through school-based and school-linked programs. These two departments also organized the National Coordinating Committee on School Health, made up of important national voluntary agencies with an interest in child and youth services in schools. The Office of Disease Prevention and Health Promotion, within the Public Health Service, provides staff support for these committees, coordinates the Healthy People 2000 Initiative, and produces materials that help communities implement the Year 2000 Objectives (indicators that health has improved).[19]

Although school-based services never reached high priority in the agendas of previous administrations, several important initiatives were launched that provided support for services for adolescents, programs with great potential for reaching high-risk youth in schools as well as in community-based programs. Through the promulgation of grants to a wide array of agencies, they have facilitated the creation of program models and the training of large cadres of youth service workers who have skills in youth development and in meeting psychosocial needs. The Division of School and Adolescent Health (DASH) was organized by the Centers for Disease Control and Prevention with the goal of reducing high-risk behaviors among adolescents through enhanced school health education and other services. Under the direction of Lloyd Kolbe, one of the nation's leading health educators, DASH gathered significant data about the prevalence of youth behaviors and stimulated new approaches to prevention programs. Beginning in 1993, the scope of this agency broadened to encompass school health services, and Kolbe indicated a strong interest in moving further in that direction by funding a School-Based Health Policy project at the Columbia University School of Public Health.

Another large-scale initiative of recent vintage is the Center for Substance Abuse Prevention (CSAP), one of the five components of the Substance Abuse and Mental Health Administration. This agency, as its name indicates, has a strong orientation toward prevention and has moved far ahead of the "traditional" substance abuse field by developing multicomponent community and school programs. Research compiled by CSAP has helped practitioners understand the need for programs expanded beyond school-based curricula, and its publications have documented a number of effective broader successful interventions that include counseling, mentoring, employment services, family involvement, and treatment.

Attempts to Pass Legislation

Because most of the funds for school-based services have had to be pieced together from an array of disparate sources, advocates for school services have urged Congress to pass legislation that would directly fund these comprehensive projects. In 1986, bills in support of a federal $50 million School-Based Adolescent Health Services

Demonstration Project were introduced in the House and the Senate.[20] "It's time to move teen health off the critical list," proclaimed Representative Cardiss Collins when she introduced the bill. No hearings were held that year; identical bills were reintroduced in 1987, but none of these bills ever reached the floor of the Congress for a vote.

In 1990, Congress did enact the Claude Pepper Young Americans Act, which held out some hope for funds to support comprehensive school-based service programs. Pepper was trying to do for young people what he did for senior citizens, namely, to give their cause visibility and focus, but funds were never authorized. Finally, in 1992, a Comprehensive Services for Youth Act was submitted to Congress, sponsored by Senator Edward Kennedy. This bill came the closest to supporting the concept of full-service schools, calling for partnerships between schools and community agencies, with an array of health and social services located in school or community sites. This bill never reached the floor of Congress, but it is being reintroduced in the current session (1993). The details of the legislation as currently proposed are described below.

New Visions for Federal Involvement in School-Based Services

More than twenty-five studies and reports have been produced in recent years that address the interconnectedness of children's health and education and incorporate a comprehensive approach to health and social services.[21] A huge catalogue of recommendations stem from these reports, particularly in regard to universal coverage for health costs and expansion of access through school-based programs.

Office of Technology Assessment—Adolescent Health

As discussed in the introductory chapter, the Office of Technology Assessment (OTA) issued a report, unique in its thorough review of the physical, emotional, and behavioral health status of American adolescents.[22] The report also documented the disjointed and categorical array of federal agencies and congressional committees charged with responsibility for adolescent health programs. Most important, OTA identified and proposed several major policy options to improve adolescents' health status. In essence, the report pushed for a basic change in the way adolescent health issues are dealt with in this country, so that "adolescents are approached more sympathetically and supportively, and not merely as individuals potentially riddled with problems and behaving badly." OTA's report legitimized the idea of school-based services. Specifically, it called for the following:

- Significant improvements in adolescents' financial and legal access to health services by developing comprehensive centers in schools and/or communities.
- Creation of a central locus for federal efforts (currently located in at least seven cabinet-level departments, several independent agencies, and numerous agencies within DHHS) and improvements in program development, research and demonstration projects, and collection and monitoring of data related to adolescent health.
- Improvement in the social environment in which adolescents live, through family supports, limitations on firearms, and expansion of recreational and community-service opportunities.

The second of these recommendations represents one of the few sources that specifically addressed changes that might take place in the federal bureaucracy to reduce fragmentation. In OTA's view, a new coordinating body could monitor trends and coordinate research; oversee the design, support, staffing, and evaluation of adolescent health services; and provide a focal point for planning, advisory bodies, and agency coordination. To accomplish this coordinating function, the new agency or coordinating body could be created at the cabinet level or placed within an existing department.

National Commission on Children

A panel appointed by President Bush and top congressional leaders issued a lengthy report in 1991, documenting its deliberations in arriving at a broad strategy for improving children's well-being.[23] While its recommendation on tax policy, the creation of a $1,000 refundable child tax credit for all children through age eighteen, received the bulk of the publicity, the report also proposed reforms in the health and educational systems. Although some of the panel members (nine out of thirty-four) dissented, the report calls for a universal system of health insurance coverage for pregnant women and for children through age eighteen.

Although health and education were the major areas examined, the report does not specifically discuss school-based health and social service clinics for needy children.[24] However, the panel did endorse the idea of "one-stop shopping" with integrated health services at one location in a community (including schools). Mirroring many other reports in this field, the panel had specific recommendations on "decategorization" without reduction of funding among some of the 340 separate child and family programs administered by offices and agencies in eleven cabinet-level departments. The report proposed that the federal government, through states, sponsor demonstration projects showing how to eliminate bureaucratic barriers, overcome professional turf lines, and work closely with parents in designing new initiatives.

Advisory Council on Social Security

After a two-year study of "current urgent questions of our health care system," an advisory council to the Social Security system came up with a $6.5 billion proposal to finance health care for twenty million of the thirty-five million uninsured people.[25] The major access recommendation called for the federal government to help states to establish health clinics in or near elementary schools and share with states the cost of providing preventive and primary health and dental services for poor children. State departments of health would operate the clinics and provide physicians for staffing, either directly or through arrangements with other health care providers. The report suggests that $3.6 billion be given to state health departments to develop school-based health centers over three years and $1 billion to assist states in subsidizing school-based health insurance.

The council determined that almost all elementary schools have a space that could be made into a clinic and that the average cost of renovation would be about $10,000 per school. Average equipment cost would be about $1,500 for new starts and $500 for schools that already have some equipment. Funding for these services would have come from both Medicaid and a system of school-based major medical insurance. School districts, with support from states, would offer voluntary, low-cost insurance to all students registered at schools. Coverage would continue up to age twenty-two whether the individual was in school or not.

New Legislative Proposals

Although it is impossible to predict what will happen in Congress, a review of legislative proposals to support school-based services provides insights into the thinking of congressional leaders. The proposed initiatives are equally divided between those that give the major responsibility to the health system and those that would expect the educational system to predominate. The Comprehensive Services for Youth Act, sponsored by Senator Edward Kennedy, calls for funds for state planning and small demonstration grants for special programs such as practitioner training.[26] The main thrust of the legislation is to support local community partnerships, which must include schools, a local health care provider, and at least one community-based youth-serving agency. Grants are to be targeted for low-income communities with evidence of lack of access to health care and high prevalence of multiproblem behaviors. Certain core services would be provided in a school-based, school-linked, or community-based center, including youth development and life-planning services (mentoring, peer counseling, prevention of new morbidities); health, mental health, and social services (screening, treatment, counseling, referral); and a case management system. This act would authorize the expenditure of about $250 million a year through DHHS in consultation with the secretary of education. A Federal Council for Children, Youth, and Families would be set up to recommend ways to remove barriers to coordination and to organize comprehensive delivery systems.

A similar health bill has been introduced by Congresswoman Maxine Waters of Los Angeles with a level of authorization of $2 billion per year.[27] Henry Waxman, the congressional leader on health issues, has introduced School-Based Adolescent Health Amendments of 1986, amending the Public Health Service Act and authorizing $50 million a year for four years for school-based clinic demonstration projects. Senator David Durenberger has proposed adding $100 million to $250 million over three years directly to the MCH Block Grant to provide and promote comprehensive and integrated health, social, and education services for children, to expand health education and access to primary and preventive health services, and to promote a healthy school environment. Although no legislation has been introduced, Community Health Centers may make a bid for the school-based clinic account by requesting $200 million to be added to their appropriation.

On the educational side, Congressman Harry Johnston of Florida has introduced an appropriately named Full-Service School Act that authorizes $72 million a year to organize a Federal Agency Work Group (with the secretary of education as lead), to stimulate states to develop interagency agreements, and to initiate a community planning process at the local level. Nita Lowey also has a House bill—the Link Up for Learning Act—that authorizes $250 million to the secretary of education for grants to local school systems eligible for Chapter 1 for coordinating educational support services for at-risk youth.

On the Senate side, Bill Bradley has a similar bill that authorizes $100 million. He cites the New Jersey School-Based Youth Services Programs as one of the most successful models for connecting schools with social services (health services are not mentioned). Another effort would amend the Elementary and Secondary Education Act— Chapter 1—to add a new part for "Coordinated Services for Schools, Students, and Families," with $20 million set aside for that purpose, including health, housing, nutrition, and other services.

The health care reform legislation presented to Congress in October 1993 included a broad $5 billion Public Health Service Initiative, ranging from training primary-care physicians to funding the National Institutes of Health research on adolescents.[28] Within this package is a comprehensive, school-related health services initiative through which the administration proposes to directly support the expansion of school clinics targeted to ten- to nineteen-year-olds in low-income, medically underserved communities with substantial evidence of the new morbidities. Two kinds of grantees would be acceptable: state health agencies that could apply for grants to fund local communities, and local partnerships in states where the health department did not apply.[29] In addition to schools, applicant partnerships would include a local health provider and a community-based agency, both with expertise in working with adolescents. The federal government would authorize $100 million for grants to school-based clinics in fiscal year 1996, increasing to a total of $400 million by the year 2000. Grants could be used for planning, staffing, developing agreements with local health alliances, and providing health services such as diagnosis and treatment of illnesses and injuries, screenings and physical examinations, medications, counseling, treatment of STDs, mental health, and outreach. Family planning services would be optional. In order to receive a grant, the applicant would have to have agreements with all regional and corporate alliance health plans in the service area, be a certified Medicaid provider, and not charge for any services. It is not clear what

would happen after the first five years or whether it would be expected that school clinics be integrated into such alliances. In addition to supporting clinics, the health reform legislation proposes additional grants to states to develop comprehensive K-12 health
education.

Moving the Vision to Reality

These reports and legislative initiatives, in addition to those of numerous other commissions, task forces, and panels in and out of government, have made recommendations about how to shape the federal involvement in improving adolescent and child health. A strong
consensus is forming around the concepts of a centralized child and
adolescent health agency, the consolidation of fragmented congressional committees, and federal support for school-based clinics and
other forms of "one-stop shopping." The call for a universal health insurance scheme that provides coverage to children and adolescents is
an important first step toward financing. Everyone agrees that more
dollars are needed to achieve this, but there is not a lot of agreement
about where the new dollars will come from. Possible sources include
higher dedicated taxes, reconfiguration of existing funds, decategorization and elimination of some programs, increased use of Medicaid,
and a new legislative initiative.

In response to these articulated demands, one or two incipient
steps have been taken. For example, in 1992, Congress authorized
the creation of the Office of Adolescent Health in the Office of the
Assistant Secretary of Health (DHHS), charged with national planning for adolescent health care. The Office was given a small budget
($2 million) to coordinate programs across HHS, develop a national
plan for the improvement of adolescent health, convene an expert
advisory committee, and act as a clearinghouse on relevant issues.
The decision about where to place this office is still up in the air,
awaiting the appointment of senior staff in the DHHS.

A new funding stream is clearly required to expedite the necessary expansion. The $250 million authorization contained in the Comprehensive Services for Children and Youth Act would be sufficient for at most 2,500 new sites in middle schools and high schools, only a fraction of the 16,000 critically needed sites. But new money would at least give the concept of full-service schools a home in the U.S. budget, a "title" that recognized the importance of these emerging programs. One might question the creation of a new categorical program with dedicated funds as an antidote to the existing fragmentation of services. However, this new program would at least represent a higher order of integration, since its primary purpose would be to give schools, communities, and states the funds they need to begin to package existing programs.

It is not possible to discuss the future of school-based centers outside of the context of national health care reform proposals. Full-service schools would be exemplary providers under national health reform. They bring services directly to disadvantaged youth and families, who otherwise might be difficult to reach; emphasize preventive and primary care; and provide mental health and social services, which can have a decisive impact on health status for this population. Even under a reformed health care system with universal health insurance coverage, it is difficult to imagine that health care provider networks will be able to offer cost-effective care to disadvantaged young people and their families. The services they need—in one place, confidential, with ample provision for individual and group counseling and adequate coverage of reproductive health care and mental health services—can best be provided in school-based health and social services or community-based adolescent care or family resource centers.

9

▲▲▲

A Call for Action

One in four children growing up in America cannot become a healthy, self-sustaining adult without immediate attention. The primary institutions that have traditionally carried the responsibilities for raising and teaching children—families and schools—cannot fulfill their obligations without immediate and intensive assistance. We must call on schools and community institutions to come together in an organized movement to help young people gain equal opportunities to grow into responsible adults. Schools have to become places where all children can learn. Community agencies must become more responsive to their constituencies as part of effective unfragmented school-based networks of care where families can go to strengthen their powers to help their children and themselves. I have proposed the concept of full-service schools to convey the spirit of this movement—a revolution in the delivery of health and social services for this nation's children, youth, and families.

Significant Questions

In this final chapter, we must address critical issues raised through-out the book. If we had to summarize all of our concerns, we might ask, "Are full-service schools for real?" Given the enormous bud-getary problems being encountered by school districts, cities, states, and the nation, does it make sense to recommend large-scale repli-cation of these various models?

Are Full-Service Schools the Wave of the Future?

Extensive testimony has been cited on these pages about the sepa-rate streams of program development in school-based services flow-ing across the country. A whole array of events, some serendipitous, some interrelated, have resulted in the creation of hundreds of cen-ters in schools that bring together health and social services and make them more accessible to students and their families. An entire new literature has emerged that states the case for devising inte-grated educational, health, and welfare initiatives. Exciting one-of-a-kind demonstration projects are springing up simultaneously. Each new entry uses its own building blocks following extended appraisals of community needs, vicissitudes, and resources.

The shape and design of programs at the local level have been in-fluenced by several significant factors. State funding has been a pow-erful factor, and each state has its own adaptation of requirements for school-based services. Foundations have their particular specifica-tions; for example, Robert Wood Johnson places emphasis on the medical model, Annie Casey is interested in new "oversight collab-oratives," Stuart looks toward case management, Carnegie works with middle schools, Hogg is building "Schools of the Future," Pew is aiming toward a total system change in family and school-centered service delivery, and BellSouth is supporting innovative school dis-tricts that tie health and education together. Most important, despite all odds, committed individuals have fashioned unique programs in their own communities that are tailored to certain schools or special agencies.

As these streams of human endeavor come together, I believe that the phenomenon can be called a wave. It is appropriate to group all of these events under the label full-service schools because that term is broad enough to include the many variants that we have examined. Whatever we call "it," an enormous amount of activity and a modest amount of mostly state funding is being directed at new administrative arrangements to bring support services into schools. The question for social policy is whether the concept of full-service schools has long-term viability or whether it is just another fad that will disappear when its advocates find another direction or grow weary of chasing after scarce resources.

Evidence that the concept has durability is suggested by the fact that many school-based clinics and family resource centers have been up and running for more than two decades. More than half a million students use the clinics and an equal number of families are probably utilizing family centers. In a few states, dedicated funds are firmly situated in the state budget, and in others, efforts are underway to certify schools as fiscal agents for reimbursements. In human terms, students and families have indicated their high satisfaction with the accessibility, convenience, and caring attention. Teachers and school administrators have attested to the improvement in the school environment with the addition of these programs. Community agencies have been stimulated by the opportunity to become active partners with schools in trying to address the overwhelming problems of today's children and their parents.

The full-service concept allows for diversity and flexibility. Emergencies can be met with dispatch; for example, massive immunization campaigns can be launched through school-based centers. One school-community needs legal services; another wants computer training for Spanish-speaking residents. Every community wants its schoolhouse doors open evenings, weekends, and over the summer.

The concept of full-service schools may founder because of other circumstances. Funding, of course, is the bottom line. Uncertainty prevails because most sources of support currently being used are not secure. Health reformers have embraced the idea of school-based clinics, but it may be years before legislation is enacted and funds authorized. In any case, money isn't the only barrier. A significant segment of the American people are not convinced that all of these subsidized support services are needed by low-income families. And others are opposed to the extension of the domain of schools beyond the provision of basic skills. The fact that almost all of these health and social services are neither operated nor paid for by school systems is poorly understood. Although the controversy over the provision of birth control in schools is perceived as a barrier, the record shows that this issue can be negotiated (as is happening now in many systems) and is not a major deterrent to the future of school-based services. However, the creation of new institutional arrangements will not happen overnight. The resolution of turf issues will require extensive efforts and a new willingness to change on the part of entrenched bureaucracies of all kinds. "Collaboration" and "service integration" are laudable goals that are rarely implemented.

The concept of full-service schools has high potential as an organizing principle for how schools and community agencies work together in the future. To realize that potential will take sustained and concerted activity at many different levels.

Should Every School Become Full-Service?

In one in five of this nation's 80,000 schools, more than half of the students are so poor that they are eligible for subsidized meals. Those sixteen thousand schools should receive high priority in the movement toward full-service schools. But low-income families in inner-city or rural communities are not the only ones with problems. Many suburban youth are also threatened by the new morbidities—they are deeply troubled, have unprotected sexual intercourse, abuse substances—and have no adult in whom they are willing to confide. Little children all over the country are coming to school with marks of abuse and neglect. Families may not be able to give children all the support they need to overcome these problems. As the concept of full-service schools is disseminated, parents in middle-income communities are beginning to articulate the demand for more school-based services.

As I have asserted, the actual relocation of support services into schools cannot be accomplished without additional funds. It is difficult to imagine that this society in its current fiscal mood would allocate sufficient resources to assist every school in its transition to full service. And, as a matter of social policy, the cost-benefits might be less in schools where only a few of the students need the services. It is important to note that the American Academy of Pediatrics supports the concept of school-based health service programs but only in the areas where health care needs are not being met. The AMA and the American College of Obstetricians and Gynecologists take similar stands, calling for the expansion of school-based clinics only in medically underserved areas (communities determined by national standards not to have adequate physician coverage).

Although wealthier school systems are generally not eligible for state or foundation grants for school-based services, the concept can certainly be extended to encourage all schools to link to community agencies through organized referral systems, frequent communication, and hotlines. As a minimum, one person in each school can be designated full-service coordinator.

How Can the Need for New Centers Be Met?

Sixteen thousand sites is a mind-boggling number, but it is not so extreme if one examines the state of Kentucky. Within a three-year period, the state stimulated the creation of family and youth centers in

400 schools, with a goal of placing a center in each of 1,100 eligible schools in the near future. Although the level of funding is relatively low (less than $75,000 per school), the centers signify a firm foot in the door, with the potential to bring in additional services as other resources are identified. The state of Kentucky has made a clear commitment to the concept of youth and family centers as a component of school restructuring. In Florida, where Governor Chiles embraced the concept of full-service schools, financing has been found for hundreds of starts, including new physical facilities. In Arkansas, the health department made state public health nurses available to local school districts to operate school site clinics in some locations. But in no state can we expect that the governor and the legislature will come up with the necessary level of funding to assure quality programs that are cost-effective.

Assuming that the price for initiating sixteen thousand centers around the country would be a minimum of $1.6 billion (at least $100,000 each to get started), where would these funds come from? I have estimated that at the most $100 million in public and private funds is currently being spent on identified programs in schools. Passage of new legislation for comprehensive school-based services might possibly yield $250 million to $500 million more, depending on which bill passes. Other existing federal programs could be tapped to use more of their resources for these efforts. At the most, two percent of the Maternal and Child Health Block Grant is being used (very creatively) to initiate school-based programs spread over more than twenty states. If 10 percent of the block grant were dedicated for child and adolescent health services in schools, more than $60 million would become available. One quarter of Chapter 1 funds (more than $6 billion) would pay the whole bill. Many program developers believe that Medicaid could pick up the major part of the expenditures for services rendered to children, adolescents, and their parents in schools.

But these programs are limited, Medicaid could be capped, and there is no assurance that either administrators or legislators are interested in using these resources differently than in the past. Just as states with a commitment to school-based services are finding at least minimal resources to get programs started, so must the federal government make a commitment to appropriate new resources for these important new initiatives. It would be foolhardy to suggest that the entire $1.6 million has to be added to the budget. At the outset, a set amount of new funds has to become available to support what programs call "seed" money to make better use of existing resources. Many options have been presented, and practitioners are waiting in the wings with many more.

Going to scale—opening thousands of new sites—requires more than money. A lot of work has to be done to turn this array of serendipitous programs into a solid field of endeavor. As Lloyd Kolbe, director of the Division of Adolescent and School Health at CDC, has attested, "If schools are to provide preventive health services, we will need to help them establish the necessary organizational means, personnel, and legal authority and the mechanisms for integrating and financing such services."[1] The same message comes through in regard to mental health, social services, parent education, child care, and employment programs. Providers, actual and potential, require help. Staff has to be trained and hired. Program managers have to know how to plan and manage. The entire educational establishment has to be consulted, reoriented, and significantly involved in these enterprises.

I have observed in some communities a kind of mystical belief that if everyone talks to everyone else, a collaborative project will emerge; but when the discussion turns to the technical expertise needed to manage complex programs, interest flags. This reflects the "it" problem—many potential community agencies and school systems have not a clue as to what this thing is that they might put together. If the full-service school movement is to grow, much greater access to technical assistance must be developed, with specific training in issues such as accounting, reporting, quality control, personnel management, and outreach. For the medical practitioners, protocols have to be developed and monitored. Skills in psychosocial counseling are required by everyone who comes in contact with young people in these clinical settings. Providers must learn about cultural and ethnic diversity.

I believe that it is entirely possible and feasible to develop centers in sixteen thousand schools within a short period of time. Creative packaging of funds can be accomplished by putting together pieces from existing categorical programs and adding new state and federally generated dollars. I repeat that money alone will not accomplish this task. Plans must be made and assistance provided to ensure that all interested parties in schools and community agencies know what they are doing.

Can There Be a Viable Marriage Between Education and Health?

A consensus that schools and community agencies must come together to create a movement toward full-service schools is apparent. However, the rhetoric has not solved everything; it never does. The main problem that emerges is the inability to bridge the distance between the educational and the health and social service establishments, a situation experienced at the community site, in local government, in state initiatives, and, most of all, at the top level of government. The higher up the authority, the greater the distance between the domains. In unique communities, local schools and health and social service agencies have welded together innovative partnerships, but in Washington and some state capitals the oratory of cooperation gets bogged down in meetings and never seems to be translated into comprehensive funding schemes. As a result, local educators and practitioners are left to grapple with the bureaucratic quagmire, trying to piece together what is needed to maintain critical services for disadvantaged children, youth, and families.

Repeated commissions, task forces, and governmental as well as nongovernmental panels have observed that health and educational institutions must work closely together. Nonetheless, whatever organizational changes are taking place are largely restricted to one institution or the other. School restructuring does not generally comprehend the concept of full-service schools. The restructuring efforts are concentrated mostly on curriculum and school management issues. At the same time, primary health programs coming into schools do not usually focus on the importance of quality education. As we have seen, a few demonstration schools have proven that the marriage between health and education can take place, but not without a lot of commitment, compromise, and organizational skill. The national goal of school readiness may help bridge the domains, with the recognition that preparing every child for school requires extensive support services along with early educational interventions. Clearly, new kinds of institutional arrangements are within the realm of possibility.

What Next?

The cumulative experience in developing school-based services suggests a number of actions that could be taken at the community, state, and federal levels to create new institutional arrangements. I believe that without these actions, the concept of full-service school-based centers will remain in the demonstration mode, with a scattering of "wonderful" programs throughout the country. For the students in the model schools, the quality of life should improve, but the sum total of all the efforts will have little effect on educational achievement, poverty, or the new morbidities. Ideas can only "bubble up" so far; then they have to be translated into staff and equipment, tangible items that have costs.

What Communities Can Do

New ways of organizing services can only be achieved if the people who live in the community want and accept the changes. In the case of school-based services, the local schools have to be willing to participate in collaborative relationships with community agencies, and the community agencies have to be prepared to deal with the realities of working on school turf. Decision makers—school boards, local governmental authorities, volunteer boards—have to allow these efforts to get off the ground.

A number of publications provide detailed guidelines for developing integrated and coordinated school-based efforts.[2] A serious planning process is the first step toward creating any kind of collaborative arrangement. The process of developing integrated school-community programs typically begins with an assessment of needs among students in the schools, their families, and in the community and of the existing resources for meeting those needs. All the players, current and potential, schools and community agencies, have to be brought to the conference table to develop a shared vision of what kinds of new institutions they hope to create in their schools that will be more effective. Inclusivity is paramount—for example, representation from community-based organizations, local medical societies, media, churches, businesses, and, above all, parents, students, and teachers. Different divisions of the school system should be represented, including pupil personnel, special education, adult education, vocational programs, and preschool programs such as Head Start. Universities have a potential that should not be overlooked in the program development process. Much of the impetus for innovative programming is coming from institutions of higher learning, not only in curriculum design, classroom managment, and school reorganization but also in health and psychosocial prevention and treatment interventions. Universities are the bases for research and development centers and clearinghouses, with staff that should be called upon for technical assistance.

This program development process typically starts with an individual in a school, health, social agency, or university who takes the initiative to bring people together to organize an effort to develop a comprehensive program. Once the relevant actors come together, various strategies can be used. One strategy is to form a community-wide youth development committee, which might ultimately turn into a freestanding nonprofit organization.[3] Another strategy is for one organization to take the responsibility to develop a proposal to a foundation or a state agency. Sometimes public officials such as school board members or county commissioners take the initiative.

Full-service schools emerge out of extended negotiations with health, social service, and other agencies. Each agency has a specific contribution to make, through relocating personnel, training, supervision, or accepting referrals. Experience has shown the importance of having a full-time person designated as coordinator of the program at a very early stage in development. Most communities have local settlement houses or chapters of national youth organizations, such as Girls Inc., Boys and Girls Clubs, and Y's, that anticipate expansion in the coming years, particularly in neighborhoods with many low-income families.[4] Rather than spending scarce resources on new buildings, these youth organizations can be encouraged to place their services in school buildings or to work in conjunction with local school boards to create new community-schools. And any new school construction should allow room for the provision of on-site health and social services suitable for students and their families.

Communities have a much better chance of developing school-based centers in states that stimulate program development with grants. Communities in states that have not begun to encourage new programs can be assisted if the federal government moves on proposals for new national initiatives.

What States Can Do

Certain states are leading the nation in developing innovative models of full-service community-schools. (See Appendix A.) All states should be encouraged to create the capacity to assist communities with direct funds appropriated through line items in health or human service budgets, special taxes on cigarettes and alcohol, or dedicated taxes on recreational facilities such as spas and gyms.

To implement the movement toward full-service schools, states should designate a lead agency (or create one) with the mandate to bring the appropriate state agencies together. The choice in most states is limited to the departments of education, health, or human services, although a few states have special children and youth agencies or cabinets that could perform the lead function. In a number of states, the creation of the position of adolescent health coordinator in the Department of Maternal and Child Health has led to more rapid program development of school-based health services. Connecticut can serve as a model with a strong central school-based services office that follows well-defined standards for the placement and operation of services. In California, the Healthy Start initiative is administered out of the Department of Education in conjunction with a private organization set up by foundations to provide technical assistance and evaluation for comprehensive programs.

Few states have sufficient staff to meet the demand for assistance needed by schools and community agencies. The central agency should be adequately supported and staffed to provide technical assistance in planning, program models, staff training, and evaluation. Grant making should be phased so that communities have at least a year to learn about different models and plan for comprehensive school-based services. Local agencies particularly need help in accessing state Medicaid systems, in negotiating for changes in regulations related to eligibility and reimbursement levels, and in understanding new state health insurance schemes. A statewide uniform data system such as in Michigan or Kentucky is an essential tool for planning, monitoring, and evaluation. State legislators and the public must be kept informed about state-funded programs through media, annual reports, and clinic open houses.

The leadership of the governor, strong support in the legislature, and responsive administrators can expedite the development of a coordinated state initiative to support full-service community-schools. Whatever arrangements are made, they have to survive changes in government. Programs can die with the end of a gubernatorial term unless they are firmly fixed in the budget. Statewide task forces, commissions, and voluntary state advocacy groups can push for legislation that provides funding to communities and allows them the flexibility to make their own decisions about the service mix. State universities should be encouraged to produce new kinds of comprehensive youth service workers and teachers with cross-disciplinary approaches involving schools of education, psychology, public health, medicine, nursing, and social work.

What the Federal Government Can Do

The movement toward full-service schools took hold during the past decade with little leadership from the federal government, despite the fact that almost every major national organization in health, education, youth, and family services pressed for action to implement the concept of comprehensive integrated school-based programs. In 1991, Congress's own Office of Technology Assessment spelled out alternatives for giving young people access to the services they need, with particular emphasis on school-based centers. Their findings reflect a powerful consensus that national movements to reform health and social services and reorganize education have to be joined, that the interests of young people and their families can best be served by new forms of full-service schools that weld together nurturing and teaching.

After a new administration moved into Washington in 1993, with many new faces in Congress, advocates believed that the climate was finally ripe for action on the legislative level. In future sessions, Congress will have the opportunity to vote on several pieces of significant legislation that address the need for school-based services. The health reform legislation recognizes school-based clinics as legitimate providers of primary health care and social services, and if passed as proposed, would authorize millions of dollars to states and local partnerships to plan and implement programs. However, it may be years before Congress approves of the plan, and there is no assurance that the school-health initiative will survive the battles to come. In the meantime, advocates for school-based services will probably reintroduce the Comprehensive Services for Children and Youth Act, which would authorize the Department of Health and Human Services, in consultation with the Department of Education, to award $250 million in grants to support state efforts and local partnerships in low-income communities involving schools, health care providers, and community-based youth-serving agencies. Other proposed legislation adds money directly to the Maternal and Child Health Block Grant, the Community Health Centers program, or the Department of Education to integrate health and social services into educational systems. One bill is even called the Full-Services Schools Act.

The president can give this movement toward full-service schools visibility and legitimation through leadership, advancement of legislation that produces new funding for services, administrative arrangements that promote better and more integrated use of existing funding sources, and support of research and evaluation. In regard to leadership, the president, cabinet members, and others in his administration must give high priority to the creation of full-service schools. In addition to the placement of school-based clinics in the health reform package, a White House conference, press conferences, and publicized visits to school-based services would solidify public support. The passage of legislation such as the Comprehensive Services for Children and Youth Act would be an important first step.

I have estimated that about $1.6 billion would be required to finance the sixteen thousand centers that are urgently needed. But even a small amount of dedicated federal funding would legitimize this movement and give it a base in the federal bureaucracy. The flow of funding from the federal government to comprehensive programs could also be expedited by increased flexibility in eligibility requirements and provider certification procedures. Incentives should be offered for states to appropriate state-budget dollars for full-service schools or to creatively use such categorical funds as the Maternal and Child Health Block Grant, Drug-Free Schools, and Chapter 1.

We do not know what impact health reform will have on the full-service school movement. It would be misguided federal policy to withhold support from school centers now in hopes that they will develop as an outgrowth of managed-care and regional health care networks. This would delay their start-up on a large scale for three to five years. The school-based health center is a proven model for widening access to health care, the need is critical now, and the public good will be best served by immediate federal support for these programs.

In regard to administrative arrangements at the federal level, OTA strongly recommends the creation of a central locus in the executive branch to insure comprehensive services for children and adolescents. A number of organizational alternatives have been advanced for the placement of this central office, all in DHHS. For the short term, the new Office of Adolescent Health has been authorized in DHHS and charged with national planning for adolescent health care. It appears that this office will be placed in the Public Health Service under the direction of Joycelyn Elders, surgeon general, who is strongly committed to the concept of school-based services. This office should be extended to cover broader youth development issues, with mandated coordination functions that bridge with the Departments of Education, Labor, Justice, and Agriculture. It could be authorized to award the Comprehensive Services for Children and Youth grants or whatever grants become available.

Unless a source of funds is designated, the movement toward broad development of school-based centers will remain forever in the demonstration phase. A new funding stream is clearly required to move to "scale," to expedite the necessary expansion described above. The Comprehensive Services funds, though meager, could stimulate the development of a "field" of school-based services that has the capacity to draw funds from many other sources. Many people from different disciplines who work in school-based services feel the lack of a defined field that would give them visibility and legitimation. Practitioners would benefit from a national organization for school-based service providers to develop guidelines for quality care; set performance standards; provide training in program models, management, data collection, and evaluation; and facilitate interchange.

Where new program funds are located in the government bureaucracy may not be as important as that the new funds be generated. Wherever they are located, funds should be appropriated to support data collection, monitoring, and evaluation. The many government agencies that are responsible for research should be mandated to support large-scale demonstration projects, with program-oriented research that includes cost-benefit studies, compares the relative effectiveness of school-based and community-based efforts, and identifies culturally relevant approaches for diverse population groups. Attention should be given to the dissemination of research findings among government agencies, as well as to the general public.

Staffing of school-based health, mental health, and social services is a major issue that must be addressed by federal policy. The shortage of nurse practitioners presents a serious barrier to the rapid proliferation of programs. Thousands of physician assistants, program coordinators, health educators, and social workers will also be necessary. All staff require specialized training in dealing with the complexities of the new morbidities and for coping with multiple family problems. Tomorrow's youth workers need a sophisticated understanding of two arcane worlds: the health delivery system and the educational system.

In Conclusion

The thrust toward full-service community schools has been launched at the local level by dedicated practitioners in schools and community agencies, in conjunction with families and students, who are looking for innovative and effective ways to respond to critical human needs. These initial efforts were facilitated by foundations and selected state and local agencies. Now the demonstration phase has ended, and it is time for the federal government to share in the fiscal responsibility for the establishment of these new institutional arrangements. The public must further this cause on the premise that full-service schools are potentially cost-effective investments, as well as exceptional human endeavors.

A small federal expenditure to launch a movement at the national level will yield an immense return, enabling schools and community agencies together to shift their systems to be responsive, responsible, and effective. Without a concerted effort, millions of young people will continue to fail and will have no hope of growing into responsible and productive adults. It will not be easy to reverse this situation. Although I firmly believe that this call to action can be implemented, I know that this is no "magic bullet." No one simple solution will make all the problems of young people growing up in this society go away. Whatever gets done in the future has to be strong, cost-effective, carefully planned, and responsive to the needs of the target population.

I have called for actions on every level:

- Schools and community agencies have to overcome turf barriers and envision new kinds of joint institutions. A planning process has to be initiated that yields an efficient design, utilizing the contributions of each party to building strong and durable full-service schools.
- States have to commit resources to the further development of comprehensive school-based services through funding, centralized administration, technical assistance in planning and program development, training, monitoring standards of quality care, and fostering evaluation. The governor should appoint a lead agency for full-service schools in each state.

- The federal government must move rapidly to support schools, communities, and states to further the movement toward school-based health, mental health, and social services for children, youth, and families. Legislation has to be passed and administrative arrangements worked out to create a central focus for improving the health and social conditions of children and youth. Someone has to be put in charge, and the administration has to back up its commitment to school-based services with immediate actions.

This is a period of rapid change in Washington. We cannot project what the effect of health reform will have on these recommendations, nor can we know what will happen to the budget in the process. These recommendations are presented with the hope that they will be received by sympathetic readers ready to support positive changes, primed to advocate young people's rights to grow up mentally and physically healthy, and willing to push their elected officials at every level to respond to this call to develop full-service schools.

APPENDIX A

▲▲▲

Twelve States That Support
School-Based Services

States have played an important role in stimulating the development of school-based health centers and full-service schools. Each state has a different history, with wide variations in lead agencies, timing, legislation, and most of all, in the amount of funding made available by the state legislature or from Maternal and Child Health Block Grant funds. The twelve examples cited here were selected as examples of varying approaches and levels of support as of mid 1993. The states included are Arkansas, California, Connecticut, Florida, Georgia, Kentucky, Massachusetts, Michigan, New Jersey, New Mexico, New York, and Oregon. Information is provided about origins, program standards, technical assistance (if provided), and funding. Many other states, among them Colorado, Delaware, and Louisiana, are also developing innovative school-based health programs in a rapidly changing political and social environment.

ARKANSAS

Origins
After Joycelyn Elders became director of the Arkansas Department of Health (prior to her appointment as surgeon general of the United States) in 1987, she actively encouraged communities to apply for grants for primary health services in schools. Within a two-year period, twenty-six Enhanced School Health Services clinics were organized in elementary, middle, and high schools around the state, primarily in the Mississippi Delta region.[1] In addition, the state health department supplied nurses for Early Periodic Screening, Diagnosis, and Treatment (EPSDT) in many other local schools around the state.

Program Standards
All school clinic staff are employees of the state Department of Health and follow the policies and procedures of the department. However, they are required by state law to conform to the authority of the local school boards. In 1991, the state legislature passed an act approving of school-based clinics but assuring that no school-based clinic could be established in a public school without a request signed by the local school board of directors, who would retain absolute control over the programs offered by the clinic. Local advisory groups decide what services may be offered in their schools, choosing from a wide menu, including reproductive health and dispensing of contraceptives (four school clinics offer birth control). No school is penalized if it chooses not to offer family planning services. The clinics typically provide health screening, counseling, immunizations, family planning, prenatal care, and health and family life education classes. Staffing includes nurses, social workers, nutritionists, and health educators.

Funding
Nine of the twenty-six clinics in the state are funded through a $512,000 one-time grant from the Arkansas Indigent Health Care

Advisory Council, a trust fund that is used for projects that improve access to health care. A clinic in Little Rock Central High School receives partial support from the Annie Casey Foundation in cooperation with the Little Rock New Futures Initiative. The remaining clinics are funded through Medicaid reimbursement funds and from the Maternal and Child Health Block Grant. In 1993, the Arkansas Department of Health budgeted $786,780 to continue the nine earlier programs and to fund all the rest.

CALIFORNIA

Origins
Up until 1992, all the school-based health clinics in California had been initiated by local advocates and practitioners. The first nine clinics were started with support from the Stuart Foundation, along with technical assistance and evaluation from the Center for Reproductive Health Care Policy Research of the University of California. Claire Brindis, associate director of the Center and an expert on evaluation, and Amy Loomis, program officer of the Stuart Foundation, were major leaders in the movement to expand school-based services. Repeated efforts by advocates to pass legislation or get a specific school-based clinic appropriation failed.

In 1990, Governor Pete Wilson led an effort to create a public-private partnership to develop integrated, comprehensive service systems for children and families. In 1991, the California legislature passed the Healthy Start Support Services for Children Act to establish innovative, comprehensive, school-based or school-linked health, social, and academic support services throughout the state. The California Department of Education was designated as the lead agency for the new $20 million program. Governor Wilson stated that he expected the funding to double in future years.

Program Standards

The Healthy Start legislation calls for support services including health care, mental health services, substance abuse prevention and treatment, family support and parenting education, academic support services, counseling, nutrition, and youth development services. To qualify for state grants, a site must demonstrate that more than half of its families are on welfare, have limited English proficiency, or are eligible for free meals. Half of the grants must be given to elementary school sites. To receive state funding, school systems must submit evidence of a working collaborative partnership or demonstrate that one is being created with health, mental health, social services, drug and alcohol, probation, and other public and nonprofit agencies.

Technical Assistance

A unique new nonprofit agency, the Foundation Consortium on School-Linked Services, has been set up by fifteen private foundations to provide monitoring, evaluation, and technical assistance to California communities and schools participating in the Healthy Start program, as well as to other integrated service initiatives. A formal agreement between the state of California and the Consortium provides for technical assistance in the development of a service system that restructures existing programs, cuts across a range of disciplines and agencies, and integrates state and local resources to avoid conflicting regulations, fragmentation, duplication, and inconsistent service delivery. In addition, the Consortium has contracted with Stanford Research Institute to conduct a $1.6 million evaluation of Healthy Start that will track systems changes, services, and outcomes.

Funding

The twenty original school-based clinics received funding from private foundations, state money generated from a tobacco surtax fund, and Medi-Cal (California's Medicaid program). Five were funded by RWJ, but those grants expired in 1992. Stuart Foundation continues funding nine programs at a level of $2 million. No Maternal and Child Health Block Grant funds have been used for school-based services in California. After $20 million had been appropriated by the state for the Healthy Start initiative, a request for proposals was issued to school superintendents in early 1992. The first grants—114 for planning involving 307 schools and 40 to existing programs in 121 schools—were awarded in 1992 to local school systems. (It is not known how many of the grants cover school-based health clinics.) In 1993, because of a fiscal crisis in the state, funding was reduced to $13 million, limiting the number of new starts among the grantees who had initiated planning. It is expected that $20 million will be available by 1994.

The partnership between the state and the Foundation Consortium is charged with developing a mechanism to obtain Medi-Cal and other funding sources and making it possible for local education agencies to become certified as Medicaid providers. State officials claim that Medicaid reimbursement could total $45 million in the first year alone and rise to as much as $300 million yearly. This money would be reinvested in the new service systems, freeing up state funds. Thus far, $1.75 million has been committed to the Consortium by foundations, and the state will contribute more than $1 million via in-kind services. The foundation contribution is expected to be over $5 million in the next three years.

CONNECTICUT

Origins
In the early 1980s, the Teen Pregnancy Prevention Coalition in Bridgeport, Connecticut, was eager to replicate the St. Paul school-based clinic model. The Connecticut Department of Health Services (CDHS) provided approximately $50,000 from the Maternal and Child Health Block Grant in the first year. As a result, primary health care and health education services were instituted in a Bridge-

port High School. Around the same time, RWJ awarded a grant to the school-based Body Shop program in New Haven High School.

For almost twenty years, the CDHS had been funding twelve Adolescent Pregnancy Prevention and Young Parent Programs. By 1985, it was becoming increasingly evident that adolescents had many other health, mental health, and social service needs that were not being met. As a result, the department offered small planning grants to four communities to assess the needs of their teens and to develop school-based health center models to address those needs. These grants provided the funds to hire staff to organize the community, build support, and ensure local involvement. Technical assistance was supplied by the department's maternal and child health staff. Two clinics opened the following year with MCH Block Grant funds. Several additional clinics were implemented in early 1987. Then in 1987, a line item of nearly half a million dollars was appropriated for school-based health services in the state budget.

Over the last several years, the state has made the development of school-based health centers a top priority. By mid 1993, nineteen school-based services were supported by the state, and eight more communities were planning these services. The supervisor of the School and Adolescent Health Division of the Connecticut Department of Health Services expects that within the near future thirty-one clinics will be in operation, covering most parts of the state.[2]

Program Standards

The state health department has developed a set of guidelines outlining the basic components for all school-based clinics. These include the provision of medical care and screening, counseling and social services, health education, and special services aimed at substance abuse prevention. In applying for grants, applicants must develop plans for the provision of services during nonoperational times by identifying medical and social services backup. Staff must be sufficient to operate a full-time licensed outpatient clinic, including a coordinator, a nurse practitioner, and a social worker. Several of the existing clinics in the state offer full dental clinics and provide family outreach through the employment of parents as community aides.

Funding
By 1992, the state commitment had grown dramatically, and, despite a tight budget year, $2 million in state general funds were appropriated, $410,000 was allocated from the Maternal and Child Health Block Grant, and $140,000 of the Drug-Free Schools money was committed to school-based clinics, for a total of more than $2.5 million. The grants ranged in size from $80,000 to $100,000. Clinics were expected to become certified as Medicaid providers. An additional $500,000 is proposed for school-based health centers in the governor's budget for next year and an equal amount for the year after, implying a total commitment of $3 million in state funds by fiscal year 1994–95.

FLORIDA

Origins
For a number of years, the only school-based clinic in Florida was located in a small town, Quincy. It was operated by the Gadsen County Health Department in a mobile unit on the campus of Shanks High School. In 1987, Governor Bob Martinez ordered the clinic moved off campus (a hundred yards down the road) in response to political pressure from conservatives. In the same year, the Department of Health and Rehabilitative Services (DHRS) was awarded $600,000 by RWJ to open a school-based clinic in Miami. When Governor Martinez opposed this move as well, the funds were awarded to a nonprofit organization, which went ahead and initiated services in a high school.

Then in 1991, under the leadership of newly elected Governor Lawton Chiles, the Florida legislature passed a law (SB 3006) supporting the development of full-service schools, to enhance the capacity of school health service programs to address teen pregnancy, risk of AIDS and other sexually transmitted diseases, and alcohol and drug abuse. State officials believed that school-based programs had the greatest potential for promoting the health of students and reducing teen pregnancy.

Program Standards

The full-service schools legislation requires the state Board of Education and the Department of Health and Rehabilitative Services (DHRS) to jointly establish programs to serve high-risk students in need of medical and social services. All full-service dollars go to county school districts, who then subcontract with other agencies. Full-service schools are one of four different types of "Supplemental School Health Programs" that communities can receive funds to operate. Full-service schools provide the most comprehensive set of services and are technically defined as "integrated education, medical, social and/or human services" provided in school facilities or in locations easily accessible to them. Among the services provided are nutritional services, basic medical services, assistance in applying for public benefits such as AFDC (welfare), parenting skills, counseling for abused children, and adult education. According to guidelines in the request for proposals, joint applications for funding had to be submitted by school districts along with DHRS county public health units.[3] School districts with a high incidence of medically underserved high-risk children, low-birth-weight babies, infant mortality, or teen pregnancy were targeted as having greatest priority.

The other three types of programs under the state's Supplemental School Health Program include (1) School Health Improvement Projects (SHIP), which place public health nurses and health aides in schools to conduct health appraisals and screening exams and refer to community health services; (2) Student Support Service Teams, which include a psychologist, social workers, and nurses who evaluate and counsel students with mental health, behavioral, or learning problems; and (3) Locally Designed Programs, which allow local districts to pursue unique approaches to providing health and mental health services in schools. Another provision of the law mandated comprehensive school health education, including human sexuality and pregnancy prevention (with abstinence as the expected standard). The Department of Education received $3 million to fund expansion of the curricula and to provide in-service training. Full-service schools are mandated to participate in evaluation. The Department of Education, in conjunction with the University of South Florida, is responsible for annual training conferences and provides technical assistance and program monitoring for grantees.

Funding
Florida's full-service schools program is funded in part by state appropriations and in part by a special tax on athletic, exercise, and physical fitness facilities and clubs. The program began in fiscal year 1990–91, with grants from DHRS totaling $2.9 million. This amount is expected to reach $9.3 million in 1994. Each year, $75,000 will be used to fund administration of the programs by DHRS. Grants were awarded in thirty-five counties encompassing 134 schools. Each recipient of the full-service school grants can receive up to $400,000 annually, and designated full-service schools can also apply for capital improvement funds.

Full service is a concept that has provided a real stimulus to people in Florida to develop more Interagency Collaborative Initiatives located in schools. In a sense, it is an umbrella under which several initiatives are placed. In addition to the full-service schools, the Supplemental School Health Services program provided $9 million to forty-nine projects in 192 schools through the Department of Health and Rehabilitative Services. These funds are used primarily to place a nurse and a health aide in a designated health room in a school.

Public Education Capital Outlay (PECO) funds for renovation, remodeling, and construction of facilities to house service providers were made available to school districts and university-affiliated schools through the Department of Education. These capital improvement funds come from a dedicated tax on utilities that totals about $400 million. In 1993, $12.6 million in PECO was earmarked for forty-six projects in full-service schools, with grants ranging from $60,000 to $2.5 million. The latter grant will construct a major health and mental health school center serving students in the St. Petersburg area. In the future, all new schools have to include room for full-service centers. Dade County received $12.5 million to include centers in renovations after the hurricane.

More than $30 million is being spent this year in Florida on collaborative school-based projects of varying service mixes. Although many new programs are being started, few would fit into the definition of traditional school-based clinics. Only about one-third of the full-service grantees include health services (many are family resource centers, case management, or recreational programs). Only 11 percent of the sites are high schools. The expectation is that *all* schools will be full-service in a few years, with the gradual introduction of child care, vocational education, and mental and other health services.

GEORGIA

Origins
The Georgia Department of Human Resources, an umbrella agency encompassing health, mental health, substance abuse, mental retardation, and family and children's services, started supporting school-based health services in 1987. With a one-time surplus of funds that went unspent during a fiscal year, the department responded to requests from local communities who wished to replicate the DAISY program—Diversified Agencies Involved in Serving Youth.[4] This

model program, initiated in 1986 by two physicians in the rural multicounty Southeast Health Unit, located a variety of services in or near schools to simplify the interactions between multiple agencies serving youth. The DAISY program proved to be effective in reducing the rate of teen pregnancy and school dropout. By 1992, the DAISY model was replicated in fourteen sites in eight counties, representing a substantial proportion of the thirty-eight school-based clinics currently operating in the state.

Program Standards

Up until recently, Georgia had no legislation supporting school-based clinics; the work of the Office of Adolescent Health was supported by the health department's general budget. The state requires that school-based clinics receiving state funds use a uniform reporting system for tracking utilization. Approximately twelve thousand students were enrolled in 1991 (according to submitted parent permission slips), and about thirty-one thousand visits were reported for that year. The state is providing some support, and it encourages substantial flexibility for local programs in terms of organizational models and type or scope of services provided. For example, school systems are beginning to hire registered nurses and to become certified as Medicaid providers to offer EPSDT screening on school sites. The Atlanta school system has hired a full-time physician to coordinate the utilization of Medicaid. Public health departments are discussing ways in which they can work more closely with schools.

Funding

Currently, the state allocates nearly $900,000 from the federal Maternal and Child Health Block Grant to fund school-based clinics. The DAISY project receives funding from the MCH Block Grant funds, but its budget of around $800,000 is supported largely by other categorical state funds for pregnancy prevention, substance abuse prevention, and a special line item in the health budget of $45,000 earmarked for this program. About half of the DAISY program's budget is also supported by private foundation grants. Another large foundation-supported school-based clinic is located in Savannah and is one of the Annie Casey Foundation's New Futures Initiatives.

A state budget request of $1.7 million to the Department of Human Resources to help support the development of school-based services in Atlanta was recently rejected. Funds were sought for nineteen "clusters" (neighborhoods) identified in the Atlanta Project, a major community improvement effort under the leadership of former President Jimmy Carter.

One initiative that has been funded is the Family Connection, which calls for developing collaborative community-school programs at fifteen sites and planning of an equal number. "Start-up" funds have come from the state ($2 million) and from the Joseph B. Whitehead Foundation ($5 million). The Departments of Education, Human Resources, and Medical Assistance are charged jointly with developing community-based programs including school systems, human services, private nonprofits, business, the religious community, and elected officials. It is expected that long-term funding will derive from refocusing and targeting existing resources within the partnerships and enhanced Medicaid support. An independent evaluation will measure the partnerships' effects on improving the lives of at-risk children and their families, particularly in regard to graduation from high school and prevention of teen pregnancy.

KENTUCKY

Origins
In 1988, the Kentucky Integrated Delivery System (KIDS) was initiated to help local agencies coordinate their services and make them more accessible in school-based sites. Though the program was sponsored by the state Department of Education and the Cabinet for

Human Resources, it had no funding from the state. Nonetheless, the KIDS program helped over a dozen local communities develop agreements between schools and agencies for the delivery of human services in the schools.

With this groundwork laid, the Kentucky legislature launched the state into the forefront of efforts to link family and youth service initiatives with comprehensive school reform. By enacting the Kentucky Education Reform Act (KERA) of 1990, the state not only radically changed the structure of public education but called for the creation of family resource centers and youth service centers, which would provide health and social services in or near each elementary or secondary school in which 20 percent of the students were eligible for free school meals. The centers were regarded as a critical element in the strategy to improve students' academic performance.

Program Standards

The state education reform law called for a sixteen-member Interagency Task Force to formulate a five-year plan for the establishment of family resource centers and youth service centers. The task force includes representatives from state departments and local agencies, parents, and teachers and is staffed by the state Cabinet for Human Resources. Grants are awarded by the Cabinet for Human Resources directly to school districts for individual schools, and it is the Cabinet that promulgates regulations, oversees the grants, provides technical assistance, and is charged with evaluating the centers.

Local advisory councils are required of all grantees. The family resource centers must include arrangements for access to full-time child care for two- and three-year-olds, after-school child care, summer programs, parent education components, and health services. The youth service centers must include referrals for health and social services; employment counseling, training, and placement; summer and part-time job development; drug and alcohol abuse counseling; and family crisis and mental health counseling.

Coordination is the major function currently carried out in the Kentucky centers. The staff is typically one full-time coordinator and an assistant, and the site is generally one room within the school building. Few of the centers would be defined as school-based clinics. Only one out of four are youth service centers (serving youth of age twelve or over); the majority are family resource centers. Several school-based clinics exist (and more are opening) with funding from the Kentucky Department for Health Services.

Funding

During 1990, $125,000 was appropriated to the Cabinet for Human Resources for planning purposes. Beginning in July of 1991, $9.5 million was made available for the first 125 centers, at the level of about $75,000 for each center (not including local match and other sources). As of 1993, the budget rose to $15.9 million for 223 centers serving nearly 414 schools.[5] It is anticipated that 125 new centers will open in early 1994, bringing the total to well over 500. To fully fund all approximately 1,100 eligible schools, a total of nearly $83 million must be appropriated by the Kentucky General Assembly. However, there is no assurance that this will actually occur. One of the goals of the program plan is to make schools eligible for Medicaid funding, particularly for case management services.

Kentucky has received grants of about $300,000 from the Annie Casey Foundation to support state office staff, training, technical assistance, and the development and implementation of a management information system that can be used for evaluation. This state is also one of the five sites selected by the Pew Charitable Trust for its Children's Initiative, to develop integrated family support services targeting children from birth to six.

In addition to the KERA school-centered initiatives, the Maternal and Child Health Division has rapidly expanded its funding of school-based health centers through local health departments. In 1993, almost $1 million was being expended in twenty sites, with the expectation that this activity will double within a year, to an expenditure of $2 million in a total of forty sites.

MASSACHUSETTS

Origins
The first school-based health center in Massachusetts was established in Holyoke High School in 1985 under the auspices of a private group of pediatricians.[6] Although the Department of Public Health supported a number of adolescent health and teen pregnancy prevention projects, no state funds were made available for school-based centers until 1989. In 1987, however, the Department of Public Health cosponsored the New England Regional Conference on School-Based Clinics and offered to provide technical assistance to those communities that wanted to start a center with local funds. Five additional school-based centers were organized independently. In 1989, the department began using their Maternal and Child Health Block Grant funds to award service contracts to the six existing providers and to two more sites for planning. The following year, an open RFP was issued resulting in the funding of school-based health centers in ten communities. A total of sixteen school sites have been identified in Massachusetts.

Program Standards
The Department of Public Health has the following priorities in funding centers: (1) provision of comprehensive primary health care; (2) administration of schoolwide student health behavior surveys; (3) provision of comprehensive health education in the host school; (4) coordination with other community agencies for health education, mental health, substance abuse, and sexuality counseling; and (5) utilization of a standardized management information system. The department has developed a technical assistance capacity to as-

sist centers achieve these priorities. All centers in Massachusetts are linked with a community hospital, health center, or board of health that provides year-round access and continuity with the same provider.

In addition to the requirement that each program begin with a survey of students' needs, grantees must maintain and tabulate records on each student visit. In fiscal year 1991, the ten state-funded centers reported a total of 3,188 enrollees and 7,042 visits. Almost one-third of the users were covered by Medicaid.

Funding

In 1989, the state made $144,000 available for school-based health centers, and it increased the amount to $410,000 the following year. In fiscal year 1992, the school-based clinics received a total of $390,000, 22 percent of the total adolescent health care budget of $1.775 million. Grants to individual school-based centers have remained minimal, in the $40,000 range. Programs are encouraged to seek private and foundation funding to supplement grants. The Departments of Public Health and Welfare are working together to ensure maximum reimbursement from Medicaid. Massachusetts is moving toward the development of Community Health Networks in twenty-seven regions that will be responsible for coordinating all grant applications. Massachusetts is currently considering a 25 percent tax on cigarettes. If the tax is approved, it is anticipated that school health services will receive $10 million to be used primarily for opening centers in elementary and middle schools.

In addition to the ten school-based centers, the Adolescent Health Program funds nine comprehensive community-based adolescent services and ten programs for pregnant and parenting teenagers. Over the years, the responsibility for adolescent health has been shifted around the state health department. School-based health centers have received a high priority in future planning, but funding has not yet reached the level necessary to create comprehensive programs. In a separate special initiative, the Boston Board of Education and the Boston Department of Health are working out a collaborative mechanism to expand school-based health services throughout the Boston school system.

MICHIGAN

Origins

Faced with alarming statistics about the growing incidence of "new morbidities" among Michigan teenagers, in 1985 the former state health director, Gloria Smith, commissioned a statewide Adolescent Health Committee to develop a Five-Year Adolescent Health Plan. The committee focused on the establishment of teen health centers, which members believed had proven effective in improving the health status of teens.[7]

In 1987, the Michigan Legislature responded to recommendations of the committee and the governor by appropriating $1.25 million for establishment of teen health centers and planning grants to assess adolescent health needs. The committee's original plan called for one hundred health centers around the state in middle, junior, and senior high schools, representing about 7 percent of all secondary schools. In 1987, six teen health centers were already in operation, a few of which were receiving state funds through an infant mortality reduction initiative.

As of 1992, the Michigan Department of Public Health supported the provision of services at nineteen teen health centers. Eight of the centers were located in middle or high schools, three were on school property, and the remaining eight were community-based centers. An additional seven "alternative" programs offered education, case finding, case management, and referral for health services in the schools but did not directly provide primary health care to teenagers. According to the director of the Michigan Department of Public Health, "there is general acceptance that a comprehensive school health program is an effective means of assisting the student to attain or maintain health, and that every student in Michigan, regardless of health status, handicapping conditions, and/or special education needs, should have access to a school health program that is comprehensive in nature."[8]

Program Standards

The RFP by the Department of Public Health lists a number of requirements for grant applications. A local advisory committee must be formed to assure community involvement in the development of program policies and procedures. Grantees must undertake an extensive community assessment of adolescent health status, needs, and attitudes. They must also survey parents, students, and community members to determine whether a teen health center is needed and, if so, where it should be located. The RFP allows for a center to be in a school building, adjacent to a school on its property, school-linked, or community-based with no connection to the school.

Every center designs its own service package, parental consent policy, and personnel policies. A pediatric or family nurse practitioner or a physician must staff the center as the primary care provider during all hours of operation. The selection of primary care services must be approved by the local advisory group and can include family planning and mental health counseling, in addition to regular screenings and crisis care. The only required service for all state-funded teen health centers is EPSDT exams for Medicaid-eligible students. Centers funded with state money are prohibited from providing abortion counseling, services, or referral.

The Michigan Adolescent Health Services Program maintains a comprehensive data system that tracks service utilization in each of the nineteen sites annually. The number of users and the number of visits have increased substantially each year since 1987. In 1992, 18,488 teens used services, an 11 percent increase over the previous year, and the total number of services provided was 75,351. More than 13 percent of the visits were for mental health. Some 25,959 teens received information in educational sessions conducted by teen health center staff, with the largest increases in presentations on mental health and STD/HIV prevention.

Funding

Under the initial $1.25 million appropriation in 1987, six previously existing centers, five new teen health centers, and nine planning grants were funded. In 1988, the state appropriation rose to $2 million, and the following year, to about $2.2 million. In 1990, the level was reduced slightly to $2.14 million, where it has remained. Each year since 1987, a few new health centers and planning grants have been added, but in 1990 the number stabilized at nineteen centers. In 1991, the department received eleven requests for development of new teen health centers, which could not be funded because the program did not receive additional funds. State funds equal 47 percent of the total average budget for each center's operation. Providers are required to find 20 percent local matching funds, which can include in-kind contributions by schools for maintenance, supplies, materials, and utilities.

NEW JERSEY

Origins

In 1987, the New Jersey Department of Human Services (DHS), under the leadership of Drew Altman (now president of the Henry J. Kaiser Family Foundation in California), added $6 million to its budget to develop "one-stop shopping" health and social service programs in schools. Researchers claim that the School-Based Youth Services Program (SBYSP) "was the first substantial effort by a state to link schools and social services to help ensure youngsters' success." They also cite the program as the model for other states and communities.[9] In 1991, the program received the prestigious "Innovations in State and Local Government" award by the John F. Kennedy School of Government at Harvard University and the Ford Foundation for being one of the nation's ten most innovative programs.

Program Standards

Following a competitive process, grants were awarded by DHS to twenty-nine communities (at least one in each of the state's twenty-one counties) for collaborative projects. Programs must be located in or near the school. They must be operated jointly by the school system and one or more local nonprofit organizations or the public health, mental health, or youth-serving agency. The lead agencies currently include schools (eleven), community mental health agencies (five), medical schools and hospitals (four), and other public and nonprofit agencies. Plans submitted by the agencies must demonstrate support from the local teachers' unions and PTAs. Schools must also agree to collaborate with project staff members in integrating existing school services into the program.

Each project must provide core services including mental health and family counseling, drug and alcohol counseling, educational remediation, recreation, and employment services at one site. Health services must also be available on site or by referral. In addition, child care, teen parenting, family planning examinations, referral for contraception, transportation, and hotlines can be supported by the grant, but not contraceptives or referral for abortion services. All centers must be open after school, weekends, and during summer vacations. In 1991, the twenty-nine programs provided services to nineteen thousand students. More than one-third of these students received mental health services, almost one-third health services, 22 percent employment services, 7 percent substance abuse treatment, and 7 percent for tutoring.

Because localities are free to decide what nonmandatory services they wish to provide, each program is different. For example, in New Brunswick and four other sites, the program's primary purpose is to provide mental health services on school grounds with staff from local community mental health centers. Plainfield features a school drop-in center for recreation and counseling and a comprehensive teen parents program. South Brunswick offers an extensive after-school remediation, arts, cooking, and sports program. Salem has a very strong family planning component, with counseling and clinic services, and classroom-based health education.

Funding

The state's appropriation to the Department of Human Services allows for grants to each project to be in the range of $150,000 to $250,000. Participating communities must contribute 25 percent of the cost incurred, through either direct funding or in-kind donations. Despite the budget crunch during 1991 and 1992, the SBYSP's budget, unlike that of many other programs, was not cut. In fact, it was awarded an increase of half a million dollars to begin expanding the program to middle and elementary schools, bringing the total up to $6.5 million. In 1993, the total appropriation was $6.8 million.

A new Children and Families Initiative in the DHS builds on the SBYSP to provide one million dollars for one county (Atlantic) to "reshape the social service delivery system," creating community-based family centers in or near schools. A county Children and Families Commission will be established to choose a lead agency and oversee the project. At the state level, a Cabinet Committee on Children and Families will move toward reorganizing the services provided by state departments to insure integration, easy access, and a focus on children and the family. Two additional counties will be "reshaped" in subsequent years if funds are appropriated.

NEW MEXICO

Origins

Although the governor and the legislature have been favorable to-ward school-based health services, no legislation has been passed to support expansion of these programs. Nonetheless, in 1990 the Maternal and Child Health Bureau Chief established an adolescent health initiative to help local programs develop and expand. In 1992, the bureau awarded $213,000 to thirteen sites in local communities to initiate and maintain school-based health services, bringing the total number of school-based clinics in the state to twenty-one. The remaining eight are operated by the University of New Mexico in and around Albuquerque and funded with private grants and Medicaid reimbursements.

Program Standards

The program model supported by the state requires staffing by a nurse practitioner, a physician assistant, and a backup supervising physician (frequently the public health doctor in the community). In New Mexico, nurse practitioners can diagnose, treat, and write prescriptions. If the facility is open full-time, the state will also fund a coordinator. Provider agencies are typically the local public health department or other local health agencies, rather than the school system. To receive a contract from the state, programs must also agree to provide gynecological tests and examinations, pregnancy and STD tests, and counseling. The provision of contraception is optional, but family planning information must be made available. So far, two of the thirteen state-funded sites have opted to distribute birth control on site.

Technical Assistance

The manager of the Adolescent Health Program in the Department of Health works closely with school districts and local public health offices doing "low-key marketing" on the need for greater access to care among adolescents. She offers technical assistance to communities and their School Health Advisory Committees that are ready to move ahead. At town meetings in rural areas, the growing demand for services for young people is apparent. Maternal and Child Health planning grants to communities, another Department of Health initiative, has facilitated the development of four more applications for school-based clinics.

Funding
The New Mexico Department of Health supports school-based health services through funds from the Maternal and Child Health Block Grant. In 1990, $80,000 was allocated to launch the statewide adolescent health initiative, and in 1992, $213,000 was allocated to provide seed grants to local communities. By the end of 1992, eight of the school-based clinics were certified as Medicaid providers, and the rest were expecting to be approved in the near future.

NEW YORK

Origins
In what became the first statewide school-based clinic initiative, the New York Department of Health began the School Health Demonstration Program (SHDP) in 1981 in response to legislation developed by the Black and Puerto Rican Caucus.[10] Building on experience with foundation- and Medicaid-funded demonstration projects, authority was given to the commissioner of health, with consent of the commissioners of education and social services, to establish school-based primary care clinics. In the first year, nine grants were awarded to health facilities to provide health services in Head Start centers and in elementary and junior high schools. In 1985, the Adolescent School Health Services Program was enacted to support the

development of clinics in high schools; with this state support, nine clinics were opened in New York City high schools. Since that time, the state has drawn funds from various state, federal, and private sources to rapidly extend services across the state. At the last count, 140 school-based clinic sites were identified where 180,000 visits were recorded. In New York City, ninety thousand students are enrolled in school-based clinics in fifty-five elementary, sixteen middle, and seventeen high schools. The clinics throughout the state are located mainly in primary care shortage areas characterized by physician shortages, poverty, and high rates of disease and death.[11]

Program Standards

The original elementary school model called for a health team composed of a project administrator, a midlevel practitioner (nurse practitioner or physician assistant), and a health aide, backed up by a part-time physician preceptor and supplemented by part-time social workers, health educators, and dental hygienists. When the Adolescent School Health Services Program began, only voluntary and public health facilities licensed to provide ambulatory public health services were eligible to apply, to assure twenty-four-hour access to care and continuity of the medical record. The legislation required that each new provider be approved by the Department of Health and by the Departments of Education and Social Services as well. State grant funds were to be considered seed money and facilities were expected to bill Medicaid and other third-party insurers, with the proceeds to be returned directly to the school-based clinic budget.

The current School Health Program uses a set of standards that all grantees are expected to follow. Services must meet EPSDT standards and furnish the "medical home" for the student. All New York school-based clinics are required to form advisory committees.

At the inception of the program, school-based clinics in New York state were allowed to distribute contraception on school grounds. However, controversy ensued and the New York City Board of Education mandated that school-based clinics could no longer dispense contraceptives in school. Later, following the chancellor's HIV initiative mandating condom distribution, the Board of Education has ruled that school-based clinics in city high schools may dispense condoms and provide prescriptions for contraceptives.

Funding

Starting in the mid-1980s, an initial state allocation of about $1.8 million and over $1 million in federal funds from a variety of sources (such as the Emergency JOBS Bill) have been used to support the development of school-based clinics in both elementary and secondary schools. Currently, about $7.6 million in state and federal funds are being used to support school-based clinics through project grants that are administered by the School Health Program in the Department of Health. About $4 million comes from the Maternal and Child Health Block Grant, which is combined at the state level with $3.64 million in state and local assistance funds appropriated by the legislature for this purpose. In the tight 1993 budget, school-based health services received an increase of half a million dollars. The New York City Department of Health and the RWJ have also been major supporters of these programs in New York City. In 1992, legislation to support school-based clinics and greatly increase funding was introduced to the Assembly Health Committee but never made it out of the Senate committee. Strong opposition from the Catholic clergy focused on the birth control issue. Nevertheless, the School Health Program expects its budget to increase to $6 million in the next fiscal year.

New York state has another relevant initiative called Community Schools, administered by the Department of Education. Funding is approved annually by the legislature and the governor through the budget process. In the first year (1986–87), $500,000 was appropriated to four schools. By 1993, the program had expanded to $6 million encompassing thirty-three schools and eight planning grants. The grants are awarded only to elementary schools to become the base for the provision of a wide range of community services including child care, adult education, senior citizen support, and recreation services.[12] One of the major goals of the Community Schools program is to open the doors of the school buildings throughout the day and for the entire year, including the summer months. Community-based organizations and universities are involved in collaborative programs such as Saturday school, community service projects, remediation, and cultural events. A review of the program found that it had great potential for modeling school-community services linkages but that implementation had been inconsistent and would remain marginal unless it received more attention from the state education department in regard to financing and program development strategies.[13]

OREGON

Origins

Beginning in 1984, Anne Cathey, a Multnomah County public health nurse, and her colleagues spent a year laying the groundwork for gaining public support to open a teen health clinic in a Portland school: "We knew it was a good idea; we knew it had worked in St. Paul; we knew it would work in Portland."[14] Following their recommendations, the county commissioners passed a resolution to fund a pilot school-based clinic for six months at a cost of $52,000. This action spurred state legislator Rick Bauman to introduce a bill to fund school-based clinics throughout the state by earmarking $250,000 for the Department of Human Resources to support comprehensive health services for high-risk youth. By 1988, the state was supporting six school-based clinics, and Multnomah County was supporting three of its own clinics. That year, Oregon's School-Based Adolescent Health Program was recognized by the Council of State Governments as an innovative and exemplary state effort.[15] As of June 1991, the number of school-based clinics had grown to eighteen, eleven of which were state-funded and seven county-funded.

Program Standards

In 1985, when the Department of Human Resources issued an RFP, it established funding priority for areas of the state with greatest need and sponsors that had the capability to maximize local matching funds. The state received sixteen responses and funded projects in five schools. Most of the programs are administered by local public health departments, with the exception of the clinics in Eugene, where the school district provides the services. The current governor, Barbara Roberts, recently instituted a new state policy to encourage all Oregon school-based clinics to provide comprehensive reproductive health services, including on-site dispensing of contraception, options counseling, and referral.

Funding

About half of the state's $1.4 million expenditures in 1992 on school-based clinics were funded by state general fund dollars and the rest from the Maternal and Child Health Block Grant and local contributions. The cost of operating each center was approximately $100,000 per year. Because of a dramatic reduction in the state's 1993 budget, it appeared that funding for all of the state's school-based clinics was in jeopardy.[16] Through effective organizing by program advocates, $750,000 was appropriated to fund eleven school-based clinics through June 1993. Multnomah County also restored full funding of $1.3 million to the seven clinics in the Portland area.

In a parallel effort, the Oregon Department of Human Resources is supporting a new Services Integration Initiative, to link at-risk families to human service providers. Schools are considered prime locations for social service efforts, with demonstration projects using schools as single points of entry for case management, as well as for the delivery of health services.

APPENDIX B

▲▲▲

Federal Sources for Funding School-Based Services

Department of Health and Human Services (DHHS)

Maternal and Child Health (MCH) Block Grant

The MCH Block Grant constitutes one of the nation's major sources of funds for maternal, child, and adolescent health services. The program originated in 1935, when the Social Security Act created a federal bureau to fund maternal and child health services. In 1981, this program was consolidated with nine other health programs targeted to mothers and children to form the Maternal and Child Health Block Grant (also known as Title V of the Public Health Services Act). The program is administered by the Maternal and Child Health Bureau (MCHB) in the DHHS Public Health Service, Health Resources and Services Administration.

In addition to perinatal care, the program's recent priorities have focused on the development of preventive and primary care systems for pregnant women and children and on the creation and expansion of organized networks of comprehensive, coordinated, family-centered services for children with chronic and disabling conditions.

The federal government appropriated $665 million to the MCH
Block Grant program in fiscal year 1993. The majority of the funds
(about 85 percent) are sent directly to states. Each state receives a
predetermined amount, plus an amount dependent on the number of
live births in the state and an adjustment for financial need. Funding priorities and eligibility criteria for services are decided by each
state. In most states, MCH Block Grant funds are allocated to local
health departments, but private agencies may also receive some of
the funds through special grants. The remaining 15 percent is re-
served for federal grants in research, training, and demonstration
projects. Of the five hundred federal grants in 1991, about seventy-
five had a focus on adolescent health.

The Bureau's Division of Maternal, Infant, and Child Health recently created a separate office for adolescent health. Most state
MCH offices have also created positions for a coordinator of adolescent health services within the last few years.[1] These coordinators
often administer state programs that use MCH Block Grant and
other state dollars for school health services and provide assistance
to communities and schools that want to apply for grants. At least
twenty states report MCH Block Grant expenditures on school-
based clinics, but the amounts vary widely from $50,000 in Maine to
$3.9 million in New York. School clinics nationally receive $8.9 million in MCH support, about 17 percent of the total expenditure for
school-based primary health services.

Medicaid

The Medicaid program, also known as Title XIX of the Social Security Act, has become the primary source of financing for medical care
of poor people.[2] The program is administered by the Health Care Financing Administration within DHHS, in conjunction with state
government agencies. Within broad federal guidelines and minimum
eligibility standards, each state sets its own policies regarding benefits, eligibility, and health care provider reimbursement. Financing is
also jointly shared by the federal and state governments, with the

federal share ranging from 50 percent to nearly 80 percent, depending on the state's per capita income.

Historically, eligibility for the program was tied to requirements for receiving welfare (Aid to Families with Dependent Children or Supplemental Security Income for elderly and disabled). However, low-income pregnant women and children with family incomes too high for welfare were made eligible for the program in 1989 when Congress mandated that states cover pregnant women and children under age six living in families making less than 133 percent of the federal poverty level, an income level that is higher than regular Medicaid eligibility levels in nearly all states.[3]

In 1990, Congress required states to provide Medicaid coverage to all children ages six to nineteen living in families earning up to 100 percent of the poverty level. But federal law permits states to phase in coverage of these children on a year-by-year basis, so not until the year 2002 would all poor adolescents be covered by Medicaid. That means that today's adolescents (ages ten to eighteen) will never be covered by the program, unless they became pregnant or unless further expansions of Medicaid or other types of public health insurance program are enacted. The Office of Technology Assessment's study on adolescent health reported that the estimated number of adolescents, ages ten to eighteen, enrolled in Medicaid in fiscal year 1988 was only about 4.5 million, or only half of the estimated 8.4 million teenagers living in poverty.

As required in federal law, all state Medicaid programs cover hospitalization, physician services, laboratory and x-ray services, family planning, and Early Periodic Screening, Diagnosis, and Treatment (EPSDT) services for children under age twenty-one. States have the option to provide other services such as prescribed drugs, dental services, inpatient psychiatric care, case management, and transportation. According to Michael Kirst, "States could develop a new category of rehabilitation services to be furnished by local school districts for Medicaid eligible low income children, based upon a handicapped child's Individualized Education Plan."[4] Several states have obtained waivers that allow school systems to bill Medicaid for special education services such as speech and physical therapy and audiological services and assessments, thus freeing up some special education funds for other uses.

The EPSDT component of Medicaid was originally designed to provide comprehensive health screening for poor children, as well as subsequent diagnosis and treatment services for conditions found during the screening exams. Comprehensive screening included not only basic health, vision, hearing, and dental components but "anticipatory guidance," which could include counseling services, case management, and health prevention. Although federal law mandated EPSDT services for Medicaid-eligible children and adolescents, states have not provided sufficient outreach and follow-up to ensure that those eligible were actually screened.

The potential of Medicaid as a funding source for school-based services is ambiguous. It may be extended depending both on state and federal policy changes to cover almost all health and social services provided in schools, or it may be capped at low levels because of budgetary restrictions.

Community and Migrant Health Centers

Federally funded community and migrant health centers were organized in 1965 as part of the Johnson Administration's "War on Poverty." Located in rural and urban areas that lacked sufficient numbers of physicians or any other health resources, the centers were intended to provide needed health care to low-income communities. Community and migrant health centers can only be established in those areas designated as medically underserved, according to federal criteria.

The centers are authorized by Sections 330 and 340 of the Public Health Service Act and are managed by the Bureau of Primary Health Care in DHHS Public Health Service, Health Resources and Services Administration. A total of $616 million was appropriated for these centers in 1993. To receive funding, centers must offer a comprehensive set of health services and be governed by a board whose members include a majority of users or consumers of the services. Approximately six hundred grantees currently operate two thousand clinics that serve about six million clients. In addition, a number of grants were awarded to centers to provide health care to homeless people living in shelters or on the streets.

A recent survey conducted by the Bureau of Primary Health Care revealed that many more community health centers were providing school-based and school-linked health services than had previously been recognized. At least two hundred centers claimed that they had some linkages to schools and thirty-five were identified as operating school-based clinics. The bureau is in the process of defining the role of neighborhood health centers in the provision of school health service. A request for $6 million to expand the school-linked capacity of thirty-five to fifty community health centers was not funded in 1993, but additional support will be requested in forthcoming appropriations.

National Health Service Corps
A program closely related to the community and migrant health centers is the National Health Service Corps, which is also managed by the Health Services and Resources Administration. The program provides scholarships and loans and arranges for low-interest loan repayments for physicians, nurses, and other health professionals who are willing to provide care in medically underserved communities. The program helps urban and rural communities recruit staff to needy areas.

During the 1980s, the program was severely cut (from 3,300 placements in 1986 to 1,100 in 1990), but it was revived in the early 1990s and has received renewed interest by the Clinton administration. In 1993, $119 million was appropriated for the corps. It is not known whether any school-based clinic personnel are directly supported by the NHSC, but community health centers are more likely than other health agencies to employ NHSC-sponsored staff, so it is possible that some corps members are currently working in schools.

Indian Health Service

The Indian Health Service (IHS) operates clinics or provides funding to deliver health care to Native Americans and Alaska Natives. According to the OTA report, in 1989 the IHS decided to target its prevention efforts on adolescent health problems, such as teen pregnancy, alcohol and substance abuse, suicide and violence, and mental health problems. The IHS has also awarded some grants to tribal governments to develop comprehensive school-based health programs that included both education and services. OTA reported that the IHS also helps to support adolescent health centers in or near four schools in the Albuquerque, New Mexico, area, which are operated by the University of New Mexico's School of Family Practice and Pediatrics. IHS recently announced a new adolescent health initiative, with an expectation of awarding nine grants of $50,000 each to school or community-based comprehensive centers.

Substance Abuse and Mental Health Services Administration

The newly reorganized Substance Abuse and Mental Health Services Administration (SAMHSA) in the DHHS Public Health Service has five components: substance abuse treatment, substance abuse prevention, mental health services, and two institutes to examine the causes, effects, and most promising treatments for substance abuse and mental health problems.

The Center for Substance Abuse Prevention (CSAP) builds on the earlier experience of the Office of Substance Abuse Prevention, which developed innovative school, family, and community demonstration projects. As part of the reorganization, CSAP altered its strategy for reducing substance abuse among adolescents by moving away from reliance on classroom-based education approaches alone. Instead, CSAP established new goals, which included empowering communities, fostering competence, encouraging collaboration, and building comprehensive prevention programs. It also recognized the importance of targeting high-risk youth and focusing on the particular needs of African-American and Hispanic communities. For example, CSAP supports a large grant program that funds demon-stration projects for high-risk youth (some of which were awarded to school-based programs), operates an information clearinghouse, pro-vides technical assistance to states, and sponsors training for coun-selors and program administrators. The budget for CSAP in 1993 was $244 million.

Beginning in 1984, the National Institute for Mental Health (NIMH) within SAMHSA initiated a grants program called the Child and Adolescent Service System Program (CASSP). It was de-signed specifically to improve services delivery for emotionally dis-turbed children and adolescents.[5] Under this program, about $10 million in grants were awarded to state governments and local com-munity organizations to develop comprehensive systems of care. The services were targeted to children and teenagers up to age eighteen who required services from multiple agencies and had been diag-nosed with a mental, emotional, or psychological problem. States were encouraged to develop cross-agency service systems (including mental health, juvenile justice, child welfare, education, and pri-mary health care services) and place more emphasis on parent in-volvement. Many school systems participated in these programs, al-though the type and level of involvement varied widely.

Centers for Disease Control and Prevention

Within the Centers for Disease Control and Prevention (CDCP), the Division of Adolescent and School Health (DASH) is among the most significant new government efforts to address comprehensive health education, promotion, and services in schools. The original charge to this agency was to facilitate the provision of AIDS educa-tion in schools through grants to state education authorities. In 1993, DASH distributed $42 million dollars to state education depart-ments, several large cities, and twenty national health and educa-tional agencies for HIV education and training of health educators. Beginning in 1993, DASH's mandate broadened to help schools prevent other health problems among adolescents and to implement school health services. Demonstration grants have been awarded for comprehensive school health programs in five states with high youth mortality rates (Arkansas, District of Columbia, Florida, West Virginia, and Wisconsin). In each of these states, DASH has funded a senior policy position in both the offices of the state school superintendent and the state health commissioner to work jointly to improve school health programs. DASH staff also started to work closely with other federal agencies and national organizations with a view toward replication of comprehensive school health program models. A grant was recently awarded to Columbia University School of Public Health for a School Health Project to develop standards for school-based clinics and to explore financing and staffing issues.

Another DASH initiative has been the Youth Risk Behavior Surveillance System. Implemented in forty states and many communities, this survey regularly monitors trends in substance use, sexual activity, violence, suicide, depression, and other risk behaviors among students in ninth through twelfth grades. Findings from this survey have been utilized to support the need for comprehensive school-based services.

Office of Population Affairs

Located in the DHHS Public Health Service, the Office of Population Affairs handles programs related to family planning and teenage pregnancy. One of its most important functions is the administration of the Family Planning Services and Research Program, created in 1970 as Title X of the Public Health Service Act. The Title X program awards family planning project grants, totaling about $175 million in 1993, directly to states and to local family planning providers. Currently, the funds are received by about four thousand family planning clinics, sponsored by local health departments, hospitals, Planned Parenthood affiliates, and other community-based centers.

About 1.5 million teenagers receive family planning counseling, examinations, and prescriptions through the clinics each year. In theory, school-based clinics can obtain Title X grants to provide birth control services on site, if they have approval from the local school board to do so. Several school-based clinics reported receiving Title X grants, but most school-based clinics are not funded from this source. Instead, most school-based clinics have arrangements to refer students to family planning clinics for reproductive health care.

The Office of Population Affairs also administers the Adolescent Family Life Program, which funds research and demonstration projects to develop effective strategies for reducing the negative outcomes associated with teenage pregnancy and childbearing. About $7 million was spent by this program in 1993, mostly to support curricula that promoted abstention. New legislation is under consideration to broaden the scope of this initiative, but its future is uncertain at this time.

During the Reagan and Bush administrations, both Title X funds and Adolescent Family Life Program funds were prohibited from being used to provide abortion counseling or abortion referrals. During the first days of the Clinton administration, the ban was lifted on the use of Title X funds to counsel and refer women to abortion services as one of several possible pregnancy alternatives. The legislation continues to prohibit these funds from being used to pay for abortions.

Administration for Children and Families

This office supports social services for a wide variety of purposes. It administers the Social Services Block Grant, Title XX of the Social Security Act ($2.8 billion in 1993), which distributes funds to states for services including emergency protective services for abused and neglected children and adults, child care, and health-related services for disabled individuals. A few school-based clinics have been able to receive funds for counseling and other social services provided to students.

The Administration for Children, Youth, and Families (ACYF) administers a number of child welfare programs to address problems related to child abuse and neglect and to runaway and homeless youth. For most of its history, the federal child welfare program tended to provide much greater support for out-of-home placement in foster care, adoptive families, or relatives' homes than for family preservation services. Recently, however, ACYF is favoring service delivery approaches that strive to keep families together and prevent out-of-home placement. Although most of these funds are targeted to programs that provide in-home services, a few school-based service programs have begun to tap these funds for family-focused social services in the schools.

Such titles as IV E of the Social Security Act are relevant to school-based services because they can be used to support preschool, after school, and summer school programs, as well as case management for children already involved with child protective services. Funds from the Family Support Act can be used for adult education and case management for programs aimed toward preventing long-term welfare dependency among teen parents and other adults.

Department of Education

Chapter 1

The Elementary and Secondary Education Act is the major federal program designed to meet the needs of economically disadvantaged children for educational remediation. Some $6.7 billion dollars was appropriated in the fiscal year 1993 budget for compensatory education grants under Title I of the Act, also known as Chapter 1. These funds are distributed by the Department of Education annually to state education departments, which then allocate the funds to local school districts. In 1992, the program served more than five million children, or about one in every nine school-aged children in the country. Currently, about 9,300 schools are eligible to be schoolwide Chapter 1 projects, but only about one-quarter to one-third of those schools have such projects.[6]

In order to assess and evaluate the Chapter 1 program, an independent commission was formed in 1990. In its 1993 report, the Commission on Chapter 1 called for the development of "whole schools" that work for disadvantaged students, instead of the traditional approach to remediation that took such children out of their regular classes to attend special programs. The commission also supported the concept of full-service schools by specifically recommending that schools be allowed to use Chapter 1 funds "to coordinate the provision of health and social services." The commission encouraged states to promote the co-location of such services at school sites and use Chapter 1 funds for screening, referral, and coordination, but it did not endorse the use of such funds to directly provide the services. Instead, the commission asked governors "to accept responsibility for preparing a plan to eliminate health and social barriers to learning."[7]

Education for All Handicapped Children
In 1975, Congress enacted the landmark Education for All Handicapped Children Act, known as Public Law 94-142 and recently renamed the Individuals with Disabilities Education Act. The act requires a free and appropriate education in the least restrictive setting for all children with disabilities, aged five to twenty-one, including those with physical or mental disorders. Amendments to the act, passed in 1986 (Public Law 99-457), extended these provisions to preschool children, aged three to five, and authorized a grant program to help states implement the law. Another component of the 1986 amendments added a separate grant program to help states develop early intervention services for infants to age two, and their families in order to detect developmental delays in young children and prevent or ameliorate more severe disability.

Federal law holds all state and local education agencies responsible for formulating Individual Education Plans (IEP) for all students with disabilities and for paying for the special education services they require. These include everything from physical and speech therapy and psychological services to intensive nursing care and case management. Congress annually appropriates funds to help state and local education agencies carry out this mandate. Although the federal funds are substantial—in 1993, almost $3 billion was appropriated—many of the costs for special education services must be financed from state and local government revenues.

Because many of the services required by disabled children are medically necessary, state Medicaid and education agencies have fought over which one is responsible for paying for health services delivered to disabled children in school settings. At first, disputes increased, especially as benefits covered under the EPSDT portion of Medicaid expanded to include just about any medically necessary service. However, in most states, these disputes have waned as state officials realized the financial benefits to be gained by charging more of these services to Medicaid for children who are eligible for the program. Federal Medicaid matching funds cover at least half of the costs of medical services, funds that have often helped financially strapped state and local governments balance their budgets.

Increased use of Medicaid to finance medically necessary special education services in the schools was not just a cost savings measure. Schools began to realize the financial benefits of becoming Medicaid-certified. In particular, they discovered that they could also bill Medicaid for other health services provided in the schools to nondisabled children that qualified for the program. Thus, some schools began to bill Medicaid for screening services provided by school nurses, if they could meet rigorous EPSDT screening standards, and, in a few cases, for primary care services delivered in school-based health clinics.

Although the special education law appears to be an entitlement, in fact, not all students with disabilities are served. Those with emotional disturbances are neglected; among those identified, less than one-third received psychological, social work, or other counseling services. A 1990 amendment to the law authorized funding of $35.5 million over four years for two new competitive grant programs designed to improve this situation, and one of them is targeted to local educational agencies for collaboration with community-based mental health agencies.

Drug-Free Schools

Most of the federal government's efforts to reduce drug use and abuse have focused on cutting the supply of illegal drugs, but a few initiatives were undertaken in the name of reducing demand or preventing drug use. Among the most important was the Drug-Free Schools and Community Act, enacted in 1986 and allocated more than $600 million in fiscal year 1993.

The program, which is administered by the Department of Education (DOE), allocates funds to states based on a formula that takes into account each state's school-age population and Chapter 1 funding. In each state, half of the grant goes to the state department of education and half to the office of the governor. The grants to state education departments are to be distributed to local school districts for drug education, other substance abuse prevention strategies such as early intervention and rehabilitation referral programs, and training and technical assistance to teachers, parents, administrators, and law enforcement officials. In 1990 and 1991, the Emergency Grants program provided extra funds to school districts that could prove the need for special assistance with counseling programs, school security, after-school activities, community outreach, and alternative schools.

The governor's portion of the funds can be used to support other types of anti–drug abuse efforts by parents' groups, community-based organizations, or other public or private groups. At least 42.5 percent of the governors' funds must be used for programs for high-risk youth and 10 percent for a police-sponsored program (DARE). Drug-Free Schools has not fared well in the current budget debate and is expected to lose about $150 million in the next fiscal year.

Comprehensive School Health Education Programs

A very small program of the Department of Education, the Comprehensive School Health Education Program, is administered by the Office of Educational Research and Improvement. The program provides about $4.5 million to schools for developing model health education programs and for training teachers.

Other Departments' Programs

Department of Agriculture

The Department of Agriculture administers several programs that target children and adolescents. Among the most significant are the Food Stamps Program, the Supplemental Food Program for Women, Infants, and Children (known as the WIC program), and the National School Lunch and School Breakfast Programs, all of which provide food assistance to low-income youth and are managed by USDA's Food and Nutrition Service. Those eligible for the WIC program must be pregnant or lactating women or children under age 6, live in families with incomes under 185 percent of poverty, and have a documented health or nutritional deficiency or other risk factors.

School-based health clinics that provide substantial prenatal care have become local WIC program sponsors. A few school-based clinics have also become WIC subcontractors to certify teens for participation, provide food vouchers, offer nutrition education, and carry out administrative work for minimal reimbursement. However, most clinics simply refer pregnant teens to another WIC agency.

Department of Justice

The Juvenile Justice and Delinquency Prevention Act, administered by the Department of Justice, was revised in 1992 to improve coordination and emphasize community-based programs and services, including family counseling. About $70 million was available in grants in 1993. The Justice Department also administers Runaway and Homeless grants ($63 million), which support both street-based and family-based services. To qualify for these grants, providers must demonstrate coordination with health and other service agencies.

Department of Labor

The Employment and Training Administration within the Department of Labor administers several programs that can directly help teenagers, especially those who are at least sixteen years old. Among these programs are the Job Training Partnership Act (JTPA), which allocates about $4 billion in funds to states to support job training and summer employment programs for young people. It also administers a federal Job Corps program, which prepares young people to work in various trades while offering educational supplementation.

APPENDIX C

▲▲▲

Glossary of Acronyms

AFDC	Aid to Families with Dependent Children
AMA	American Medical Association
CAS	Children's Aid Society
CASSP	Child and Adolescent Service System Program
CDCP	Centers for Disease Control and Prevention
CPO	Center for Population Options
CHC	Community Health Center
CIS	Cities in Schools
CSAP	Center for Substance Abuse Prevention

DAISY	Diversified Agencies Involved in Serving Youth
DASH	Division of Adolescent and School Health
DHEW	Department of Health, Education, and Welfare
DHHS	Department of Health and Human Services
DHRS	Department of Health and Rehabilitative Services
DOE	Department of Education
EPSDT	Early Periodic Screening, Diagnosis, and Treatment
HMO	Health Maintenance Organization
IHS	Indian Health Services
JTPA	Job Training Partnership Act
KERA	Kentucky Education Reform Act
KIDS	Kentucky Integrated Delivery System
LEP	Limited English Proficiency
MCH	Maternal and Child Health (Bureau, Block Grant)
NEA	National Education Association
OEO	Office of Economic Opportunity
OTA	Office of Technology Assessment
PECO	Public Education Capital Outlay
RFP	Request for Proposals
RWJ	Robert Wood Johnson Foundation

SAMHSA	Substance Abuse and Mental Health Services Administration
SBYSP	School-Based Youth Services Program
SCPP	Social Competency Promotion Program
SHDP	School Health Demonstration Program
SHIP	School Health Improvement Projects
WIC	Women, Infants, and Children
WPA	Works Progress Administration

Notes

▲▲▲

Chapter One

1. U.S. Department of Health and Human Services. *Child Health USA '92*. Washington, D.C.: U.S. Government Printing Office, 0-16-036247, 1993.

2. "Child Poverty Hits 25-Year High, Growing by Nearly 1 Million Children in 1991." *CDF Reports*, 1992, *13*(12), 2.

3. Dryfoos, J. *Adolescents at Risk: Prevalence and Prevention*. New York: Oxford Press, 1990.

4. Dornbusch, S., and others. "The Relation of Parenting Style to Adolescent School Performance." *Child Development*, 1987, *58*, 1244–1257.

5. National Adolescent Student Survey. *National Survey Reveals Teen Behavior, Knowledge, and Attitudes on Health, Sex Topics*. Washington, D.C.: American Alliance for Health, Physical Education, Recreation, and Dance, Aug. 9, 1988. Press release.

6. Panel on High-Risk Youth, Commission on Behavioral and

Social Sciences and Education. *Losing Generations: Adolescents in High Risk Settings.* Washington, D.C.: National Academy Press, 1993.

7. An additional 5.5 million children are enrolled in 26,800 private schools.

8. Commissioner's Task Force on the Education of Children and Youth at-Risk. *The Time for Assertive Action: School Strategies for Promoting the Education Success of At-Risk Children.* Albany: New York State Education Department, 1988.

9. Kirst, M. "Improving Children's Services: Overcoming Barriers, Creating New Opportunities." *Phi Delta Kappa,* Apr. 1991, pp. 615–618.

10. *Turning Points: Preparing American Youth for the 21st Century.* Washington, D.C.: Task Force on Education of Young Adolescents, Carnegie Corporation, 1989.

11. Gardner, S. "Fix the Kids or Fix the Institutions?" In *Voices from the Field: 30 Expert Opinions on "America 2000," The Bush Administration's Strategy to "Reinvent" America's Schools.* Washington, D.C.: William T. Grant Foundation Commission on Work, Family, and Citizenship, 1991.

12. Meade, E. "Ignoring the Lessons of Previous School Reform." In *Voices from the Field: 30 Expert Opinions on "America 2000," The Bush Administration's Strategy to "Reinvent" America's Schools.* Washington, D.C.: William T. Grant Foundation Commission on Work, Family, and Citizenship, 1991.

13. National Commission on the Role of the School and the Community in Improving Adolescent Health. *Code Blue: Uniting for Healthier Youth.* Washington, D.C.: American Medical Association and National Association of State Boards of Education, 1990.

14. Ibid., 41.

15. Office of Technology Assessment, U.S. Congress. *Adolescent Health.* Vol. 1, *Summary and Policy Options.* Washington, D.C.: U.S. Government Printing Office, OTA-H-468, 1991.

16. Office of Technology Assessment, U.S. Congress. *Adolescent Health.* Vol. 3, *Crosscutting Issues in the Delivery of Health and Related*

Services. Washington, D.C.: U.S. Government Printing Office, OTA-H-468, 1991.

17. Reed, S., and Sutter, R. "Children of Poverty." *Phi Delta Kappan*, Kappan Special Report, June 1990.

18. Weiss, H. *Raising the Future: Families, Schools, and Communities Joining Together*. Cambridge, Mass.: Harvard Family Research Project (forthcoming).

19. E. Zigler. Speech to Westchester Mental Health Association. White Plains, New York, Nov. 1, 1990.

20. Fleisch, B., Knitzer, J., and Steinberg, Z. *At the Schoolhouse Door: An Examination of Programs and Policies for Children with Behavioral and Emotional Problems*. New York: Bank Street College of Education, 1990.

21. Levy, J. *Joining Forces: A Report from the First Year*. Washington, D.C.: National Association of State Boards of Education, 1989.

22. Gerry, M., and Morrill, W. *"Integrating the Delivery of Services to School-Aged Children at Risk: Toward a Description of American Experience and Experimentation."* Paper prepared for Conference for Children and Youth at Risk, sponsored by the U.S. Department of Education, Washington, D.C., Feb. 6, 1990.

23. Dryfoos, J., op. cit., note 3 above.

24. Anderson, J. "The Distribution of Chapter 1 Services: Which School Districts and Schools Serve Students in Chapter 1." Paper presented at annual meeting of the American Educational Research Association, Apr. 1992.

Chapter Two

1. Brown, J., Schlossman, S., and Sedlak, M. *The Public School in American Dentistry*. Santa Monica, Calif.: Rand Corporation, 1986. Levine, A., and Levine, M. *Helping Children: A Social History*. New York: Oxford University Press, 1992. Schlossman, S., and Sedlak, M. "The Public School and Social Services: Reassessing the Progressive

Legacy." *Educational Theory*, 1985, *35*(4), 371–383. Tyack, M. "Health and Social Services in Public Schools: Historical Perspectives." In *The Future of Children: School-Linked Services*. Los Altos, Calif.: Center for the Future of Children, David and Lucile Packard Foundation, Spring 1992, *2*(1), 19–31.

2. Levine, A., op.cit., note 1 above, 275.

3. Schlossman, S., and Sedlak, M., op. cit., note 1 above.

4. Cronin, G., and Young, W. *400 Navels: The Future of School Health in America*. Bloomington, Ind.: Phi Delta Kappa, 1979.

5. Duffy, J. *A History of Public Health in New York City, 1866–1966*. New York: Russell Sage Foundation, 1974.

6. Ibid., 78.

7. Lynch, A. "School Health Programs." In Levin, A. (ed.), *Health Services: The Local Perspective*. New York: Praeger, 1977.

8. Kort, M. "The Delivery of Primary Health Care in American Public Schools, 1890–1980." *Journal of School Health*, 1984, *54*(11), 453–457.

9. Steiner, G. *The Children's Cause*. Washington, D.C.: Brookings Institute, 1976.

10. Hoag, E., and Terman, L. *Health Work in the Schools*. Boston: Houghton Mifflin, pp. 10–11, 1914. Cited in Schlossman, S., and Sedlak, M. "The Public School and Social Services: Reassessing the Progressive Legacy." *Educational Theory*, 1985, *35*(4), 371–383.

11. Kort, M. "The Delivery of Primary Health Care in American Public Schools, 1890–1980." *Journal of School Health*, 1984, *54*(11), 455.

12. Starr, P. *The Social Transformation of American Medicine*. New York: Basic Books, 1982. Steiner, G., op. cit., note 9 above.

13. Kort, M., op. cit., note 11 above.

14. Yankauer, A., and Lawrence, R. "A Study of Periodic School Medical Examinations." *American Journal of Public Health*, 1955, *45*(1), 71–78.

15. *A Survey of 86 Cities*. New York: American Child Health Association, 1925.

16. Lynch, A. "Evaluating School Health Services." In A. Levin

(ed.), *Health Services: The Local Perspective*. New York: Praeger, 1977.

17. Hunt, B. *An Introduction to the Community School Concept*. Portland, Oreg.: Northwest Regional Laboratory, Field Paper no. 20, 1968.

18. Boyd, J. *Community Education and Urban Schools*. London: Longman, 1977.

19. Schmidt, W. "Physical Fitness and Health Problems of the Adolescent: Health Service in a High School—What Can It Offer?" *American Journal of Public Health*, 1945, *35*, 579–583.

20. The current expenditure per pupil is about $5,000 per year.

21. Baumgartner, L. "Some Phases of School Health Services." *American Journal of Public Health*, 1946, *36*(6), 629–635.

22. Jacobziner, H. "The Astoria Plan: A Decade of Progress." *Journal of Pediatrics*, 1951, *38*, 221–230.

23. Ibid., 228.

24. Drislane, A., Frantz, R., Katz, S., and Yankauer, A. "A Study of Case Finding Methods in Elementary Schools." *American Journal of Public Health*, 1962, *52*(4), 656–662. Yankauer, A. "An Evaluation of the Effectiveness of the Astoria Plan for Medical Services in Two New York City Elementary Schools." *American Journal of Public Health*, 1947, *37*(7), 853–859.

25. Steiner, G. op. cit., note 9 above.

26. Ibid., 113.

27. Millstein, S. *The Potential of School-Linked Centers to Promote Adolescent Health and Development*. Washington, D.C.: Carnegie Council on Adolescent Development, 1988.

28. Cronin, G., and Young, W., op. cit., note 4 above.

29. Lynch, A. "There Is No Health in School Health." *Journal of School Health*, Sept. 1977, pp. 410–413.

30. Cronin, G., and Young, W., op. cit., note 4 above.

31. Califano, J., Secretary of Health, Education, and Welfare. "School Health Message." *Journal of School Health*, Sept. 1977, pp. 395–396.

32. Ibid., 396.

33. Schlossman, S., and Sedlak, M. op. cit., note 1 above.

Chapter Three

1. Editorial. "Report Card in Chelsea." *Boston Globe*, Sept. 14, 1992, p. 23.

2. Celis, W. "Tough Time for Private Manager of Public Schools." *New York Times*, Sept. 23, 1992, p. B9.

3. Center for the Future of Children. *The Future of Children: School-Linked Services*. Los Altos, Calif.: Center for the Future of Children, David and Lucile Packard Foundation, 2(1), 1992.

4. Mathis, N. "School Nurses Seek Broader Role in Wake of New Health Concerns." *Education Week*, Aug. 3, 1988, p. 3.

5. Tyack, D. "Health and Social Services in Public Schools: Historical Perspective." *The Future of Children*, 1992, 2(1), 27.

6. Beth Moore. Maternal and Child Health nursing supervisor, Catawba County Health Department. Interview, Mar. 1992.

7. Poehlman, B., manager, Comprehensive School Health Programs Project, National School Boards Association. Listings of schools provided. Alexandria, Va. 1992.

8. Igoe, J., and Giordano, B. *Expanding School Health Services to Serve Families in the 21st Century*. Washington, D.C.: American Nurses, 1992.

9. Burtnett, F. "Move Counseling Off the Back Burner of Reform." *Education Week*, Apr. 28, 1993, p. 32.

10. Adelman, H., and Taylor, L. "Mental Health Facets of the School-Based Health Center Movement: Need and Opportunity for Research and Development." *Journal of Mental Health Administration*, 1991, *18*, 272–282.

11. Gail Reynolds, "School-Based Youth Services Program," Report of the New Brunswick Public Schools, n.d. Also, author visits to program and discussion with director (May 1991 and Nov. 1991).

12. *Children's Mental Health Program*. South Orange County, N.Y., Health Care Agency, May 1989.

13. Caplan, M., Sivo P., and Weissberg, P. "A New Conceptual

Framework for Establishing School-Based Social Competency Promotion Programs." In L. Bond, and B. Compas, (eds.), *Primary Prevention and Promotion in the Schools*. Newbury Park, Calif.: Sage, 1989.

14. Freedman, M. *The Kindness of Strangers: Adult Mentors, Urban Youth, and the New Voluntarism*. San Francisco: Jossey-Bass, 1993.

15. Ibid.

16. Freedman, M. *Partners in Growth: Elder Mentors and At-Risk Youth*. Philadelphia, Pa: Public/Private Ventures, 1988.

17. Hara, S., and Ooms, T. *The Family-School Partnership. A Critical Component of School Reform*. Washington, D.C.: Family Impact Seminar, 1992.

18. State of Connecticut. "Family Resource Centers." Pamphlet prepared by the Office of the Commissioner, Department of Human Services.

19. Kagan, S. L. *United We Stand: Collaboration for Child Care and Early Education Services*. New York: Teachers College Press, 1991.

20. "Helping Families Grow Strong: New Directions in Public Policy." Paper from the Colloquium on Public Policy and Family Support, Apr. 1990, p. 240. Available from the Center for the Study of Social Policy, Washington, D.C.

21. Family Impact Seminar. *Promoting Adolescent Health and Well-Being Through School-Linked, Multi-Service, Family-Friendly Programs*. Washington, D.C.: American Association for Marriage and Family Therapy Research and Education Foundation, 1991.

22. Institute of Responsive Education. "League of Schools Reaching Out." Boston: Institute for Responsive Education, 1992.

23. Carnegie Council on Adolescent Development. *A Matter of Time: Risk and Opportunity in the Nonschool Hours*. New York: Carnegie Corporation, 1992.

24. "The Beacons: A School-based Approach to Neighborhood Revitalization," *AEC Focus*. Greenwich, Conn.: Annie E. Casey Foundation, 1993.

25. Office of Substance Abuse Prevention. *Breaking New Ground*

for Youth at Risk: Program Summaries. Washington, D.C.: Alcohol, Drug, and Mental Health Administration, United States Department of Health and Human Services, OSAP Technical Report 1, 1990.

26. "Fact Sheet" and "Questions About Cities in Schools." Washington, D.C.: Cities-in-Schools, 1988.

27. Leonard, W. "Keeping Kids in School." *Focus.* Greenwich, Conn.: Annie E. Casey Foundation, June 4–5, 1992, 2, pp. 3–4.

28. *Pinal County Prevention Partnership, Year End Report FY 1988–1989.* Pinal County Human Services, Arizona, 1990.

29. Freedman, M. "No Simple Dream." *Public/Private Ventures News.* Philadelphia, Pa: Public/Private Ventures, Winter 1987.

30. Baratta, A., Baecher, R., and Cicchelli, T. "Dropout Prevention Strategies for Urban Children at Risk: A Longitudinal Analysis." Paper presented at annual meeting of the American Education Research Association, Boston, Apr. 1990.

31. *State and Communities on the Move: Policy Initiatives to Create a World-Class Workforce.* Washington, D.C.: William T. Grant Foundation on Work, Family, and Citizenship, 1991.

32. *The Forgotten Half: Pathways to Success for America's Youth and Young Families.* Washington, D.C.: William T. Grant Foundation Commission on Work, Family, and Citizenship, 1988.

33. Materials provided by Nancy Johnson, executive director of Youth Guidance, Chicago, Ill., 1992.

34. Materials provided by Edwin Ridgway, director, Program Development, WAVE, Inc., Washington, D.C., 1993.

35. Rigden, D. *Business and the Schools: A Guide to Effective Programs, Second Edition.* New York: Council for Aid to Education, 1992.

36. Conrad, D., and Hedin, D. *High School Community Service: A Review of Research and Programs.* Madison, Wis.: National Center on Effective Secondary Schools, Dec. 1989.

37. Allen, J., Hoggson, N., McNeil, W., and Philliber, S. "Teen Outreach: A Three-Year Evaluation of a Program to Prevent Teen Pregnancy and School Dropout." Report to Association of Junior Leagues, New York, 1988.

38. Lewis, A. *Youth Serving the Young*. Washington, D.C.: Youth Service America, 1987.

39. Levin, H. "California Researchers 'Accelerate' Activities to Replace Remediation." *Education Week*, Nov. 30, 1988, p. 12.

40. Comer, J. "Improving American Education: Roles for Parents." Hearing before the Select Committee on Children, Youth, and Families. Washington, D.C.: U.S. Government Printing Office, June 7, 1984.

41. Center for Research on Elementary and Middle Schools. "Success for All." *CREMS Report*, Johns Hopkins University, Feb. 1989, pp. 1–7.

42. Sizer, T. *Horace's Compromise*. Boston: Houghton Mifflin, 1984.

43. Mathtech, Inc., and Policy Studies Associates, Inc. *Selected Collaborations in Service Integration*. Report for the U.S. Department of Education and U.S. Department of Health and Human Services, ED Contract LC89089001, Feb. 1, 1991.

44. *Focus*, Quarterly Report from the Annie E. Casey Foundation, Spring 1992, 2(2).

45. Holtzman, W. (ed.). *School of the Future*. Austin, Tex.: American Psychological Association and Hogg Foundation for Mental Health, 1992.

46. Blank, M., and Melaville, T. *Together We Can: A Guide for Grafting a Profamily System of Education and Human Services*. Washington, D.C.: U.S. Government Printing Office, 0-16-041721, Apr. 1993.

47. Peder Zane, J. "Teacher, Doctor, Counselor in One." *New York Times*, Feb. 26, 1992, p. B1.

Chapter Four

1. Dryfoos, J. "Review of Interventions in the Field of Adolescent Pregnancy." Preliminary Report to the Rockefeller Foundation, New York, Oct. 1983.

2. An earlier school-based clinic was started in 1965 to provide comprehensive health services primarily to younger children in Cambridge, Massachusetts. See Philip Porter, "School Health Is a Place, Not a Discipline." *Journal of School Health*, 1987, 57(10), 417–418.

3. Edgington, A., and Ralph, N. "An Evaluation of an Adolescent Family Planning Program." *Journal of Adolescent Health Care*, 1983, *4*, 158–162.

4. Arnold, K., Edwards, L., Hakanson, E., and Steinman, M. "Adolescent Pregnancy Prevention Services in High School Clinics." *Family Planning Perspectives*, 1980, *12*, 6–14.

5. Dryfoos, J. G. "School-Based Health Clinics: A New Approach to Preventing Adolescent Pregnancy." *Family Planning Perspectives*, 1985, *17*(2), 70–75.

6. Ibid., 72.

7. Glascow, R. "Abortion and the Rise of School-Based Clinics (Part 3)." *National Right-to-Life News*, Oct. 9, 1986.

8. Council on Scientific Affairs, American Medical Association. "Providing Medical Services Through School-Based Health Programs." *Journal of American Medical Association*, 1989, *261*, 1939–1942.

9. Elam, S., Gallup, A., and Rose, L. "The 24th Annual Gallup/Phi Delta Kappa Poll of Public's Attitude Toward the Public Schools." *Phi Delta Kappan*, Sept. 1992.

10. *We the People...* Charlotte, N.C.: North Carolina Coalition on Adolescent Pregnancy, 1993.

11. Lear, J., Gleicher, H., St. Germaine, A., and Porter, P. "Reorganizing Health Care for Adolescents: The Experience of the School-Based Adolescent Health Care Program." *Journal of Adolescent Health*, 1991, *12*, 450–458.

12. Pittsburgh Board of Public Education, *School Health Partnerships*. Pittsburgh Board of Public Education, Apr. 5, 1993.

13. *School-Based Clinics: Update 1990*. Washington, D.C.: Center for Population Options, 1991.

14. Klein, J., and others. *Comprehensive Adolescent Health Services in the United States, 1990*. Chapel Hill, N.C.: Cecil Sheps Center for Health Services Research, Center for Early Adolescence, and Center for Health Promotion and Disease Prevention, 1992.

15. Lear, J., Gleicher, H., St. Germaine, A., and Porter, P., op. cit., note 11 above.

16. Ibid., 452.

17. Neidell, S., and Waszak, C. *School-Based and School-Linked Clinics: Update 1991.* Washington, D.C.: Center for Population Options, 1992.

18. Goldsmith, M. "School-Based Health Clinics Provide Essential Health Care." *Journal of American Medical Association,* 1990, 265(19), 2458–2460.

19. English, A., and Tereszkiewicz, L. *School-Based Health Clinics: Legal Issues.* Washington, D.C.: Center for Population Options and San Francisco: National Center for Youth Law, 1989.

20. Legally emancipated minors are generally those under eighteen who are married, serving in the armed forces, or living apart from their parents and managing their own financial affairs.

21. Lear, J., Gleicher, H., St. Germaine, A., and Porter, P., op. cit., note 11 above.

22. Neidell, S., and Waszak, C., op. cit., note 17 above.

23. Center for Population Options, op. cit., note 13 above.

24. Kirby, D., Waszak, C., and Ziegler, J. *An Assessment of Six School-Based Clinics: Services, Impact, and Potential.* Washington, D.C.: Center for Population Options, 1989.

25. A Community Partnership for Children and Youth. *Denver School-Based Clinics Annual Progress Report: School Year 1991–92.* Denver: University of Colorado Health Sciences Center, 1992.

26. Brindis, C. "Funding and Policy Options." In *Condoms in Schools.* Menlo Park, Calif.: Kaiser Forum, 1993, pp. 37–62.

27. Brindis, C., and others. "Utilization Patterns Among California's School-Based Health Centers: A Comparison of the School Year 1989–90 with the Baseline Year of 1988–1989." Paper from Center for Reproductive Health Policy Research, University of California, San Francisco, Feb. 1991.

28. For example, see *San Jose School Health Centers 1990–91 Annual Report.* San Jose, Calif.: San Jose Medical Center, 1991.

29. Goldsmith, M., op. cit., note 18 above.

30. Ibid.

31. Secord, L., clinic manager, Ensley High School Health Center, Birmingham, Ala. In *Helping America's Youth in Crisis*. Testimony presented at hearing of the Committee on Labor and Human Resources, U.S. Senate, Washington, D.C., July 28, 1992.

32. McCollough, J. Forrest City, Ark. In *Helping America's Youth in Crisis*. Testimony presented at hearing of the Committee on Labor and Human Resources, U.S. Senate, Washington, D.C., July 28, 1992.

33. Bradford, J., State Senator, Pine Bluff, Ark. In *Helping America's Youth in Crisis*. Testimony presented at hearing of the Committee on Labor and Human Resources, U.S. Senate, Washington, D.C., July 28, 1992.

34. Minneapolis (Minnesota) Public Schools. Adolescent Health Program Annual Report, 1990–91.

35. Adlesheim, S., and others. "Innovation, Peer Teaching, and Multidisciplinary Collaboration: Outreach from a School-Based Clinic." *Journal of School Health*, 1991, 61, 367–369.

36. L. Tiezzi, director of Community and Health Education, Center for Population and Family Health, Columbia University School of Public Health, New York. Interview, May 1993.

37. Hechinger, F. *Fateful Choices: Healthy Youth for the 21st Century*. New York: Hill and Wang, 1992.

Chapter Five

1. Dryfoos, J. "Operating School-Based Clinics in Inner-City Junior High Schools." Submitted for publication Sept. 1993.

2. Information supplied by Philip Coltoff, director, and Warren Moses, associate director, Children's Aid Society; Mark Kavarsky, principal of IS 218; Richard Negron, community school director; and other staff during site visits in early 1993. Also Peder Zane, J. "Teacher, Doctor, Counselor in One." *New York Times*, Feb. 26, 1992, p. B1.

3. *Building a Community School: A Revolution in Public Education*. New York: Children's Aid Society, 1993.

4. In Hastings-on-Hudson, New York, where the author lives, the annual cost per student is more than $12,000.

5. W. Moses, associate director, Children's Aid Society. Memo to author, Jan. 1993.

6. Enochs, J. *Hanshaw Middle School Healthy Start SB 620 Operational Grant Letter of Commitment.* Memorandum from superintendent to Stanislaus County (California) Interagency Children's Services Coordinating Council, Apr. 23, 1992.

7. "School as a Community." *Modesto Bee,* Sept. 2, 1991, p. 14.

8. Leonard, G. "The End of School." *Atlantic Monthly,* May 1992, 269(5), 24–28.

9. *Hanshaw Middle School, Healthy Start Support Services for Children Act (SB 620), Operational Grant Proposal.* Submitted by Modesto City Schools, Apr. 30, 1992.

10. Flores, D. "School Board Accepts Grants for Student Care." *Modesto Bee,* Aug. 24, 1992, p. B1.

Chapter Six

1. Gomby, D., and Larsen, C. "Evaluation of School-Linked Services." In *The Future of Children: School-Linked Services.* Los Altos, Calif.: Center for the Future of Children, David and Lucile Packard Foundation, Spring 1992, 2(1), 68–84.

2. Dryfoos, J. *Adolescents-at-Risk: Prevalence and Prevention.* New York: Oxford Press, 1990. Moskowitz, J. "The Primary Prevention of Alcohol Problems: A Critical Review of the Literature." *Journal of Studies of Alcoholism,* 1989, 50(1), 54–88.

3. Leitenberg, H. "Primary Prevention in Delinquency." In J. Burchard and S. Burchard (eds.), *Prevention of Delinquent Behavior.* Newbury Park, Calif.: Sage, 1986.

4. Burt, M., and Resnick, G. "Youth At Risk: Evaluation Issues." Washington, D.C. Urban Institute, paper prepared for DHHS, 1992.

Zabin, L., and Hirsch, M. *Evaluation of Pregnancy Prevention Programs in the School Context*. Lexington, Mass.: Lexington Books, 1991.

5. Dryfoos, J. "School and Community-Based Prevention Programs." In Coupey, S., and Klerman, L. *Adolescent Sexuality: Preventing Unhealthy Consequences*. Philadelphia: Hanley and Belfus, 1991.

6. Downes, B., and others. "The Effects of School-Based Health Clinics in St. Paul on School-Wide Birthrates." *Family Planning Perspectives*, 1993, *25*(1), 12–16.

7. Hardy, J., and others. "Evaluation of a Pregnancy Program for Urban Teenagers." *Family Planning Perspectives*, May/June 1986, *18*(3), 123.

8. Dryfoos, J. "School-Based Health Clinics: Three Years of Experience." *Family Planning Perspectives*, 1988, *20*(4), 193–200.

9. Kitzi, G. Presentation at Third Annual Conference of the Support Center for School-Based Clinics, Denver, 1986.

10. Hardy, J., and others, op. cit., note 7 above.

11. Galavotti, C., and Lovick, C. "The Effect of School-Based Clinic Use on Adolescent Contraceptive Effectiveness." Paper presented at National Conference on School-Based Clinics, Kansas City, Mo., Nov. 1987.

12. Edwards, L., and Arnold-Sheeran K. Unpublished data from St. Paul. Presented at annual meeting of American Public Health Association, New York, Nov. 1985.

13. Furstenberg, F., Herceg-Baron, R., and Shea, J. "Clinic Continuation Rates According to Age, Method of Contraception, and Agency." Paper presented at annual meeting of National Family Planning and Reproductive Health Association, Mar. 1982.

14. Philliber Research Associates. *Annual Progress Report: Year IV Process and Product*. Accord, N.Y.: Philliber Research Associates, 1991.

15. Kirby, D., and Waszak, C. *An Assessment of Six School-Based Clinics: Services, Impact, and Potential*. Washington, D.C.: Center for Population Options, 1989.

16. Adams, B., senator. In *Helping America's Youth in Crisis*. Testimony presented at hearing of Committee on Labor and Human Resources, U.S. Senate, Washington, D.C., July 28, 1992.

17. Bureau of Primary Health Care. *School-Based Clinics That Work*. Washington, D.C.: Division of Special Populations, Health Resources and Services Administration, HRSA 93-248P, June 1993.

18. Thomas, T. *Dallas Children and Youth Project*. Presentation at third annual conference of Support Center for School-Based Clinics, Denver, Oct. 1986.

19. *Evaluation of Quincy Neighborhood Health Center at Shanks High School*. Tallahassee, Fla.: Center for Human Services Policy and Administration, Florida State University, Aug. 1988.

20. Center for Reproductive Health and Policy Research. *Annual Report to the Carnegie Corporation of New York and the Stuart Foundations, July 1,1991–June 3, 1992*. San Francisco: Institute for Health Policy Studies, University of California, 1993.

21. Chapar, G. "School-Based Adolescent Health Care." *American Journal of Diseases in Children*, May 1992, *146*, 615–621.

22. Bureau of Primary Health Care, op. cit., note 17 above.

23. Center for Reproductive Health and Policy Research, op. cit., note 20 above, p. 87.

24. Presentation at annual meeting of Support Center for School-Based Services. Dearborn, Mich., Oct. 1991.

25. Anthony, D. Michigan Department of Public Health. Remarks to annual meeting of Support Center for School-Based Clinics. Dearborn, Mich., Oct. 1991.

26. Kitzi, G., op. cit., note 9 above.

27. Bureau of Primary Health Care, op. cit., note 17 above.

28. *Clinic News*. Support Center for School-Based Clinics, Apr. 1986, *2*(1).

29. Stout, J. "School-Based Health Clinics: Are They Addressing the Needs of the Students?" Thesis for Master of Public Health, University of Washington, 1991.

30. National Adolescent Health Resource Center. *Evaluative Review: Findings from a Study of Selected High School Wellness Centers in Delaware*. Dover, Del.: Division of Public Health, Delaware Health and Social Services, Apr. 1993.

31. Welfare Research, Inc. *Health Services for High School Students*. Report to New York City Board of Education, June 3, 1987.

32. Fothergill, K., Foy, J. M., Klein, J. D., and McCord, M. T. "School-Based Clinic Use and School Performance." *Journal of Adolescent Health*, 1993, *14*.

33. Dolan, L., and Haxby, A. *The Role of Family Support and Integrated Human Services in Achieving Success for All in the Elementary School*. Johns Hopkins University, Center for Research on Effective Schooling for Disadvantaged Students, Report no. 31, Apr. 1992.

34. Center for the Future of Children. *The Future of Children: School-Linked Services*. Los Altos, Calif.: Center for the Future of Children, David and Lucile Packard Foundation, 1992, *2*(1), Appendix A, 1992.

35. Ibid., 139.

36. W. R. McKennie, project director, Ballou Adolescent Health Center, Washington, D.C. site visit, Nov. 11, 1992.

37. Bureau of Primary Health Care, op. cit., note 17 above.

38. Center for Human Services Policy and Administration. *Shanks Health Center Evaluation. Final Report: Third Year of Program Operation*. Tallahassee, Fla.: Florida State University, 1990.

39. Bosker, I., and others. "A School-Based Clinic Immunization Outreach Project Targeting Measles in New York City." Paper presented at annual meeting of American Public Health Association, Washington, D.C., Nov. 1992.

40. Emihovich, C., and Herrington, C. D. *Florida's Supplemental School Health Services Projects: An Evaluation*. Tallahassee, Fla.: Florida State University, 1993.

41. Ibid., 11.

42. The *School Health Care—Online!!!* system and documentation is available from David Kaplan, M.D., The Children's Hospital, 1056 E. 19th Ave., Denver, Colo., 80218.

Chapter Seven

1. Melaville, A., Blank, M., and Asayesh, G. *Together We Can: A Guide for Crafting a Profamily System of Education and Human Services*. U.S. Department of Education and U.S. Department of Health and Human Services, 1993, p. vii.

2. Coye, M., Commissioner of Health. Speech at Conference on School Linked Integrated Services, Oakland, Calif., Oct. 1992.

3. Morrill, W. "Seeking Better Outcomes for Children and Families," *NCSI News*. National Center for Service Integration, Spring 1993, pp. 1–2.

4. See, for example, Melaville, A., and Blank, M., op. cit., 1993, note 1 above; Berends, M. *A Description of Restructuring in Nationally Nominated Schools*. Madison: University of Wisconsin, Center on Organization and Restructuring of Schools, 1992; Kahn, A., and Kammerman, S. *Integrating Services Integration: An Overview of Initiatives, Issues, and Possibilities*. New York: National Center for Children in Poverty. Columbia University, 1993.

5. L. Groves, Office of Interagency Affairs, Florida Department of Education. Presentation at the Council of Chief State School Officers' School Health Conference, Washington, D.C., June 2, 1992.

6. Klein, J., and others. *Comprehensive Adolescent Health Services in the United States, 1990*. Chapel Hill, N.C.: Cecil Sheps Center for Health Services Research, Center for Early Adolescence, and Center for Health Promotion and Disease Prevention, 1992.

7. Fox, H., Lipson, D., and Wicks, L. *Improving Access to Comprehensive Health Care through School-Based Programs*. Washington, D.C.: Fox Health Policy Consultants, Jan. 1992.

8. *School-Based Health Center Questions and Answers*. Department of Health Services, State of Connecticut, 1992, pp. 2–3.

9. Tetelman, E. "New Jersey's School-Based Youth Services Program." Newsletter, National Dropout Prevention Center, Spring 1993, p. 4.

10. English, A., and Tereszkiewicz, L. *School-Based Health Clinics: Legal Issues*. San Francisco: National Center for Youth Law, 1989.

11. Burch, P., Davies, D., and Palanki, A. *Mapping the Policy Landscape*. Report 7. Boston: Center on Families, Community, Schools, and Childrens' Learning, Mar. 1992.

12. Cohen, D. "Reality Tempers New Futures' Leaders' Optimism." *Education Week*, Sept. 25, 1991, *11*(4), 1.

13. *The Medically Fragile Child in the School Setting*. Washington, D.C.: American Federation of Teachers, AFL-CIO, 1992.

14. School-Based Adolescent Health Care Program. *The Answer Is at School: Bringing Health Care to Our Students*. Washington, D.C.: Robert Wood Johnson Foundation, 1993.

15. Proposal Committee of the Kahuku High and Intermediate School and the Community of Koolauloa and the North Shore. Proposal to the State of Hawaii Department of Education and Department of Health for funding for a school-based health service center, June 5, 1991.

16. Haggerty, R., professor emeritus, University of Rochester Medical Center, Rochester, New York. Letter to author, May 7, 1993.

17. R. Stone, communications director, Ounce of Prevention Program, Chicago. Letter to author, Nov. 18, 1992.

18. English, A., and Tereszkiewicz, L. *School-Based Health Clinics: Legal Issues*. San Francisco: National Center for Youth Law, 1989.

19. National Health Policy Forum. "Creating a Vision for Child Health: School-Based Clinics Confront Access, Training, Coordination, and Funding Issues." George Washington University, June 26, 1992.

20. Gadsen County Shared Service Network Stakeholder Analysis Report, Gadsen County (Florida) Shared Service Network Umbrella Council, Oct. 13, 1992.

21. Lawson, H. "Informing, Nurturing, Protecting, and Empowering Children Through Human Services Collaboration: A Planning Document." Oxford, Ohio: School of Education and Allied Professions, Miami University, 1992.

22. National Health Policy Forum. *Community and System Responses to Symptoms of Distress*. Washington, D.C.: National Health Policy Forum, July 1992, p. 11.

23. Hunt, S. "School-Based Clinics: The Politics of Values." Thesis, Department of Government, Wesleyan University, June 1992.

24. School-Based Adolescent Health Care Program. *Access to Comprehensive School-Based Health Services for Adolescents*. Washington, D.C.: Robert Wood Johnson Foundation, Spring 1991.

25. Ibid., 3.

26. Center on Organization and Restructuring of Schools. *Brief to Policymakers, No. 4*, Fall 1992.

27. Sedlak, M., and Schlossman, S. "The Public School and Social Services: Reassessing the Progressive Legacy." *Educational Theory*, 1985, 35(4), 371.

28. Chira, S. "In Plans to Improve Schools, a Grab Bag of Ideas and Ideologies." *New York Times*, July 15, 1992, p. B7.

29. "NASDC Project Summaries." *Education Week*, Aug. 4, 1993, pp. 50–52. Descriptions of the projects made available by the New American Schools Development Corporation, Arlington, Va., Aug. 1992.

Chapter Eight

1. School-Based Adolescent Health Care Program. *Access to Comprehensive School-Based Health Services for Adolescents*. Washington, D.C.: Robert Wood Johnson Foundation, Summer 1990, p. 1.

2. Farrow, F., and Joe, T. "Financing School-Linked Integrated Services." In *The Future of Children: School-Linked Services*. Los Altos, Calif.: Center for the Future of Children, David and Lucile Packard Foundation, 1992, 2(1), 60.

3. Center for Reproductive Health Policy Research. "School Based Clinics: A Closer Look—Revenue Generating Capacity and Potential." San Francisco: Institute for Health Policy Studies, University of California at San Francisco, Sept. 10, 1991.

4. School-Based Adolescent Health Care Program. *Access to*

Comprehensive School-Based Health Services for Adolescents. Washington, D.C.: Robert Wood Johnson Foundation, Summer 1993.

5. Office of Inspector General, Health and Human Services. "School-Based Health Services Design." OEI-05-92-00680, 1992.

6. Center for Population Options. *School-Based Clinic Policy Initiatives Around the Country: 1986.* Washington, D.C.: Support Center for School-Based Clinics, 1986.

7. Brellochs, C. *Background Information for National Workgroup Meeting One.* New York: School Health Project, Center for Population and Family Health, Columbia University School of Public Health, June 1993.

8. State of Louisiana. *Adolescent School Health Initiative, Request for Proposals to Establish Health Centers in Schools.* Baton Rouge, La.: Department of Health and Hospitals, 1992.

9. Meeropol, I. "The Full Service Schools Act." *Summary of Proceedings: Florida Full Service Schools Training Conference.* Tallahassee, Fla.: Florida Department of Education, 1992, p. 87.

10. *Bringing Health to School: Policy Implications for Southern States.* Washington, D.C.: Southern Governors' Association, June 1991.

11. Klink, H. "Eye on Oregon: Support at the Grassroots Carries SBCs through Crisis." *Clinic News*, Spring 1992, vol. 7, p. 5. Washington, D.C.: Center for Population Options.

12. Office of Technology Assessment, U.S. Congress. *Adolescent Health*, vol. 3: *Cross-cutting Issues in the Delivery of Health and Related Services.* Washington, D.C.: U.S. Government Printing Office, OTA-H-467, June 1991.

13. Brellochs, C., op. cit., note 7, above.

14. Comparable budget data for all states are not available from any source. Also note that total spending by school-based service programs in any one state is considerably more than the amount of state appropriations because nearly every school-based clinic also receives funds from other sources.

15. Clinton, W. "The Clinton Health Care Plan." *New England Journal of Medicine*, Sept. 10, 1992, *327*, 804–807.

16. American Academy of Pediatrics. "A Federal Look at Integrated Services." Washington, D.C.: Report to the Workgroup on Integrated Services, 1993.

17. Neidell, S., and Waszak, C. *School-Based Clinics—Update 1991*. Washington, D.C.: Center for Population Options, 1991. This estimate was derived from the reported average of 17 percent of clinics' budgets from the Maternal and Child Health Block Grant, about 5 percent from Medicaid including EPSDT, 7 percent from Community Health Centers, and 3 percent from the Social Services block grant.

18. The six organizations were the National Center for Children in Poverty; the National Governors' Association; Mathtech, Inc; the Child and Family Policy Center; Policy Studies Associates; and the Bush Center in Child Development and Social Policy of Yale University.

19. Office of Disease Prevention and Health Promotion. *Healthy Schools: A Directory of Federal Programs and Activities Related to Health Promotion Through the Schools*. Washington, D.C.: Department of Health and Human Services, 1992.

20. HR 5377 To amend the Public Health Service Act to establish school-based adolescent health services demonstration projects. House of Representatives, Aug. 8, 1986.

21. Lavin, A.; Shapiro, G., and Weill, K. *Creating an Agenda for School-Based Health Promotion: A Review of Selected Reports*. Cambridge: Harvard School of Public Health, 1992.

22. Office of Technology Assessment, U.S. Congress. *Adolescent Health*. Vols. 1–3. Washington, D.C.: U.S. Government Printing Office, OTA-H-476, June 1991.

23. National Commission on Children. *Beyond Rhetoric: A New American Agenda for Children and Families*. Washington, D.C.: U.S. Government Printing Office, 1991.

24. In an implementation guide, issued after the commission report, the Jackson-Hinds Comprehensive Health Center is cited as a model, including its satellite health centers located in schools.

25. *Commitment to Change: Foundation for Reform*. Washington, D.C.: 1991 Advisory Council on Social Security, Dec. 1991.

26. Kennedy, E., chairman. *Comprehensive Services for Youth Act of 1992 (S3088)*. Washington, D.C.: Committee on Labor and Human Resources, July 28, 1992.

27. *Quick Notes*. Washington, D.C.: National Organization of Adolescent Pregnancy and Parenting, May 1, 1993.

28. Portner, J. "Substantial Funding for Clinics Expected in Health Plan." *Education Week*, Oct. 13, 1993, p. 10.

29. 103rd Congress. *Health Security Act*. Washington, D.C.: U.S. Government Printing Office, 1993.

Chapter Nine

1. Kolbe, L. "An Essential Strategy to Improve the Health and Education of Americans in the Twenty-First Century." *Preventive Medicine*, 1993, *22*, 544–560.

2. Healthy Start Field Office. *Guide to Creating Comprehensive School-Linked Supports and Services for California Children and Families*. Davis: University of California, 1993; Melaville, T., and Blank, M. *Together We Can: A Guide for Crafting a Profamily System of Education and Human Services*. Washington, D.C.: U.S. Department of Education and U.S. Department of Health and Human Services (available through Institute for Educational Leadership), 1993; National School Boards Association. *Link-Up: A Resource Directory—Interagency Collaborations to Help Students Achieve*, Alexandria, Va.: National School Boards Association, 1991; NCSI Information Clearinghouse, National Center on Services Integration, National Center on Children and Poverty, 154 Haven Avenue, New York, NY 10032; Support Center for School-Based Services. *A Guide to School-Based and School-Linked Health Centers* (3 vols.), Center for Population Options, 1025 Vermont Avenue NW, Suite 210, Washington, DC 20005.

3. For assistance, contact the Youth Development Division, Academy for Educational Development, 1255-23rd Street NW, Washington, DC 20037.

4. Carnegie Council on Adolescent Development, Task Force on Youth Development and Community Programs. *A Matter of Time: Risk and Opportunity in the Nonschool Hours*. New York: Carnegie Corporation, 1992.

Appendix A

1. *Arkansas School-Based Clinics: General Information*. Little Rock: Arkansas Department of Health, 1992.

2. Letarte, L. *School-Based Health Centers*. Hartford: Department of Health Services, State of Connecticut, 1990. Updated by L. Letarte, personal communication, May 1993.

3. Department of Health and Rehabilitative Services and Department of Education, State of Florida. *Request for Program Designs for Supplemental School Health Programs, Feb. 1–June 30, 1991*. Instructions.

4. Porter, P. "Conquering the Public Health Bureaucracy: A Lesson from Rural Georgia." *Healthy Children*. Boston: Division of Health Policy, Harvard University. Undated.

5. Roeder, P. "Assessment of Family Resource and Youth Centers." *First Year Reports to the Prichard Committee*. Lexington Ky., July 1992.

6. *Adolescent Health Program for Fiscal Year 1992, Annual Report*. Boston: Massachusetts Department of Public Health, 1992.

7. Schrock, K. "Adolescent Health a Priority for Michigan Says Michigan Department of Public Health." *Michigan Medicine*, Sept. 1988, pp. 529–532.

8. Anthony, V. D., Michigan Department of Public Health. Remarks to Support Center for School-Based Clinics Annual Meeting, Dearborn, Mich., Oct. 1991.

9. Levy, J., and Shepardson, W. "A Look at Current School-linked Service Efforts." *The Future of Children: School-Linked Services*. Los Altos, Calif.: Center for the Future of Children, David and Lucile Packard Foundation, Spring 1992, 2(1).

10. Hughes, J. Description of School Health Demonstration Program. Albany: New York State Department of Health, 1984.

11. Coalition for School-Based Primary Care. Handout. New York: Center for Population and Family Health, Columbia University School of Public Health, 1992.

12. Pires, L. *New York State Community Schools Pilot Project, Summary Update*. New York: Edwin Gould Foundation for Children, June 1989.

13. State Community Aid Association. *School-Services Linkages: The Community Schools Program as a Tentative Effort*. Albany, N.Y.: State Community Aid Association, 1992.

14. Porter, P. "Oregon: Pioneers for Children." *Healthy Children*. Boston: Division of Health Policy, Harvard University. Undated.

15. Oregon Department of Human Resources. *School-Based Adolescent Health Program: Report 1987–88*. Salem, Oreg.: Health Division, Adolescent Health Program, 1988.

16. Klink, H. "Eye on Oregon: Support at the Grassroots Carries SBCs through Crisis." *Clinic News*, Spring 1992, 7. Washington, D.C.: Center for Population Options.

Appendix B

1. *Adolescent Health: Abstracts of Active Projects FY 1991*. Washington, D.C.: National Center for Education in Maternal and Child Health, 1991 (contains list of state adolescent health coordinators).

2. Johnson, K. *Building Health Programs for Teenagers*. Washington, D.C.: Children's Defense Fund, 1986.

3. In 1990, the poverty level for a family of four was $13,300.

4. Kirst, M. "Financing School-Linked Services." *Policy Brief*. University of Southern California, Center for Research in Education Finance, no. 7, Jan. 1992, p. 4.

5. Family Impact Seminars. *Integrated Approaches to Youths' Health Problems: Federal, State, and Community Roles*. Background briefing report, Washington, D.C., July 7, 1989.

6. *National Assessment of the Chapter 1 Program: The Interim Report*. Washington, D.C.: U.S. Department of Education, June 1992.

7. *Making Schools Work for Children in Poverty*. Washington, D.C.: Commission on Chapter 1, 1993.

Index

▲▲▲

Salome Urena Middle Academies
(Washington Heights, New York).
See IS 218 (Salome Urena Middle
Academies) (Washington Heights,
New York)
San Fernando High School (San
Fernando), 128
Schlossman, S., 41, 168–169
Schmidt, W., 31
School-Based Adolescent Health
Amendments of 1986, 200
School-Based Adolescent Health
Program (Oregon), 248
School-Based Adolescent Health
Services Demonstration Project,
195–196
School-based clinics: administration
of, 145–148; background information regarding, 78–83; collaborative
efforts regarding, 149–150; description of, 77; distributed by state,
179–182; dropout rate and utilization of, 127, 128; funding of,
88–90, 172–179, 185–188,
192–193, 195–196; group counseling and health promotion offered
by, 96–98; growth and distribution
of, 83–88; in IS 218, 104–105; opposition to, 26–28, 39, 82, 124,
165, 184–185; organization and
funding for, 88–90; parental consent and, 90–92, 158–159; providing prenatal care, 263; quality of
care issues related to, 160–162; reported effects of, 124–134; services
provided by, 92–96, 153; sexual activity and, 124–128; staffing of,
162–164; state management responsibility for, 189–192; student
support for, 95; utilization of,
93–94, 127–129, 131–135. *See also*

Health services; School health
services
School-based services: categories of,
141–142; comprehensive multicomponent, 71–75; evaluation of
benefits of, 123–124; explanation
of, 46, 143–144; provision of mental health care through, 53–55; reported effects of, 124–134; research
needs regarding, 135–137; school-
linked vs., 46–47; state management responsibility for, 189–192;
summary evaluation findings regarding, 134–135; utilization of,
93–94, 127–129, 131–135; yearly
cost of, 171. *See also* Family resource centers; School-based
clinics
School-Based Youth Services Program
(New Jersey), 53, 167, 178, 183,
201, 241–243
School boards, role in establishing
school-based clinics, 150–151
School Development Program, 69–70
School dropout rate: programs geared
to reduce, 63–66, 144; school clinic
utilization and, 127, 128, 130, 131;
for teen mothers, 131
School Health Care—Online!!!, 137
School Health Partnerships
(Pittsburgh), 87
School health services: description of,
51; forerunners of contemporary,
36–41; opposition to, 26–28, 39,
82, 124, 165, 184–185; during
Progressive Era, 24–25; recommendations and support for, 6–9, 26,
31–34, 39, 42, 196–199, 202–203,
217–222; role of school nurses in,
47–48. *See also* Health services;
School-based clinics